SIXTH EDITION

MOSAIC 2

Listening/Speaking

Jami Hanreddy

Elizabeth Whalley

Lawrence J. Zwier
Contributor, Focus on Testing

Mosaic 2 Listening/Speaking, Sixth Edition

Published by McGraw-Hill ESL/ELT, a business unit of The McGraw-Hill Companies, Inc., 1221 Avenue of the Americas, New York, NY 10020. Copyright © 2014 by The McGraw-Hill Companies, Inc. All rights reserved. Printed in the United States of America. Previous editions © 2007, 2001, and 1995. No part of this publication may be reproduced or distributed in any form or by any means, or stored in a database or retrieval system, without the prior written consent of The McGraw-Hill Companies, Inc., including, but not limited to, in any network or other electronic storage or transmission, or broadcast for distance learning.

Some ancillaries, including electronic and print components, may not be available to customers outside the United States.

This book is printed on acid-free paper.

2 3 4 5 6 7 8 9 0 DOW / DOW 1 0 9 8 7 6 5 4 3

ISBN: 978-0-07-759521-0
MHID: 0-07-759521-1

Senior Vice President, Products & Markets: Kurt L. Strand
Vice President, General Manager, Products & Markets: Michael J. Ryan
Vice President, Content Production & Technology Services: Kimberly Meriwether David
Director of Development: Valerie Kelemen
Marketing Manager: Cambridge University Press
Lead Project Manager: Rick Hecker
Senior Buyer: Michael R. McCormick
Designer: Page2, LLC
Cover/Interior Designer: Page2, LLC
Senior Content Licensing Specialist: Keri Johnson
Manager, Digital Production: Janean A. Utley
Compositor: Page2, LLC
Printer: RR Donnelley

Cover photo: Demetrio Mancini/Shutterstock.com

www.mhhe.com

www.elt.mcgraw-hill.com

The *McGraw·Hill* Companies

A Special Thank You

The Interactions/Mosaic Sixth Edition team wishes to thank our extended team: teachers, students, administrators, and teacher trainers, all of whom contributed invaluably to the making of this edition.

Maiko Berger, **Ritsumeikan Asia Pacific University**, Oita, Japan • Aaron Martinson, **Sejong Cyber University**, Seoul, Korea • Aisha Osman, Egypt • Amy Stotts, **Chubu University**, Aichi, Japan • Charles Copeland, **Dankook University**, Yongin City, Korea • Christen Savage, **University of Houston**, Texas, USA • Daniel Fitzgerald, **Metropolitan Community College**, Kansas, USA • Deborah Bollinger, **Aoyama Gakuin University**, Tokyo, Japan • Duane Fitzhugh, **Northern Virginia Community College**, Virginia, USA • Gregory Strong, **Aoyama Gakuin University**, Tokyo, Japan • James Blackwell, **Ritsumeikan Asia Pacific University**, Oita, Japan • Janet Harclerode, **Santa Monica College**, California, USA • Jinyoung Hong, **Sogang University**, Seoul, Korea • Lakkana Chaisaklert, **Rajamangala University of Technology Krung Thep**, Bangkok, Thailand • Lee Wonhee, **Sogang University**, Seoul, Korea • Matthew Gross, **Konkuk University**, Seoul, Korea • Matthew Stivener, **Santa Monica College**, California, USA • Pawadee Srisang, **Burapha University**, Chantaburi, Thailand • Steven M. Rashba, **University of Bridgeport**, Connecticut, USA • Sudatip Prapunta, **Prince of Songkla University**, Trang, Thailand • Tony Carnerie, **University of California San Diego**, California, USA

Dedications

To my charming and indomitable students, who constantly inspired me to find ever fresher, more challenging, and "funnier" ways to meet their needs, met every challenge head on, and provided so many wondrous, hilarious, and inspiring stories. To Valerie Kelemen at the helm, who had the vision to go for a Sixth Edition, making our books quite likely the longest lived series in our niche, if not in all of creation, never lost her cool, and got going when it was toughest. To Anita Raducanu, editor extraordinaire, who, though still remaining "faceless" at the time of this writing, is the embodiment of grace, good humor, intelligent solutions, and "how to just get it done." To Gracie, Fred, and Emma, who curled up and waited patiently, until they decided I needed my exercise. And to Joe, top chef never to be chopped, whose love consummately provides the context for these efforts.

—Jami Hanreddy

Thanks and props to Jami who met all the deadlines and did most of the work, grueling and otherwise. To Mary Dunn whose light still shines. "Time is a gift in which to learn." And, of course, to the folks at the Plant.

—Elizabeth Whalley

Photo Credits

Table of Contents

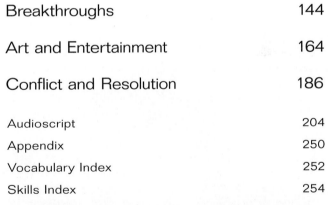

A 21st-Century Course for the Modern Student

Interactions/Mosaic prepares students for university classes by fully integrating every aspect of student life. Based on 28 years of classroom-tested best practices, the new and revised content, fresh modern look, and new online component make this the perfect series for contemporary classrooms.

Proven Instruction that Ensures Academic Success

Modern Content:
From social networking to gender issues and from academic honesty to discussions of Skype, *Interactions/Mosaic* keeps students connected to learning by selecting topics that are interesting and relevant to modern students.

Digital Component:
The fully integrated online course offers a rich environment that expands students' learning and supports teachers' teaching with automatically graded practice, assessment, classroom presentation tools, online community, and more.

- **3 Revised Chapters**, updated to reflect contemporary student life:
  Chapter 1: Language and Learning
  Chapter 3: Gender and Relationships
  Chapter 9: Art and Entertainment
- **40% new Listenings** that focus on global topics and digital life
- **Over 60 new vocabulary words** that enhance conversational proficiency
- **New photos** that showcase a modern, multi-cultural university experience

Emphasis on Vocabulary:

Each chapter teaches vocabulary intensively and comprehensively. This focus on learning new words is informed by more than 28 years of classroom testing and provides students with the exact language they need to communicate confidently and fluently.

Practical Critical Thinking:

Students develop their ability to synthesize, analyze, and apply information from different sources in a variety of contexts: from comparing academic articles to negotiating informal conversations.

Highlights of *Mosaic 2 Listening/Speaking* 6th Edition

Part 1: Building Background Knowledge
Each chapter begins with facts and figures pertaining to an interesting contemporary topic. The activities that follow prepare students for developing important listening skills.

Did You Know?

- There are more people in the world who use English as a second language than there are native speakers of English. English now has more than 500 million second-language speakers and that number is growing rapidly.

- In 1989, Sir Richard Francis, a former director of the British Council, stated that "Britain's real black gold is not North Sea oil, but the English language."

- When English is absorbed into the culture of the country in which it is used, it takes on a distinct flavor or characteristic based on the native language of that country. Thus, while the total number of languages in the world is diminishing, the number of different "Englishes" is increasing.

- According to Mark Abley, author of numerous books and articles about language in the 21st century, some rich Koreans pay for their children to have an operation that lengthens the tongue. These parents believe that it will help their children produce better English *l* and *r* sounds even though there is no research to support this idea. In fact, Korean children who are born and/or grow up in English-speaking countries never seem to have much trouble pronouncing *l* or *r*.

1 **What Do You Think?** Discuss the following questions in pairs.

1. Did the fact that there are now more speakers of English as a second language than there are native speakers of English surprise you? Why or why not?
2. What does the phrase "black gold" refer to? What do you think Sir Richard Francis meant when he said that it was not North Sea oil, but English that was the real "black gold" of Britain?
3. Why do you think that the number of languages spoken in the world is decreasing? Why do you think the number of different "Englishes" is increasing?
4. Why do you think parents (such as the Korean parents Mark Abley refers to) might take extreme measures to help their children learn to speak English better? What would you be willing to do to help your children speak a second language?

Sharing Your Experience

2 **Recollecting Language-Learning Experiences** Think about your entire English-language-learning experience up to now and share your recollections in small groups. Use the questions on page 5 to guide your discussion.

---

1. How old were you when you were first expected to learn some words in English? Who taught them to you? What method did they use to teach you?
2. How many years did you study English in school? Why?
3. What things helped you the most to learn English?
4. What things do parents do in your native country to ensure that their children will learn English well? Why?
5. How is English used in your native country? How do you think your native culture and language has influenced the way English is used in your native country?

Vocabulary Preview

3 **Determining Meaning from Context** The following words are used in the lecture. Complete each statement with the appropriate word from the list. Then compare your answers with your classmates' answers.

Words	Definitions
bound to	cannot be avoided
capacity	the ability to do or learn something
contender	a candidate or contestant that has a chance to win
devotee	a loving follower or supporter
diluted	mixed with a liquid (usually water) to reduce its strength
diplomacy	peacekeeping negotiations
exponentially	increasing by doubling in number again and again
hare	a wild animal that is similar to a rabbit, but has longer legs and longer ears
insatiable	having an appetite that never seems to be satisfied
lingua franca	any language used as a common language between speakers who do not have the same native language
neutralize	to reduce a negative effect to zero or almost zero
prestigious	having high status
royal decree	a judgment or law declared by the ruling king or queen
settlers	people who make a home on land previously occupied by a native population; colonizer
sheer	great or large
symptoms	signs or indicators of a problem or disease
usurp	to take or seize for one's own

Emphasis on Vocabulary Each chapter presents, practices, and carefully recycles vocabulary-learning strategies and essential words.

Strategy

Listening for Main Ideas in a Lecture

In most lectures, several main ideas are presented. These are the important concepts the speaker wants the audience to remember. Most often, the lecturer also provides a general statement, called the thesis statement, which identifies the overall purpose or argument of the lecture. When a lecturer is not well organized or is long-winded (taking a long time to come to the point), understanding the gist, or general idea, of what is being said can be difficult. However, when a lecturer is well organized, and the lecture has a clear beginning, middle, and end, you will have three chances to pick out the main ideas in the introduction, body, and conclusion.

1. **Introduction**
   Most often a good lecturer will begin with a statement that grabs the audience's attention and stimulates interest in the topic. This opening is followed by some background information and then a thesis statement. Sometimes, the main ideas are mentioned in the thesis statement but are not fully explained.

2. **Body**
   The main ideas and examples supporting the thesis are presented here. If you didn't catch what the thesis was in the introduction, you might be able to figure it out from the main ideas and supporting details.

3. **Conclusion**
   The conclusion most often begins with a restatement of the thesis followed by a brief summary of the main points supporting the thesis. This provides another chance to confirm your understanding of the thesis and main supporting points. This section often ends with a concluding statement that stimulates interest in further exploration of the topic or other related topics, and can serve as another hint about the main points.

Before You Listen

1 Considering the Topic Discuss the following questions in small groups.

1. What is the language that typical families in your country speak at home? Are there many dialects of the language? Why do you think this is so?

2. What is the lingua franca of commerce and higher education in your country? Why do you think this is so?

Language and Learning   7

Part 2: Understanding Main Ideas
Each chapter teaches crucial skills such as listening for main ideas in a lecture.

Listen

2 Listening for Main Ideas Listen to the lecture once all the way through. Then listen again. The second time, listen for the main ideas in the introduction, the body, and the conclusion of the lecture. Stop the recording after you hear each of the following sentences and write the main idea of the part of the lecture that you have just heard.

Stop 1 Yet, even in India, where English is definitely associated with the negative aspects of colonialism, it is still the dominant language of the media, administration, education, and business; and the number of its uses and speakers continues to increase exponentially.

_____

_____

Stop 2 Indeed, all of you in this room are more likely to be familiar with Klingon, which was originated by Marc Okrand for the *Star Trek* films, or the wonderful language… oh, I've forgotten the name… but it was spoken by the blue-skinned Na'vi in the 2009 film *Avatar*. Remember?

_____

_____

Sometimes we know more about the languages of fictional aliens than about the origins of our own languages.

8   CHAPTER 1

Impactful exercises Engaging assignments draw students in, making learning more efficient and fun.

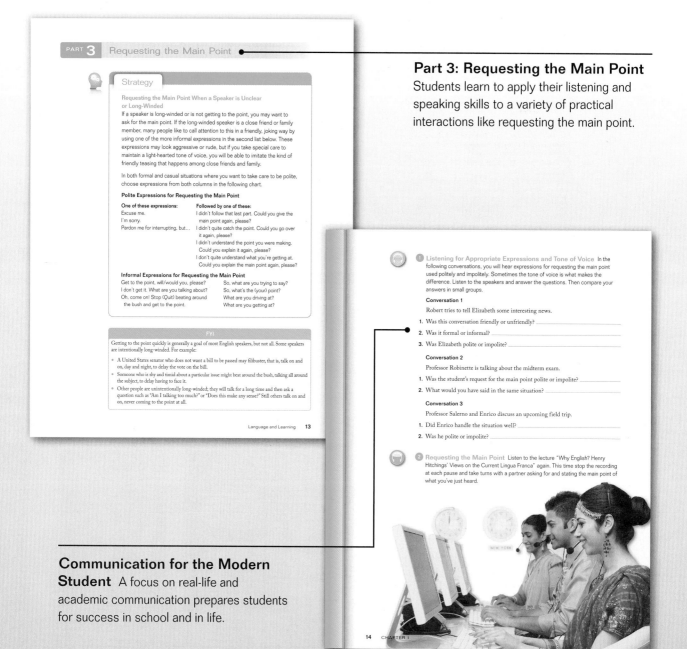

PART 3 — Requesting the Main Point

Strategy

Requesting the Main Point When a Speaker is Unclear or Long-Winded

If a speaker is long-winded or is not getting to the point, you may want to ask for the main point. If the long-winded speaker is a close friend or family member, many people like to call attention to this in a friendly, joking way by using one of the more informal expressions in the second list below. These expressions may look aggressive or rude, but if you take special care to maintain a light-hearted tone of voice, you will be able to imitate the kind of friendly teasing that happens among close friends and family.

In both formal and casual situations where you want to take care to be polite, choose expressions from both columns in the following chart.

Polite Expressions for Requesting the Main Point

One of these expressions:	Followed by one of these:
Excuse me.	I didn't follow that last part. Could you give the main point again, please?
I'm sorry.	
Pardon me for interrupting, but…	I didn't quite catch the point. Could you go over it again, please?
	I didn't understand the point you were making. Could you explain it again, please?
	I don't quite understand what you're getting at. Could you explain the main point again, please?

Informal Expressions for Requesting the Main Point

Get to the point, will/would you, please?	So, what are you trying to say?
I don't get it. What are you talking about?	So, what's the (your) point?
Oh, come on! Stop (Quit) beating around the bush and get to the point.	What are you driving at?
	What are you getting at?

FYI

Getting to the point quickly is generally a goal of most English speakers, but not all. Some speakers are intentionally long-winded. For example:

- A United States senator who does not want a bill to be passed may filibuster, that is, talk on and on, day and night, to delay the vote on the bill.
- Someone who is shy and timid about a particular issue might beat around the bush, talking all around the subject, to delay having to face it.
- Other people are unintentionally long-winded; they will talk for a long time and then ask a question such as "Am I talking too much?" or "Does this make any sense?" Still others talk on and on, never coming to the point at all.

Language and Learning **13**

---

1 **Listening for Appropriate Expressions and Tone of Voice** In the following conversations, you will hear expressions for requesting the main point used politely and impolitely. Sometimes the tone of voice is what makes the difference. Listen to the speakers and answer the questions. Then compare your answers in small groups.

Conversation 1

Robert tries to tell Elizabeth some interesting news.

1. Was this conversation friendly or unfriendly? _____
2. Was it formal or informal? _____
3. Was Elizabeth polite or impolite? _____

Conversation 2

Professor Robinette is talking about the midterm exam.

1. Was the student's request for the main point polite or impolite? _____
2. What would you have said in the same situation? _____

Conversation 3

Professor Salerno and Enrico discuss an upcoming field trip.

1. Did Enrico handle the situation well? _____
2. Was he polite or impolite? _____

2 **Requesting the Main Point** Listen to the lecture "Why English? Henry Hitchings' Views on the Current Lingua Franca" again. This time stop the recording at each pause and take turns with a partner asking for and stating the main point of what you've just heard.

14 CHAPTER 1

Part 3: Requesting the Main Point
Students learn to apply their listening and speaking skills to a variety of practical interactions like requesting the main point.

Communication for the Modern Student
A focus on real-life and academic communication prepares students for success in school and in life.

x

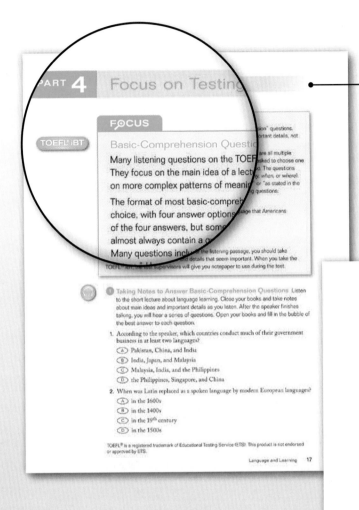

Part 4: Focus on Testing Students learn how to prepare for typical college exams and international assessments.

Results for Students A carefully structured program presents and practices academic skills and strategies purposefully, leading to strong student results and more independent learners.

Scope and Sequence

Chapter	Features	Listening

Speaking	Critical Thinking	Vocabulary Building	Focus on Testing
Expressing ideas and opinions on the role of English as a world language	Speculating about why the number of world languages is decreasing	Using definitions and context to place new vocabulary into appropriate sentences	Taking notes to answer basic-comprehension questions
Recollecting language-learning experiences	Utilizing introduction, body, and conclusion to discern the main ideas in a lecture	Understanding and using new vocabulary in discussions about language learning	
Comparing answers to questions about main points	Evaluating a lecturer's style		
Presenting your English-language-learning autobiography	Evaluating speakers' effectiveness in getting to the main point		
Comparing main points in English-language-learning autobiographies	Evaluating appropriateness of expressions and tone of voice		
Requesting the main point during lectures and situation role-plays	Selecting context-appropriate expressions for requesting the main point		
Sharing prior knowledge of thrill-seekers and thrill-seeking activities	Identifying thrilling experiences and common reasons for thrill seeking	Using definitions and context to place vocabulary words into appropriate sentences	Using notes to answer basic-comprehension questions about specific details
Sharing opinions about reasons for thrill seeking	Choosing a note-taking strategy that works best for you	Understanding and using new vocabulary in discussions about danger and daring	
Sharing personal thrilling experiences	Speculating about which people are more likely to be thrill seekers than others		
Sharing speculations about which people are more likely to be thrill seekers than others	Using a graphic organizer to reorganize information from notes that might be on a test		
Comparing note-taking methods and results with classmates	Using a prepared outline to give a presentation		
Giving a presentation about a daredevil stunt	Using a graphic organizer to rate strength of *yes* and *no* expressions		
Responding to questions with a variety of *yes* and *no* expressions	Selecting *yes* and *no* expressions that match feelings		
Giving and taking a survey on risk taking			

Speaking	Critical Thinking	Vocabulary Building	Focus on Testing
Discussing the changing roles of women in education and the workplace	Identifying the qualities of a "perfect" husband and "perfect" wife	Using definitions and context to place new vocabulary into blanks in an email	Answering questions involving pragmatic understanding of things such as tone of voice, hesitations, and word stress to interpret a speaker's attitudes, feelings, and intentions
Discussing your family's economic arrangement	Identifying ways to abbreviate when taking notes	Understanding and using new vocabulary in discussions about household roles played by a husband and wife	
Discussing the most important qualities of the "perfect" wife and "perfect" husband	Using symbols to communicate messages		
Sharing and comparing note-taking symbols	Using tone of voice as a cue to distinguish sincerity from insincerity		
Guessing and explaining the meanings of abbreviations and symbols	Choosing appropriate expressions of congratulations and condolences		
Sharing expressions of congratulations and condolences from your communities/cultures			
Expressing congratulations and condolences in a role-play			
Sharing ideas about the importance of aesthetics in developing products	Speculating about why standards of beauty seem to change from era to era, generation to generation	Using definitions and context to place new vocabulary into appropriate sentences	TOEFL iBT Answering comprehension questions with multiple answers
Discussing how cultural values affect ideas of beauty and aesthetic choices	Ranking adjectives according to personal aesthetic values	Understanding and using new vocabulary in discussions about aesthetics and beauty	
Sharing personal aesthetic values	Speculating about the role of aesthetics in the effectiveness of a device		
Speculating about why there are so many designs for a one-function object	Identifying reference words that provide cohesion and their referents		
Speculating about why a beautiful device is often more effective than an ugly one	Speculating about what makes a product beautiful		
Discussing the lecture about aesthetics and beauty	Distinguishing when and how to admit a lack of knowledge		
Using formal and informal expressions to admit a lack of knowledge	Collaborating to design a more appealing product		
Role-playing an industrial design project team			

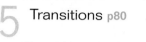

Scope and Sequence

Speaking	Critical Thinking	Vocabulary Building	Focus on Testing
Sharing feelings about life stages Sharing ideas about E. Rogers's five levels of willingness to try new things Recalling and sharing experiences of transitions in life Sharing personal experiences relating to new vocabulary concepts Sharing ideas about free will, fate, and time Discussing the meanings of analogies and metaphors in a radio program Brainstorming analogies Role-playing characters that "tell it like it is"	Speculating about why some people are more willing to try new things than others Understanding and using figurative language Theorizing about free will and fate Interpreting quotes Completing analogies and metaphors Deciphering the meanings of analogies and metaphors Choosing appropriate tone of voice and expressions when "telling it like it is" Identifying what is revealed when speakers "tell it like it is" Inferring speakers' attitudes from tone and expressions used Using a graphic organizer to sort and categorize information	Using context to match new vocabulary words to definitions Understanding and using new vocabulary in discussions about transitions	**TOEFL® iBT** Answering classification questions that require sorting, classifying, or categorizing of information
Discussing advantages and disadvantages of a virtual reality experience Sharing ideas about the nature, purpose, and effects of dreams Discussing the content of dreams and when and how often they occur Discussing dreams that look back and dreams that seem to look forward Comparing and discussing answers to exercises with classmates Comparing and contrasting dreams Role-playing a team of psychoanalysts analyzing patients' dreams Interviewing people about their dreams Debating dream-related topics as an optimist or a pessimist Role-playing seeing the "bright side" of bad situations	Speculating about the nature, purpose, and effects of dreams Comparing and contrasting dreams Analyzing and interpreting dreams Summarizing or paraphrasing the positive view of the lecturer Recognizing the "bright side" of a bad situation	Pooling knowledge and collaborating with classmates to match definitions to new vocabulary words Using context and definitions to match new vocabulary words to their synonyms Understanding and using new vocabulary in discussions about the mind	**TOEFL® iBT** Answering a realistic mix of question types (including basic-information questions, pragmatic-information questions, and classification questions)

Speaking	Critical Thinking	Vocabulary Building	Focus on Testing
Sharing personal experiences of good or bad jobs and ideas about the "perfect" job	Speculating about what would be a "perfect" job	Pooling prior knowledge with classmates to match definitions to new vocabulary words	**TOEFL® iBT** Taking notes for and responding to speaking questions involving the integration of skills (listening, speaking, and reading)
Discussing W. Edwards Deming's principles of quality improvement	Ranking criteria for job satisfaction	Using definitions and context to fill in blanks in a paragraph with new vocabulary words	
Discussing criteria for job satisfaction	Researching assumptions about job satisfaction	Understanding and using new vocabulary in discussions about working	
Discussing assumptions about U.S. workers' job priorities	Hypothesizing about the best ways to run a company		
Sharing opinions about cooperation in the workplace	Identifying causes and effects given directly or implied in a lecture		
Discussing the effects of innovations	Identifying and sorting the effects of innovations		
Presenting and giving in to persuasive or enticing arguments	Collaborating to come up with an innovation to make things easier		
Debating work-related issues	Identifying and using expressions used to introduce persuasive arguments, enticing offers, and giving in		
Role-playing people persuading and giving in	Formulating convincing arguments in a debate		
Sharing prior knowledge about the laws of nature	Speculating about the practical uses of a theory	Using definitions and context to choose sentences that use new vocabulary with multiple meanings in the same way as in the lecture	**TOEFL® iBT** Answering questions about biographical narratives by paying special attention to the chronology of events
Sharing personal breakthroughs	Paraphrasing/summarizing notes		
Pooling knowledge about complex scientific concepts	Selecting strategies for dealing with difficult concepts	Using definitions and context to choose sentences that use new vocabulary words correctly	
Discussing strategy preferences when dealing with difficult concepts	Describing scientific processes		
Role-playing giving and receiving compliments and "buttering someone up"	Analyzing situations in which compliments are given and received		
Sharing experiences of receiving inappropriate compliments			
Role-playing a team of scientists working on and explaining a breakthrough device			

Scope and Sequence

Speaking	Critical Thinking	Vocabulary Building	Focus on Testing
Sharing prior knowledge and opinions about reality TV	Speculating about the popularity of reality shows and why people want to be on them	Using clues to complete a crossword puzzle containing new vocabulary	**TOEFL iBT** Recognizing and answering questions about speaker's opinions
Discussing the effects of reality TV on its audience	Speculating about the positive and negative effects of reality TV	Understanding and using new vocabulary in discussions about reality TV	
Sharing reality TV show preferences	Identifying the effects of reality TV shows on their audience		
Role-playing a reality TV show producer	Completing a crossword puzzle		
Expressing doubt or disbelief in formal and informal situations	Using specific strategies to distinguish between fact and opinion		
Completing conversations with appropriate expressions of doubt or disbelief	Choosing appropriate ways to express doubt or disbelief		
Presenting "facts" (real or imaginary) and expressing doubts in a challenge game about personal experiences			
Sharing why quotes "speak" to you and/or are funny	Solving a decoding puzzle	Pooling knowledge to match definitions to new vocabulary words	**TOEFL iBT** Taking notes on and answering questions about information and point of view in classroom interactions
Sharing experiences with conflicts	Speculating about RA duties and types of conflicts they might deal with	Placing new vocabulary into a "decoding" puzzle, decoding the quotes about conflict in the puzzle, and discussing their meanings	
Discussing RA duties and conflicts in dorms	Evaluating possible exam questions		
Discussing what might/might not be included on an exam	Using notes to answer exam questions	Understanding and using new vocabulary words in discussions about dealing with conflicts	
Sharing notes to answer exam questions	Analyzing differences in tests for different courses		
Discussing possible differences in tests constructed for different courses	Writing good exam questions		
Collaborating to write exam questions	Determining how and when to acquiesce or express reservations		
Asking and answering exam questions			
Discussing when and how to acquiesce or express reservations			
Role-playing characters who must acquiesce or express reservations			

CHAPTER 1

Language and Learning

"One language sets you in a corridor for life. Two languages open every door along the way."

Frank Smith
Psycholinguist, Professor
of Education and author
Received PhD in Psycholinguistics
from Harvard in 1967

In this
CHAPTER

Lecture Why English? Henry Hitchings' Views on the
Current Lingua Franca

Learning Strategy Listening for Main Ideas

Language Function Requesting the Main Point

Connecting to the Topic

1. Imagine yourself walking down a corridor or hallway that is very long and very straight. There do not seem to be any obstacles in your way, but there are no doors or other ways out of the corridor either. How is this like speaking only one language?

2. Imagine yourself walking down another corridor that is also very long and very straight, but this time there are thousands of doors along each side. How is this like speaking a second or even a third language? What could be behind those doors?

Did You Know?

- There are more people in the world who use English as a second language than there are native speakers of English. English now has more than 500 million second-language speakers and that number is growing rapidly.

- In 1989, Sir Richard Francis, a former director of the British Council, stated that "Britain's real black gold is not North Sea oil, but the English language."

- When English is absorbed into the culture of the country in which it is used, it takes on a distinct flavor or characteristic based on the native language of that country. Thus, while the total number of languages in the world is diminishing, the number of different "Englishes" is increasing.

- According to Mark Abley, author of numerous books and articles about language in the 21st century, some rich Koreans pay for their children to have an operation that lengthens the tongue. These parents believe that it will help their children produce better English *l* and *r* sounds even though there is no research to support this idea. In fact, Korean children who are born and/or grow up in English-speaking countries never seem to have much trouble pronouncing *l* or *r*.

1 **What Do You Think?** Discuss the following questions in pairs.

answer

1. Did the fact that there are now more speakers of English as a second language than there are native speakers of English surprise you? Why or why not?

2. What does the phrase "black gold" refer to? What do you think Sir Richard Francis meant when he said that it was not North Sea oil, but English that was the real "black gold" of Britain?

3. Why do you think that the number of languages spoken in the world is decreasing? Why do you think the number of different "Englishes" is increasing?

4. Why do you think parents (such as the Korean parents Mark Abley refers to) might take extreme measures to help their children learn to speak English better? What would you be willing to do to help your children speak a second language?

Skip

Sharing Your Experience

2 **Recollecting Language-Learning Experiences** Think about your entire English-language-learning experience up to now and share your recollections in small groups. Use the questions on page 5 to guide your discussion.

1. How old were you when you were first expected to learn some words in English? Who taught them to you? What method did they use to teach you?

2. How many years did you study English in school? Why?

3. What things helped you the most to learn English?

4. What things do parents do in your native country to ensure that their children will learn English well? Why?

5. How is English used in your native country? How do you think your native culture and language has influenced the way English is used in your native country?

Vocabulary Preview

learn

3 **Determining Meaning from Context** The following words are used in the lecture. Complete each statement with the appropriate word from the list. Then compare your answers with your classmates' answers.

Words	Definitions
bound to	*cannot be avoided*
✓ capacity	*the ability to do or learn something*
✓ contender	*a candidate or contestant that has a chance to win*
✓ devotee	*a loving follower or supporter*
✓ diluted	*mixed with a liquid (usually water) to reduce its strength*
✓ diplomacy	*peacekeeping negotiations*
✓ exponentially	*increasing by doubling in number again and again*
✓ hare	*a wild animal that is similar to a rabbit, but has longer legs and longer ears*
✓ insatiable	*having an appetite that never seems to be satisfied*
✓ lingua franca	*any language used as a common language between speakers who do not have the same native language*
✓ neutralize	*to reduce a negative effect to zero or almost zero*
✓ prestigious	*having high status*
✓ royal decree	*a judgment or law declared by the ruling king or queen*
settlers	*people who make a home on land previously occupied by a native population; colonizer*
✓ sheer	*great or large*
✓ symptoms	*signs or indicators of a problem or disease*
✓ usurp	*to take or seize for one's own*

1. The _settlers_ in America and in Australia pushed the native populations, Native Americans and Aborigines, out of their territory.

2. He has a great _capacity_ to learn languages. That's why he can speak so many fluently.

3. The popularity of English around the world makes it a _contender_ for the most widespread language in history.

4. Even though most people think of English as a _prestigious_ language, there are some who are trying hard to _neutralize_ any negative aspects associated with it.

5. Since English had already become the _lingua_ of commerce, education, and _diplomacy_, the queen made a _royal decree_ that only English would be spoken in her country.

6. The students' hunger for information is _insatiable_ and their knowledge is therefore growing _exponentially_.

7. If you study all day and all night, you are _bound to_ pass the vocabulary test simply because of the _sheer_ amount of time you spent studying.

8. Even though the _hare_ was usually a very fast runner, the turtle still won the race.

9. Because she _diluted_ the medicine, it was not able to relieve her cold _symptoms_.

10. The president was sure that his friend was a _devotee_ of his programs, so he did not expect him to try to overthrow him and _usurp_ his power.

Strategy

Listening for Main Ideas in a Lecture

In most lectures, several main ideas are presented. These are the important concepts the speaker wants the audience to remember. Most often, the lecturer also provides a general statement, called the thesis statement, which identifies the overall purpose or argument of the lecture. When a lecturer is not well organized or is long-winded (taking a long time to come to the point), understanding the gist, or general idea, of what is being said can be difficult. However, when a lecturer is well organized, and the lecture has a clear beginning, middle, and end, you will have three chances to pick out the main ideas in the introduction, body, and conclusion.

1. **Introduction**

   Most often a good lecturer will begin with a statement that grabs the audience's attention and stimulates interest in the topic. This opening is followed by some background information and then a thesis statement. Sometimes, the main ideas are mentioned in the thesis statement but are not fully explained.

2. **Body**

   The main ideas and examples supporting the thesis are presented here. If you didn't catch what the thesis was in the introduction, you might be able to figure it out from the main ideas and supporting details.

3. **Conclusion**

   The conclusion most often begins with a restatement of the thesis followed by a brief summary of the main points supporting the thesis. This provides another chance to confirm your understanding of the thesis and main supporting points. This section often ends with a concluding statement that stimulates interest in further exploration of the topic or other related topics, and can serve as another hint about the main points.

Read about ← *(handwritten note)*

Before You Listen

1 Considering the Topic Discuss the following questions in small groups.

look on this (handwritten note)

1. What is the language that typical families in your country speak at home? Are there many dialects of the language? Why do you think this is so?

2. What is the lingua franca of commerce and higher education in your country? Why do you think this is so?

2 Listening for Main Ideas Listen to the lecture once all the way through. Then listen again. The second time, listen for the main ideas in the introduction, the body, and the conclusion of the lecture. Stop the recording after you hear each of the following sentences and write the main idea of the part of the lecture that you have just heard.

Stop 1 Yet, even in India, where English is definitely associated with the negative aspects of colonialism, it is still the dominant language of the media, administration, education, and business; and the number of its uses and speakers continues to increase exponentially.

_____

_____

_____

Stop 2 Indeed, all of you in this room are more likely to be familiar with Klingon, which was originated by Marc Okrand for the *Star Trek* films, or the wonderful language… oh, I've forgotten the name… but it was spoken by the blue-skinned Na'vi in the 2009 film *Avatar*. Remember?

_____

_____

_____

Sometimes we know more about the languages of fictional aliens than about the origins of our own languages.

Stop 3 He says... and you're gonna love this... "English is both the language of rock 'n' roll and royal decree."

_____

_____

_____

_____

Stop 4 And as I told you last week, while the number of languages in the world is diminishing overall, the number of different Englishes is increasing.

_____

_____

_____

_____

3 Listening for Details Listen to the lecture again. Answer the questions and complete the statements below about details supporting the main points in the lecture. Then compare answers with a partner.

1. Who is Henry Hitchings?

_____

2. According to Hitchings, the adoption of English as the lingua franca of

_____ and _____ is just a symptom of the

world becoming more _____ and more _____.

3. English has become the dominant language in the general areas of higher

education, commerce, economics, and science and technology in many, many

countries around the world. English has also become dominant in the specific

areas of (name at least 6) _____, _____,

_____, _____, _____,

_____, _____, _____.

4. Hitchings says that English has spread around the world because of a

complex set of circumstances which include _____,

_____, and _____.

▲ Native American

▲ Australian aborigine

5. Whose language dominated the language of the native people in America and Australia?

_____

_____

6. What happened in India that is surprising about English there?

_____

_____

7. Where does the term _lingua franca_ come from? Why was it first used?

_____

_____

8. What is Globish?

_____

_____

9. Describe at least three other invented languages and how they have been used.

_____

_____

_____

10. What does Pennycook say about the paradoxical nature of English as a world

language? _____

_____

11. What does McCrum say about the paradoxical nature of English as a world

language? _____

_____

12. What languages are the top contenders for *usurping* the place of English as the lingua franca? Is this likely to happen soon? Why or why not?

_____

_____

13. What type of writers have the greatest possibility of changing English from the inside out? _____

_____

_____

After You Listen

④ Evaluating a Lecturer's Style Discuss the following questions about the lecture in small groups.

1. Do you think the lecture was well organized? Poorly organized? Why?

2. Was the lecturer long-winded and taking too much time to get to the point? Did the lecturer *ever* get to the point?

⑤ Comparing Notes In the same small groups, share the main ideas that you wrote down in Activity 2. Did you find it easy or difficult to pick out the main ideas? Why?

Talk It Over

⑥ Sharing Your English-Language-Learning Autobiography Think about the variety of experiences you've had as you've been learning English. Begin with the point at which you didn't know a single word and continue through to the present. In small groups, use the following questions as a guide to present your "English-language-learning autobiography." Speak for two to three minutes. As you listen to your classmates' autobiographies, write down the main points.

1. When and where were you first exposed to English? How old were you?

2. Have you been learning English continuously since then, or were you interrupted for some reason?

3. Why did you want to learn English? If you didn't want to, why not?

4. Did you study English in school? If so, where and when?

5. What approaches or methods did your teachers use? Were they effective?

6. Were any of your teachers native English speakers? Do you think this made a difference? Why or why not?

7. Have you had opportunities to speak English outside the classroom with friends or family? Have you had a close boyfriend or girlfriend or perhaps a husband or wife who spoke English?

8. Were you exposed to more than one dialect of English? Do you think this helped or hindered your English-language acquisition? Why?

9. Is English used in your native country as a lingua franca in any way? If so, how? How do you think this has influenced how/what you were taught or chose to learn in English?

10. Do you now speak English on a daily basis to anyone or for any particular purpose?

7 **Comparing English-Language-Learning Autobiographies** Discuss the following questions with the whole class.

1. What were some of the most interesting points in the English-language-learning autobiographies shared in your group?

2. Did the main points shared have similarities or were they very different? In what ways?

3. Did any type of experiences emerge as being important for almost everyone?

8 **Evaluating Speakers in Context** Choose three people from the following list and find an opportunity to listen to each one speak without interruption for several minutes (in person or on the radio or TV).

artist	parent	scientist	teacher
businessperson	politician	shopkeeper	teenager
news reporter	religious speaker	talk show host	young child

As you listen, note the main points and then consider these questions:

1. Which of the three speakers was the most long-winded?

2. Which one got to the point in the shortest amount of time?

3. Did any of the speakers talk on and on so much that you felt they never got to the point? If so, which one(s)?

4. With which speaker was it easiest to get the gist of what was being said?

5. With which speaker was it hardest to get the gist of what was being said?

With your classmates, give brief descriptions of your three subjects, including approximate ages, educational backgrounds, and your answers to the previous questions. Then discuss the following:

1. Did you notice any patterns? For example, did you and your classmates discover a relationship between profession and long-windedness? Or perhaps between age and not getting to the point?

2. Were there any particular topics about which most subjects tended to "beat around the bush"?

FYI

In everyday interactions with friends, family, or co-workers, there are times when we are well organized and we express our main points clearly. There are also times when we all have difficulty getting to the point, or we "beat around the bush" (talk around the subject, but not exactly on the subject).

Strategy

Requesting the Main Point When a Speaker is Unclear or Long-Winded

If a speaker is long-winded or is not getting to the point, you may want to ask for the main point. If the long-winded speaker is a close friend or family member, many people like to call attention to this in a friendly, joking way by using one of the more informal expressions in the second list below. These expressions may look aggressive or rude, but if you take special care to maintain a light-hearted tone of voice, you will be able to imitate the kind of friendly teasing that happens among close friends and family.

In both formal and casual situations where you want to take care to be polite, choose expressions from both columns in the following chart.

Polite Expressions for Requesting the Main Point

One of these expressions:	Followed by one of these:
Excuse me.	I didn't follow that last part. Could you give the main point again, please?
I'm sorry.	
Pardon me for interrupting, but…	I didn't quite catch the point. Could you go over it again, please?
	I didn't understand the point you were making. Could you explain it again, please?
	I don't quite understand what you're getting at. Could you explain the main point again, please?

Informal Expressions for Requesting the Main Point

Get to the point, will/would you, please?	So, what are you trying to say?
I don't get it. What are you talking about?	So, what's the (your) point?
Oh, come on! Stop (Quit) beating around the bush and get to the point.	What are you driving at?
	What are you getting at?

FYI

Getting to the point quickly is generally a goal of most English speakers, but not all. Some speakers are intentionally long-winded. For example:

- A United States senator who does not want a bill to be passed may filibuster, that is, talk on and on, day and night, to delay the vote on the bill.
- Someone who is shy and timid about a particular issue might beat around the bush, talking all around the subject, to delay having to face it.
- Other people are unintentionally long-winded; they will talk for a long time and then ask a question such as "Am I talking too much?" or "Does this make any sense?" Still others talk on and on, never coming to the point at all.

1 **Listening for Appropriate Expressions and Tone of Voice** In the following conversations, you will hear expressions for requesting the main point used politely and impolitely. Sometimes the tone of voice is what makes the difference. Listen to the speakers and answer the questions. Then compare your answers in small groups.

Conversation 1

Robert tries to tell Elizabeth some interesting news.

1. Was this conversation friendly or unfriendly? _____

2. Was it formal or informal? _____

3. Was Elizabeth polite or impolite? _____

Conversation 2

Professor Robinette is talking about the midterm exam.

1. Was the student's request for the main point polite or impolite? _____

2. What would you have said in the same situation? _____

Conversation 3

Professor Salerno and Enrico discuss an upcoming field trip.

1. Did Enrico handle the situation well? _____

2. Was he polite or impolite? _____

2 **Requesting the Main Point** Listen to the lecture "Why English? Henry Hitchings' Views on the Current Lingua Franca" again. This time stop the recording at each pause and take turns with a partner asking for and stating the main point of what you've just heard.

3 Role-Playing Conversations With a partner complete the following role-plays. The first one has been partially completed as an example.

1. Take turns being Speaker A and Speaker B to create a variety of conversations.

2. Speaker B will ask for the main point on his or her first turn. Speaker A can choose to answer right away or to continue the conversation for a while before giving the main point.

3. When you have completed these conversations, try making up a few conversations of your own, using these as models.

4. Select the conversation that you and your partner enjoyed most (either one here or one you made up) and present it to the class.

Conversation 1

A: Good morning, professor. Did you hear about that terrible accident on the highway last night? The traffic was backed up for hours. I hope everyone was OK. I'll bet a lot of people were late getting home, too. Probably a lot of people couldn't do some of the things they'd planned to do 'cause they got home so late. You know, almost everything closes by nine o'clock—like the public library and everything and…

B: Stop beating around the bush, Goran. What's your point?

A: Well, so I was one of the people, and I was late and…

B: Get to the point, please. I'm late for class.

A: I don't have my homework.

B: _____

A: _____

Conversation 2

A: Yes—about your English project—well, rap music is an interesting medium of expression; and, sure, hip-hop dancing seems to go along with it. And your outfit—yes, that jacket does have some interesting possibilities. And those drums… it never occurred to me to use them like this. So your sister told me you're not sure whether you're going to major in English literature or not. Emma Cotib went through the same thing. Have you ever met Emma? She works over in the career counseling center now.

B: _____

A: _____

B: _____

Conversation 3

A: Dad, I'd like to talk to you about something. I went over to the registrar's office yesterday. And, you know, Jeremiah works over there. The line was really long—all the way out the door and around the building. I hadn't decided which classes to sign up for yet, but I figured that I had plenty of time to do that while I waited in line. And then I bumped into Jeremiah, you know, that really interesting guy I was telling you about, and we started talking. You know, he's had the most fascinating life, and he never even went to college!

B: _____

A: _____

B: _____

Conversation 4

A: Do you remember that autobiography you loaned me last week? _The Hunger of Memory_ by Richard Rodriquez? Well, I was reading the chapter about how he lost the ability to communicate with his parents and grandparents because he never learned how to speak his native language well, and then the phone rang. It surprised me because it was so early. No one usually calls before eight o'clock. I didn't want to get up to answer it because the chapter was so interesting. But I did and…

B: _____

A: _____

B: _____

FOCUS

Basic-Comprehension Questions

Many listening questions on the TOEFL® iBT are "basic-comprehension" questions. They focus on the main idea of a lecture or conversation and on important details, not on more complex patterns of meaning.

The format of most basic-comprehension questions is familiar. They are all multiple choice, with four answer options (A, B, C, and D). Usually, you are asked to choose one of the four answers, but some questions may ask you to choose two. The questions almost always contain a question word (*who, what, how, which, why, when,* or *where*). Many questions include a phrase like "according to the professor" or "as stated in the lecture." Here are two examples of basic-comprehension listening questions:

Sample Question 1:

According to the lecture, what is the most common language that Americans study as a foreign language?

Sample Question 2:

When was the first ESL textbook published?

Because you get only one chance to hear the listening passage, you should take notes about both the main ideas and details that seem important. When you take the TOEFL® iBT, the test supervisors will give you notepaper to use during the test.

 1 Taking Notes to Answer Basic-Comprehension Questions Listen to the short lecture about language learning. Close your books and take notes about main ideas and important details as you listen. After the speaker finishes talking, you will hear a series of questions. Open your books and fill in the bubble of the best answer to each question.

1. According to the speaker, which countries conduct much of their government business in at least two languages?
   - (A) Pakistan, China, and India
   - (B) India, Japan, and Malaysia
   - (C) Malaysia, India, and the Philippines
   - (D) the Philippines, Singapore, and China

2. When was Latin replaced as a spoken language by modern European languages?
   - (A) in the 1600s
   - (B) in the 1400s
   - (C) in the 19th century
   - (D) in the 1500s

3. Why was Latin kept in the school curriculum until the 18th century?

   Ⓐ because it had always been the dominant language of commerce, education, and religion

   Ⓑ because it was believed that the study of Latin increased a person's intellectual abilities

   Ⓒ because people didn't want to give up speaking it

   Ⓓ because that is when the grammar schools were established

4. What did John Comenius include in his *Opera Didactica Omnia* in 1657?

   Ⓐ a theory of modern language

   Ⓑ a curriculum for teaching English

   Ⓒ a theory of language acquisition

   Ⓓ rules for studying English grammar

5. In the grammar-translation method, what are students required to do a lot of?

   Ⓐ listening and speaking

   Ⓑ reading and writing

   Ⓒ memorizing vocabulary

   Ⓓ learning grammar and translating texts

6. What is the main focus of current language-acquisition methodologies?

   Ⓐ using language for everyday purposes

   Ⓑ getting a good job in today's economy

   Ⓒ learning to become a native

   Ⓓ acquiring perfect grammar and pronunciation

Self-Assessment Log

Check (✓) the words in this chapter you have acquired and can use in your daily life.

Nouns		Adjectives	Verbs
▨ capacity	▨ lingua franca	▨ diluted	▨ bound to
▨ contender	▨ royal decree	▨ exponentially	▨ neutralize
▨ devotee	▨ settlers	▨ insatiable	▨ usurp
▨ diplomacy	▨ symptoms	▨ prestigious	
▨ hare		▨ sheer	

Check (✓) your level of accomplishment for the skills introduced in this chapter. How comfortable do you feel using these skills in everyday situations?

	Very comfortable	Somewhat comfortable	Not at all comfortable
Listening for main ideas	☐	☐	☐
Listening for details	☐	☐	☐
Evaluating a speaker's style	☐	☐	☐
Using formal expressions such as *I didn't follow the last part* and *Could you go over it again, please?* to request the main point	☐	☐	☐
Using informal expressions such as *What are you driving at?* to request the main point	☐	☐	☐

Think about the topics and activities in this chapter and complete the statements.

In this chapter, I learned something new about _____

_____

_____

I especially liked (topic or activity) _____

_____

_____

I would like to know more about _____

_____

_____

2 Danger and Daring

> "Life is either a daring adventure, or nothing."
>
> Helen Keller
> Deaf and blind U.S. author
> and speaker

In this
CHAPTER

Lecture Hooked on Thrills

Learning Strategy Noting Specific Details

Language Function Saying *Yes* and *No*

 **Connecting to the Topic**

1. Do you know any people who seek thrills (look for intense excitement and emotion) by facing unnecessary danger? If so, what type of thrill-seeking activity do they participate in?

2. What do you think is the most popular type of thrill-seeking activity in your native country for participants? Is this the one that draws the most spectators? If not, which activity does?

Did You Know?

- On October 24, 1901, Annie Taylor became the first person to go over Niagara Falls in a barrel. It was her 63rd birthday. You can see pictures of her and hundreds of other daredevils at the Daredevil Museum in Niagara Falls, New York.

- On September 12, 1980, stuntman and magician Tony Vera tried to jump off the Brooklyn Bridge in New York wearing only a loincloth around his hips and a straightjacket to keep his arms locked around himself.

- Freediving is an extreme sport in which divers compete to see who can swim the deepest with just one breath. Tanya Streeter, a young woman from England, says she can survive up to six minutes without breathing and freedives up to 400 feet on one breath of air, without any assistance. About 55 freedivers die each year.

- The fastest and perhaps the most dangerous team sport is freeflying. In freeflying, a team jumps out of an airplane, joins hands, and then falls through the air at an average rate of 160 to 180 miles per hour. A few teams have reached the highest speed on record of 250 miles per hour before they finally release their parachutes and float to the ground.

▲ Freeflying is an extreme team sport where a lack of cooperation and precision can have extreme consequences.

1 **What Do You Think?** Answer the following questions in pairs.

1. Have you ever been to Niagara Falls? Why do you think the Falls attract so many daredevils?

2. Why do you think people like to jump off of high places?

3. Why do you think freedivers and skydivers risk their lives? Is it just to break a record or do they have other reasons?

2 **What Is Thrilling to You?** Discuss the following questions in small groups.

1. What is thrilling to you? What makes your heart race?

2. What is the most thrilling thing you've ever done? Did it involve taking a risk?

3. What is the most dangerous thing you've ever done? Was it thrilling to you? Would you do it again? Why or why not?

3 **Vocabulary in Context** The following words are used in the lecture in this chapter. Read the definitions and complete the sentences below with the correct forms of the words.

Words	Definitions
daredevil	*a person who fears nothing and will attempt anything*
hullabaloo	*excitement; chaotic activity*
irresistible	*too strong to oppose or withstand*
motivate	*to give encouragement or a reason for action*
pull off	*to accomplish something very difficult*
seeker	*a person who looks for something*
stunt	*a difficult or dangerous action*
take up	*to begin a new hobby or activity*

1. Annie Taylor, Tony Vera, and Tanya Streeter all have one thing in common.

   They love danger and are _____.

2. Do you know anyone who loves climbing mountains? To such a person, an offer to be a member of an expedition to Nepal to climb Mount Everest would

   probably be _____.

3. Have you ever seen a rock star whose fans scream and jump up and down whenever they see the star?

   This star causes a lot of _____ wherever he or she goes.

4. When magician David Blaine decided to freeze himself into a block of ice on a New York City street, he claimed that he wasn't doing it for the publicity or the money. Therefore, no one, not even his girlfriend, could figure out what could possibly

   have _____ him to do such a thing.

▲ How long did David Blaine survive in this block of ice?

5. Do you know someone like Tony Vera who looks for thrilling experiences all the time? This person could be called a thrill _____.

6. What is the most important factor that helps you to _____ difficult tasks?

7. What is the most exciting thing you do on a regular basis and when did you first _____ this activity?

8. Because people love to watch other people do dangerous things, many people are able to earn a lot of money doing _____ for an audience. Unfortunately, this wasn't the case for Annie Taylor, who died poor.

PART 2   Noting Specific Details

Strategy

Using Lecture Organization as a Guide to Note Specific Details

Once you have learned to pick out the main ideas in a lecture, your next step is to note the specific details. You will need these details later to answer questions on all types of exams: multiple choice, short answer, and essay. To listen for and note specific details, it is helpful to notice how the lecture is organized.

If the lecture is organized in the standard way, that is, if it contains three sections—introduction, body, and conclusion—listen for and note the main ideas in each of these sections. Then try to fill in the main ideas with supporting details. The following information will help you decide which specific details you should write down in your notes.

1. If the introduction to the lecture is a summary of what you learned in the previous class session, take notes on this material again. These notes will be an added reminder of what the lecturer thinks is important.

2. If the introduction to the lecture is just a general introduction or an attention getter (a fact, a saying, a story, or a joke), you don't need to write this material down unless you might like to tell it to your friends later.

3. Next, listen for information in the body of the lecture. You will probably hear the most details in this section. Write down as much information as you can in your notes, but don't worry if you can't get everything. Just put a question mark in the margin for anything you missed and ask questions later.

4. As you listen to the conclusion, continue to make your notes as complete as possible. Most conclusions won't contain any new information, but be ready in case the instructor has forgotten to include an important detail earlier and decides to mention it in the conclusion.

One good way to organize the main points and specific details of a clearly organized lecture is to use a formal outline. Look at the examples below. The one on the left is more commonly used, but many note takers find the one on the right easier to use because they don't need to remember when to use the capital and lowercase letters or Roman and Arabic numerals.

Examples of Formal Outlines

Outline Using Roman Numerals, Arabic Numerals, and Letters	**Outline Using Only Arabic Numerals**
I. Introduction	Introduction (In paragraph form, a paraphrase of the lecturer's introductory remarks.)
A. Main point	1. Main point
B. Main point	1.1. Specific detail
C. Main point	1.2. Specific detail
II. Discussion/body	1.3. Specific detail
A. Restatement of main point A	1.3.1. Further detail of 1.3
1. Specific detail	1.3.2. Further detail of 1.3
2. Specific detail	2. Main point
3. Specific detail	2.1. Specific detail
a. Further detail of A3	2.1.1. Further detail of 2.1
b. Further detail of A3	2.1.2. Further detail of 2.1
B. Restatement of main point B	2.2. Specific detail
1. Specific detail	3. Main point
a. Further detail of B1	3.1. Specific detail
b. Further detail of B1	3.2. Specific detail
2. Specific detail	3.2.1. Further detail of 3.2
C. Restatement of main point C	3.2.2. Further detail of 3.2
1. Specific detail	3.3. Specific detail
2. Specific detail	Conclusion
a. Further detail of C2	(In paragraph form, a paraphrase of the lecturer's concluding remarks.)
b. Further detail of C2	
3. Specific detail	
III. Conclusion	
A. Summary of IIA	
B. Summary of IIB	
C. Summary of IIC	

Choosing Alternatives to Formal Outlines

Formal outlines, such as the previous examples, work best for note-taking when the lecturer carefully organizes the material into an introduction, body, and conclusion, but many lecturers do not follow these rules. Some lecturers do not use an outline format to help them to stay organized when speaking and others, even if they do use an outline, add bits of information here and there as they think of them during the lecture. In these cases, you may need alternatives to the formal outline in order to note main points and specific details well. Here are six different ways to organize your notes. Use the one that feels the most comfortable and useful to you.

Alternative 1

This method of note taking is most useful when the main points and details are long phrases and sentences.

```
Main point
    Detail
    Detail
    Detail
Main point
    Detail
    Detail
    Etc.
```

Alternative 2

This method of note taking is most useful when details are symbols, statistics, single words, or very short phrases.

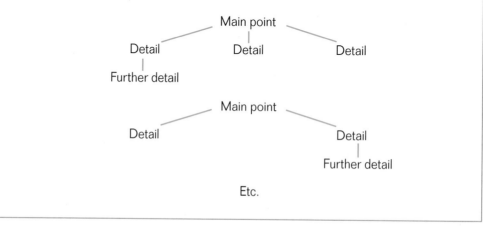

Alternative 3

This method is especially useful when the lecturer tends to back up and give specific details on points mentioned earlier in the lecture. If you leave enough space to add more details later, note-taking during this type of lecture should not be difficult.

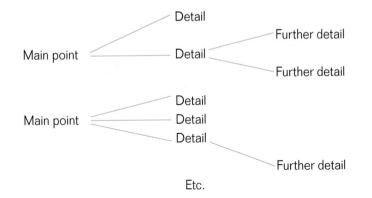

Etc.

Alternative 4

This method is useful when the details precede the main point.

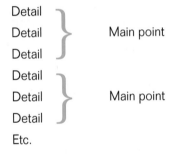

Etc.

Alternative 5

This method is especially useful if the lecture is not well organized or if the lecturer does not state the main points clearly or digresses frequently. By putting all of the main points on the left and details on the right, you can match them up with arrows later and double check to see if something you thought was a main point was really a detail, and vice versa.

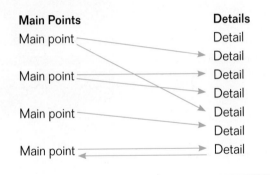

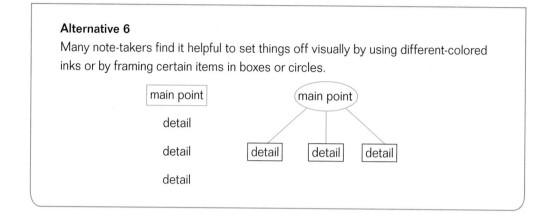

Alternative 6

Many note-takers find it helpful to set things off visually by using different-colored inks or by framing certain items in boxes or circles.

main point	main point
detail	
detail	detail detail detail
detail	

1️⃣ **Considering the Topic** Discuss the following questions in small groups.

1. Many thrill seekers claim that they engage in dangerous activities only for personal satisfaction—that they are concerned only with increasing their self-esteem. Some critics say, however, that money is the real motive behind the most daring of these activities and that if there were no publicity or fame and fortune, there would be no daredevils to perform dangerous stunts. Which of these explanations do you think is more accurate? Why? Can you think of examples to back up your answer?

2. Which groups do you think are more likely to engage in thrill-seeking activities and why?

   - Men or women?
   - Young children or teenagers?
   - Young adults or middle-aged people?
   - Rich people or poor people?
   - A visitor in a foreign country or a person at home?

Extreme skateboarding has become popular ▶ with thrill-seeking men and women.

2 Listening to Note Specific Details Listen to the beginning of the lecture about people who choose to face danger and what it means to be "hooked on thrills," and decide whether you should take notes on the introduction.

Your decision: I should _____ should not _____ take notes on the introduction because _____.

Listen to the lecture from the beginning to the midpoint. Take notes using one of the two traditional outline forms on page 25 or one of the six alternative note-taking methods shown on pages 26–28. Note as many specific details as you can.

Did the note-taking method that you chose work well for this part of the lecture? Listen again to check your notes. If the note-taking method you chose did not work well, choose another method and listen again to note the main points and specific details in the first half of the lecture.

Now listen to the rest of the lecture and continue taking notes. Use the note-taking method that has worked best for you so far or you may try out another one for practice. Listen again to check your notes.

3 Reorganizing Your Notes to Prepare for Tests Compare notes in small groups and share your feelings about the note-taking methods you used. Then work together, using your notes to fill in the following chart on specific details in the lecture that could be on a test.

Four types of high-level sensation seekers	Characteristics of each type of high-level sensation seeker	Examples of activities for each type of high-level sensation seeker	Which gender and which age group forms the majority in each category?

Talk It Over

4 Speaking from a Prepared Outline Prepare a brief talk on a daredevil stunt that you have read about and present your talk to the class. You may need to use the Internet or make a trip to the library to get enough information to make your talk interesting to your classmates.

As you speak:

- Use notes that you have made in outline form.
- Have your classmates take notes in outline form.

After you have finished speaking:

- Compare the notes you spoke from with the notes other students made.
- Do you and your classmates have the same main points and details? If not, discuss the differences and why you think they occurred.

Strategy

Understanding and Using *Yes* and *No* Expressions

When we are asked if we would like to do or have something, we have three basic ways to respond: *yes*, *no*, and *maybe*.

Maybe is a neutral word meaning that at a later time your answer may be *yes* or *no*. *Maybe* is exactly in the middle of the scale between *yes* and *no*, and there are no ways of saying *maybe* that are either stronger or weaker. Some alternative expressions for *maybe* are *perhaps*, *possibly*, and *I'll think about it*.

Yes and *no* can be expressed in a variety of ways. Depending on how close to or far away from *maybe* your feelings are, you may choose either a weaker or stronger expression to say *yes* or *no*.

Expressions for Saying *Yes* and *No*

Stronger *Yes*

Absolutely!
Definitely!
For sure!
Great!
I'll say!
Of course!
OK! (with excited intonation)
Sure thing!
You bet!

Weaker *Yes*

I think so.
I'm considering it.
Most likely I will/would.
OK. (with unenthusiastic intonation)
OK, if you really want me to.
Probably.
Sure. Why not?
  (with unenthusiastic intonation)
That might be a good idea.

Stronger *No*

Are you kidding?
Forget it!
Never!
Never in a million years!
No way!
Not for all the tea in China!
Not on your life!
Nothing doing!

Weaker *No*

I don't think so.
I doubt it.
I'd rather not.
Not especially.
Not likely.
Not really.
Probably not.
That's probably not such a good idea.

1 **Listening for *Yes* and *No* Expressions** Listen to the following conversations and note the various ways in which the speakers say *yes* and *no*. Fill in the blanks for each conversation. Note that only a line or two of each conversation is given as a cue before each blank. When you are finished, compare your answers in small groups.

Conversation 1

Ted and Paul are discussing their plans for the weekend.

Ted: ... You want to go with us?

Paul: _____

_____

Ted: ... Take it and you'll be ready to go with us.

Paul: _____

_____

Ted: ... I know lots of people who've done it.

Paul: _____

_____

Ted: ... The course is only 20 bucks.

Paul: That's not too bad.

_____

_____

Ted: ... You have the money, don't you?

Paul: _____

_____

Conversation 2

Terry and Lynn are discussing vacation possibilities.

Terry: ... Wouldn't that be great? Let's go!

Lynn: _____

_____

Terry: ... Think how strong and brave you'll feel at the end.

Lynn: _____

_____

Terry: ... You'll be a better person for it.

Lynn: I won't climb a mountain! _____

_____

Lynn: ... Want to go out to dinner?

Terry: _____

_____

2 **Rating** *Yes* **and** *No* **Expressions** Listen to the conversations again. This time write down as many of the expressions used for saying *yes*, *no*, and *maybe* as you can in the spaces provided under the following five categories.

Stronger *Yes*	Weaker *Yes*	*Maybe*
Stronger *No*	Weaker *No*	

3 **Using** *Yes* **and** *No* **Expressions** In the lecture, there are four statements from Marvin Zuckerman's Sensation Seeking Survey. Listen to this part of the lecture again. When you hear one of these statements, write it down. Then write the expression (from the list on page 32) that best indicates how strongly you agree or disagree with the statement. Discuss your answers with your classmates.

▲ A young woman enjoying the thrill of rock climbing

1. **Statement:** _____

   Your response: _____

   _____

2. **Statement:** _____

   Your response: _____

   _____

3. **Statement:** _____

   Your response: _____

   _____

4. **Statement:** _____

   Your response: _____

   _____

Talk It Over

4 Answering Survey Questions Do you like to take risks and try new things? Or are you more cautious and not particularly interested in new adventures? Working with a partner, take turns giving and taking the Risk-Taker Test on page 36 to find out. Follow these directions to see how you "measure up" on the Risk-Taker Ruler on page 37.

1. The test giver reads each item to the test taker.
2. The test taker responds to each item, using expressions from page 32.
3. The test giver puts a check in the appropriate column for each answer.
4. When you both have completed the test, look in the Appendix on page 250 for scoring instructions.
5. Add up your scores and see how you each "measure up" on the Risk-Taker Ruler on page 37.
6. Share your ratings with the class—if you dare!

For further practice, make up a few of your own risk-taker test questions to ask each other. Answer the questions using the expressions that best represent your immediate reactions to the questions. Then share your questions and answers with your classmates. Begin your questions with the following or similar phrases:

- Would you ever...?
- How would you like to...?
- How about...?

Risk-Taker Test					
Question	**Response**				
Would you ever...	**Strong yes**	**Weak yes**	**Maybe**	**Weak no**	**Strong no**
1. try a new haircut that is popular but unusual?					
2. try a very unusual food with a familiar name (for example, chocolate-covered ants)?					
3. try a very unusual food with an unfamiliar name?					
4. explore a recently discovered island?					
5. go alone to see a band at a club?					
6. play in a band that goes on tour to another country?					
7. volunteer to be the first passenger in a newly designed two-seater airplane?					
8. try skysurfing?					
9. try to climb a 15,000-foot mountain?					
10. try motocross mountain biking?					
11. parachute from a plane onto a beautiful, sweet-smelling meadow?					
12. parachute from a plane onto the top of a skyscraper?					
13. try skydiving stunts?					
14. sail across the Pacific Ocean from San Francisco to Japan in a boat without a motor?					
15. dive off a 40-foot cliff in Hawaii into the cool blue water below?					
16. go out on a blind date?					
17. go to a small party where you know only two of the seven people there?					
18. go to a party of 60 people where you know only the host?					
19. drive a race car at 150 miles per hour?					
20. volunteer to take part in an experiment to test the effects of a new drug on humans?					
21. go to a country where you could not read, write, or speak the language at all and where you did not know anyone?					
22. cross the street against a red light?					
23. eat a dessert for breakfast?					
24. take part in a traditional cultural dance while visiting another country?					
25. volunteer to make a speech in front of a large group of people?					

Risk-Taker Ruler

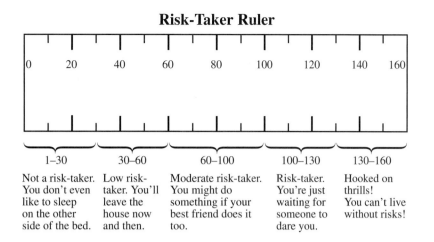

1–30	30–60	60–100	100–130	130–160
Not a risk-taker. You don't even like to sleep on the other side of the bed.	Low risk-taker. You'll leave the house now and then.	Moderate risk-taker. You might do something if your best friend does it too.	Risk-taker. You're just waiting for someone to dare you.	Hooked on thrills! You can't live without risks!

FOCUS

TOEFL® iBT

Basic-Comprehension Questions about Specific Details

In the Focus on Testing section in Chapter 1, you practiced taking notes on the main ideas and most important details for tests such as the TOEFL® iBT. On other tests, such as those that instructors write for their own courses, you might be asked questions about very specific and somewhat less important details in addition to the main ideas and most important details. For both the TOEFL® iBT and teacher-made tests, it is always best to take notes to help you remember main ideas and details and to pay special attention to negative words such as *no*, *not*, and *never* when examples are given so that you understand the exact nature of the example.

1 **Taking Notes to Answer Basic-Comprehension Questions about Specific Details** Listen to the sports news feature about extreme sports. Close your books and take notes about main ideas and specific details as you listen, paying particular attention to any negatives you hear. After the speaker finishes talking, you will hear a series of questions. Open your books and fill in the bubble of the best answer to each question.

1. In what year were the first X Games held?

- (A) 1919
- (B) 1990
- (C) 1995
- (D) 1999

2. What do all extreme sports have in common?

   Ⓐ dangerous stunts executed at high speed

   Ⓑ technological advances

   Ⓒ an element of danger

   Ⓓ heavy equipment

3. Skateboarding is a prime example of what?

   Ⓐ a group activity

   Ⓑ a child's recreational sport

   Ⓒ a dangerous game

   Ⓓ an extreme sport that grew out of a recreational activity

4. Why are some extreme sports called "outlaw sports"?

   Ⓐ because they are illegal in some places

   Ⓑ because only daredevils participate in them

   Ⓒ because they are done outside

   Ⓓ because they are very dangerous

5. Why do the Pentecost Islanders leap from towers?

   Ⓐ to test the strength of their ankles

   Ⓑ to test the strength of the vines

   Ⓒ to show courage and ensure a good crop of yams

   Ⓓ to be daredevils and thrill seekers

6. What kind of a sport is bungee jumping?

   Ⓐ a popular sport among all young people in California

   Ⓑ a very dangerous sport invented in France

   Ⓒ a sport for young daredevils and thrill seekers

   Ⓓ a sport that requires a lot of special training

7. What do bungee jumpers do?

   Ⓐ jump feet-first from high places

   Ⓑ jump from bridges, cranes, and balloons

   Ⓒ jump into the water below

   Ⓓ jump up into the sky

8. What equipment must bungee jumpers use?

   Ⓐ hot air balloons at great heights

   Ⓑ parachutes up in the air

   Ⓒ special suits on their bodies

   Ⓓ cords like giant rubber bands

9. In the speaker's opinion, what draws people to bungee jumping?

   (A) the special skill involved

   (B) the discipline of the special training

   (C) the fact that anyone can try this dangerous sport

   (D) the physical strength that is needed

Self-Assessment Log

Check (✓) the words in this chapter you have acquired and can use in your daily life.

Nouns	Verbs	Adjective
▦ daredevil	▦ motivate	▦ irresistible
▦ hullabaloo	▦ pull off	
▦ seeker	▦ take up	
▦ stunt		

Check (✓) your level of accomplishment for the skills introduced in this chapter. How comfortable do you feel using these skills?

	Very comfortable	Somewhat comfortable	Not at all comfortable
Noting specific details using formal outlines, diagrams, and visual cues	☐	☐	☐
Using your detailed notes to prepare for tests	☐	☐	☐
Speaking from a formal outline	☐	☐	☐
Using expressions such as *Absolutely!* and *OK, if you really want me to* to say *yes*	☐	☐	☐
Using expressions such as *Never in a million years!* and *Not especially* to say *no*	☐	☐	☐

Think about the topics and activities in this chapter and complete the statements.

In this chapter, I learned something new about _____

_____

_____

I especially liked (topic or activity) _____

_____

_____

I would like to know more about _____

_____

_____

Gender and Relationships

> "We've begun to raise daughters more like sons… but few have the courage to raise our sons more like our daughters."

Gloria Steinem
Author, lecturer, journalist, activist

Lecture I Want a Wife

Learning Strategy Using Abbreviations

Language Function Extending Congratulations and Condolences

Connecting to the Topic

1. What does the quote by Gloria Steinem mean to you? Do you agree with it? Why or why not?

2. What might be some of the consequences of having, as Steinem says, "the courage to raise our sons more like our daughters"?

3. Do you think that men's and women's roles are changing in your culture? If so, how? If not, why not?

Did You Know?

- In the U.S., about 57 percent of bachelors degrees, 60 percent of masters degrees, and 52 percent of doctoral degrees are currently earned by women.

- In the majority of U.S. urban areas, single, childless women in their 20s now earn from 10–20 percent more than their male peers. However, women overall (all ages and geographical areas) still lag behind and generally earn 20 percent less than their male peers for the same or similar work.

- In the U.S., less than 1 in 5 married-couple families are supported by the husband alone. Within the large majority of dual-earner couples (or double-income families), women contributed an average of 44 percent of the family income in 2008—up from 39 percent in 1997. At this rate, it is expected that women will be contributing more than 50 percent of the average family income by 2015.

1 **What Do You Think?** In pairs, discuss the following questions.

1. What do you think is the most important consequence of the education of women in general? In particular, what are the consequences of the high percentage of advanced degrees awarded to women?

2. Why do you think women are generally paid less than their male peers for the same work? What might be some of the reasons that this does not seem to be true for single women in their 20s?

3. Do you think that the increasing earning power of women is changing society in any way? How?

4. If you are a male, how would you feel if your spouse earned more than you? If you are a female, how would you feel if your spouse earned less than you?

Sharing Your Experience

2 **Recalling Your Family's Economic Arrangement** In small groups, discuss the following questions.

1. Did you grow up in a one- or two-parent family? Or perhaps in an extended family?

2. What did your parent(s) or other caregivers do for a living?

3. Who left the home to go to work each day? Who stayed home?

4. What were your parent(s)' duties at home?

5. What changes in responsibilities (if any) do you remember occurring as you grew up? What things might have influenced these changes?

Vocabulary Preview

3 **Vocabulary in Context** The following words are some of the key terms used in the lecture. Use the correct forms of the words to complete the sentences in the letter from Jake to Marti on page 44.

Words	Definitions
envious	*jealous*
highlights	*the most important or best parts*
hold to a standard	*to expect to follow generally accepted rules*
in its entirety	*all of it*
launch into	*to get into; to get started on*
meat	*the main part; core*
nurturing	*encouraging*
parody	*a satirical or comic version*
perspective	*a point of view*
rebuttal	*an opposing argument*
refresh	*to recharge or renew*
run into	*to meet by chance*
sympathetic	*kind and concerned*

To: martiwifey@mailbox.com

From: jakehubby@moremail.com

Date: Thursday, October 16

Dear Marti,

    I'm really glad that this business trip is almost over. I miss you and the kids and must admit I'm a little _____ of the time that you get to spend with them when I'm away. Before you _____ your usual complaints about how little I appreciate what you do for the kids, let me assure you that I know that it's hard work, too, and not all fun and games. You are an incredibly _____ and _____ mother and I think everyone should be _____ that you set.

    I know that we've argued about the fact that you essentially do two full-time jobs, while I only do one, but I want to tell you that something happened on this trip that opened my eyes a little and changed my _____. I _____ your friend Judy yesterday at the conference and she invited me to go see a play in the evening with her boyfriend, Jimmy. It was a really funny play, a _____ of the common arguments that couples have. I hope that sometime you can see it _____, but I'll share some of the _____ with you now. And after you have a chance to see it, we can really discuss the _____ of it.

    The men and women in the play were always bickering about whose lives are more difficult, who earns more money, who should be responsible for household duties, who needs to change, etc. I'm sure you get the idea. Each argument a person made was always countered with a hilarious _____. It really made me laugh.

    In addition to giving me another view of things, the play made me realize that we don't take the time for each other that we used to. When I get home, let's try to lighten up a little and simply let go of the same old arguments. Let's just hit the _____ button. What do you say?

Love,

Jake

P.S. Give the kids a hug from me.

Strategy

Taking Notes Using Abbreviations

The best way to accurately note a lecturer's ideas is to use the same words the lecturer uses as often as possible. However, writing down every word the lecturer says is almost impossible. Knowing when and how to abbreviate, or shorten, certain words will help you quickly and accurately take down the information. Later, when you are writing exams or papers, you can put the information into your own words.

Four Main Ways to Abbreviate

1. Leave out whole words, word endings, vowels, or other letters.

   Example Men's and women's roles in relationships are going through a metamorphosis.
   Male & female roles go thru metmorph.

2. Use only the first letter, or first two or three letters, of a word.

   Example M/F roles metmorph.

3. Use symbols to replace words or letters.

   Example ♂ + ♀ roles = metmorph.

4. Change word order.

   Example roles of M/F metmorph.

Cautions When Using Abbreviations

1. Be careful not to use the same abbreviation for two different things. For example, if the instructor is talking about *transitions* in life and *transmission* of knowledge, you shouldn't use *trans.* as the abbreviation for both words. Similarly, you should not use *ord.* as the abbreviation for both the words *ordinary* and *order.*

2. Make sure that the symbols you use are specific enough to avoid confusion. For example, if an anthropology lecturer is discussing particular differences between what boys and men in a particular tribe are allowed to do, it would be confusing to use the symbol ♂ for both *men* and *boys.*

3. Don't forget what your abbreviations mean, otherwise you will not be able to decode your notes. To avoid this problem, you can keep a key to your abbreviations at the top of your notes. For example:

   M = male   max. = maximum
   m. = married   min. = minimum
   man. = manage   mx. = mix

Commonly Used Abbreviations

a.	answer		**g.**	gram
alt.	altitude, alternative		**gal.**	gallon
Amer(s).	American(s)		**id.**	the same, identical (from Latin *idem*)
atm.	atmosphere, atmospheric			
avg.	average		**i.e.**	that is (from Latin *id est*)
ave.	avenue		**jr.**	junior
b.	born		**m.**	married
b.p.	boiling point		**mod.**	modern
bc.	because		**n.b.***	note well (from Latin *nota bene*)
c.	about (from Latin *circa*)		**no(s).**	number(s)
cf.	compare (from Latin *confer*)		**pd.**	paid
co.	company		**pop.**	population
ct.	count		**re.**	regarding, concerning
cu.	cubic		**rel.**	religion
d.	deceased, died		**ret.**	retired, returned
dept.	department		**riv.**	river
doz.	dozen		**s.**	son
Dr.	doctor		**sc.**	science
ea.	each		**sr.**	senior
e.g.	for example (from Latin *exempli gratia*)		**sq.**	square
			st.	street
ff.	following pages		**stat.**	statistics
fr.	from		**terr.**	territory
ft.	feet		**yr.**	year

*n.b. is a good abbreviation to use as a note to yourself, indicating something important

Abbreviations for Homework Assignments

assgn.	assignment		**od. #s**	odd numbers
ch.	chapter		**p.**	page
ev. #s	even numbers		**pp.**	pages
hw.	homework		**q.**	question(s)
l.	learn		**st.**	study

Mathematical and Other Symbols

1	one		**@**	at		→	means, causes
2	two		**b/4**	before		←	is caused by
1st	first		**=**	equal to		–	minus
2nd	second		**≠**	not equal to		**$**	money
3rd	third		**∫**	identical to		**¢**	cents
4th	fourth		**∴**	hence, therefore		**?**	question
~	approximately		**∪**	intersection		**%**	percent
&	and		**>**	more than		↑	increase
+	plus, and, over		**<**	less than		↓	decrease

1 **Practicing Writing and Decoding Abbreviations** In the chart below are some examples of things a professor or instructor might say and some ways to abbreviate these things in your notes. Fill in the chart by completing the third alternative abbreviation (in the right-hand column) for what the speaker said in items 1 and 2 and by decoding the abbreviations for what the speaker might have said in items 3–5 (in the left-hand column).

If the Instructor Says	You Might Write
1. You will be expected to learn all about the key ways that gender roles are changing in relationships, perhaps over fifty, by the end of the term.	know 50 ways roles are changing by end of term Or know > 50 changes in roles Or kn > 50 _____
2. Even though there are more househusbands than ever before, there are still a much greater number of females than males who are the primary child raisers and housekeepers in U.S. families.	United States: females > males as housewives/husbands Or U. S.: F > M as prim. parent and housekeep. Or <# ♂ than _____
3. Men and women are often _____ _____ _____ _____.	M & W in compet. same jbs.
4. _____ _____ _____ _____.	>W wkg. + child. +schl. than prev.
5. _____ _____ _____ _____.	>M hm. w/ no jb. than prev.

2 Discussing Abbreviations In small groups, share any note-taking abbreviations and symbols that you use.

- Write down any that are not in the boxes. Share them with the rest of the class.
- Ask your instructor what symbols and abbreviations he or she uses most often. Add these to your list.

_____

_____

_____

_____

Listen

3 Taking Notes Using Abbreviations Listen to the lecture and take notes. Abbreviate whatever you can. At the pause, stop the recording and discuss your answers to the lecturer's questions with a partner. Then continue listening to the rest of the lecture and taking notes.

_____

_____

_____

_____

_____

_____

_____

_____

_____

_____

_____

4 Filling in the Gaps in Your Notes In small groups, compare your notes from the lecture.

- If you see any abbreviations your classmates used that you think would be useful to the rest of the class, put them on the board.
- Use these new abbreviations as you listen to the lecture and take notes a second time in your notebooks.

5 **Using Notes with Abbreviations to Answer Test Questions** Share your notes from the lecture with a partner and together answer the following questions that could appear on a test about this lecture. When you are finished, compare your answers with the rest of the class.

1. *Metamorphosis* means: _____

   _____

2. Who wrote the famous essay "I Want a Wife"? _____

   _____

3. When was this essay first published? _____

   _____

4. Where was the author working when she wrote the essay? _____

   _____

5. What stimulated her to write the essay? _____

   _____

6. Give at least five reasons why the author says she would like to have a wife (presumably, like the one her husband has):

   a. _____

   _____

   b. _____

   _____

   c. _____

   _____

   d. _____

   _____

   e. _____

   _____

7. What is a parody? _____

   _____

8. Give at least five reasons why the author of "I Want a Husband" says he wants a husband (presumably, like the one his wife has):

   a. _____

   _____

   b. _____

   _____

   c. _____

   _____

   d. _____

   _____

   e. _____

   _____

9. Is the essay "I Want a Husband" a perfect parody (or mirror image) of "I Want a Wife"? Why or why not? _____

   _____

   _____

   _____

10. In what ways do you think the information in the lecture connects with the data presented in the *Did You Know?* box on page 42? _____

    _____

    _____

    _____

Talk It Over

6 **Describing the "Perfect" Wife and the "Perfect" Husband** Discuss the following questions in small groups consisting of all males or all females. Then share your responses with the rest of the class by posting lists of your answers on the wall. Then the men can see what the women think and the women can see what the men think are the qualities of the "perfect" wife and the "perfect" husband. Walk around and read all of the lists. Then discuss any differences between the lists made by the female groups and the lists made by the male groups.

1. What do you think are the most important qualities of the "perfect" wife?

2. What do you think are the most important qualities of the "perfect" husband?

7 **Decoding Symbols and Abbreviations** We encounter abbreviations and symbols in a variety of situations every day. In small groups, decide what these abbreviations stand for and then share your group's ideas with the rest of the class.

1. ASAP (on a business memo) _____

2. FYI (on a business memo) _____

3. BTW (on a note or memo) _____

4. ANML DOC (on a license plate) _____

5. SOS _____

6. Tom clld @ 7; cll bk tmorow _____

7. bday prty _____

8. H_2O _____

9. 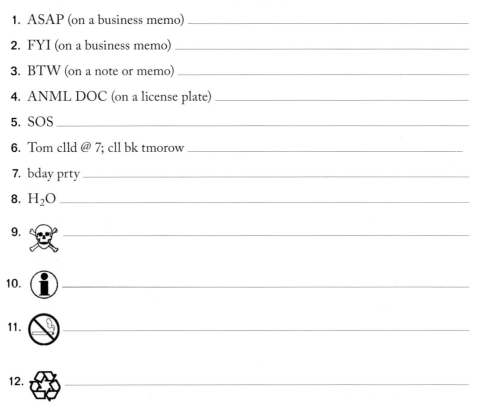 _____

10. _____

11. _____

12. _____

8 **Guessing About "Found" Symbols** Look for examples of symbols and abbreviations in your daily life or online. (You'll probably need to spend a couple of days looking.) Bring 8–10 of them to class, write them on the board, and have your classmates guess where you found them and what they mean.

9 **Creating Messages Using Abbreviations** In small groups, create some abbreviated messages like those in the pictures.

- Write at least three personal messages for car license plates. Use only the number of letters allowed in your state or area.
- Create three more messages that you could use on a coffee mug or T-shirt.
- When you are finished, write each of them in large letters on a piece of paper or on the board and have your classmates guess their meanings.

▲ People love to put abbreviated messages on everything from personalized car license plates to coffee mugs and designer T-shirts.

Strategy

Offering Congratulations and Condolences

Many events in families are happy occasions such as birthdays, graduations, marriages, and anniversaries. At these times we offer *congratulations*. Family members also congratulate each other on a "job well done," such as completing a project or doing well in school or at sports. In contrast, when someone suffers a serious loss, such as the destruction of a home due to a natural disaster or the death of a parent, spouse, child, or close friend, we offer *condolences* for the loss.

Expressions for Extending Congratulations

When you wish to congratulate someone, you can say "Congratulations" and add one of the following phrases expressing good wishes appropriate to the particular occasion. Of course, when you extend congratulations, you must use the appropriate tone of voice as well as the right words. For example, if your tone of voice is not genuinely happy or expresses indifference, your words of congratulations will never convince listeners that you are truly happy for them.

For something new, such as a baby, a job, a car, an award, a raise, an engagement or for something "well done"

I'm so happy for you!
I'm so pleased for you!
I'm so proud of you!
I'm thrilled for you!
It couldn't have happened to a nicer person! (used for something like a special award or promotion)
That's wonderful / terrific / great (news)!
You deserve it! (used for something like getting a new job, a new car, or a raise)

For birthdays

Enjoy another great year!
Have a great day!
May you have a hundred more.
May you have many, (many) more.

For weddings

(I wish you) All the best in the years to come.
All the best to you both.
May you have a long and prosperous life together.

For graduation

I know you've got a great future ahead of you.
I'm sure you'll have great success in the years to come.

Expressions for Extending Condolences

On occasions of loss and grief, you should choose the most appropriate and sensitive words to express your feelings and offer comfort.

Use one of these expressions

All my sympathy to you in this
    trying time.

I can't tell you how sorry I am.

I'm so (terribly, extremely) sorry.

My condolences to you
    (and your family).

My thoughts are with you
    (and your family).

Followed by one of these (optional)

Can I help out in any way?

If there's anything I can do to help,
    please don't hesitate to ask.

Is there anything I can do?

Let me know if there's anything you need.

*If you don't feel comfortable with any of the expressions of condolence listed above, just be honest and put it this way:

    I'm sorry. I just don't know what to say.

      or

    I can't express how sorry I am.

 1 Listening for Expressions of Congratulations Listen to the following conversation and write down all the expressions of congratulations you hear. Compare answers with your classmates.

_____

_____

_____

_____

 2 Listening for Expressions of Condolences Listen to the following conversation and write down all the expressions of condolences you hear. Compare answers with your classmates.

_____

_____

_____

_____

3 **Listening for Sincere and Insincere Congratulations** Listen to the following short conversations. In some conversations, the second speaker is sincere (his or her tone of voice is enthusiastic), and in others, he or she is indifferent (not enthusiastic) or insincere.

- Circle the word that best describes the *second* speaker.
- When you are finished, compare your answers in small groups.

Conversation 1	**Conversation 4**
sincere — insincere	sincere — insincere
Conversation 2	**Conversation 5**
sincere — insincere	sincere — insincere
Conversation 3	**Conversation 6**
sincere — insincere	sincere — insincere

Talk It Over

4 **Sharing Cultural Expressions** In small groups, think of expressions of congratulations or condolences in languages other than English for the following occasions. Then translate these expressions into English and share them with the class. Discuss any similarities or differences with their English equivalents.

1. An engagement: _____

   _____

2. A wedding (to the newly married couple): _____

   _____

3. A pregnancy: _____

   _____

4. A graduation: _____

   _____

◀ What congratulations could you offer these young men and women?

5. The birth of a baby: _____

_____

6. A job promotion: _____

_____

7. A new purchase (a car or a house): _____

_____

8. A retirement party: _____

_____

9. A job loss: _____

_____

10. The death of a friend: _____

_____

11. The death of a relative: _____

_____

12. A serious accident: _____

_____

⑤ **Writing and Role-Playing Dialogues** Work with a partner to write dialogues for a few of the following situations requiring congratulations and condolences. In each situation, you must decide what might be said *before* and what might be said *after* the offered congratulations and condolences. Rehearse and present your dialogues to the class. If time permits, change partners and write and present another dialogue or two to the class.

1. A: _____

    B: Congratulations! I'm so happy for you. When do you expect the new arrival?

    A: _____

2. A: _____

    B: I'm so sorry. How did it happen?

    A: _____

3. A: _____

    B: I'm so sorry. You must feel very sad. Is there anything I can do?

    A: _____

▲ Congratulations! I'm so happy for you!

4. **A:** _____

   B: Congratulations! Who's the lucky person?

   A: _____

5. **A:** _____

   B: Congratulations! And what are your future plans?

   A: _____

6. **A:** _____

   B: Congratulations! What's his/her name?

   A: _____

7. **A:** _____

   B: I can't tell you how sorry I am. How's your mother doing?

   A: _____

8. **A:** _____

   B: Congratulations! I'm so pleased for you! When do you start?

   A: _____

9. **A:** _____

   B: Congratulations! That's great news! What time was she born?

   A: _____

10. **A:** _____

    B: I'm sorry. I just don't know what to say. Please call me if you need anything.

    A: _____

11. **A:** _____

    B: Oh, that's terrible. I'm so sorry. Do you have any other possibilities?

    A: _____

TOEFL® iBT

Questions About Pragmatic Understanding

Standardized tests such as the TOEFL® iBT test include many "pragmatic-understanding" questions. These items go beyond basic facts and ask about things such as a speaker's attitude or intentions, how sure the speaker is of certain information, and why a speaker says a particular thing. To answer these questions correctly, you have to consider not just what the speaker says but how he or she says it. To do this, you must listen for cues, such as tone of voice, hesitations, and word stress.

Some pragmatic-understanding questions ask you to listen again to part of the lecture or conversation before you answer. The repeated portion of the listening passage focuses on an important word or phrase and gives you some context from the passage. You are expected to judge the meaning or purpose of the word or phrase in that context. Here is an example of this kind of question.

Sample Question:

Listen again to part of the conversation:

Why does the man say, "Whatever"?

1 **Pragmatic Understanding: Conversation** Listen to the conversation about men's and women's roles. Close your books as you listen, and take notes. After the conversation, you will hear a series of questions. Open your books and fill in the bubble of the best answer to each question.

1. Listen again to part of the conversation.

   Why does the woman ask, "How about you?"

   A to find out how he is

   B to find out where he is

   C to find out what he prefers

   D to find out what he thinks

2. How do you think the man feels about scrubbing the toilet?

   A that it might be dangerous

   B that it might be fun

   C that it is not a suitable task for him

   D that he can see himself doing it

3. Which of the following best states the woman's attitude toward men sharing household duties with women?

   (A) She thinks that women should not complain about doing all the housework.

   (B) She thinks that men should complain when things are not done right.

   (C) She thinks that men should share the household duties with women.

   (D) She thinks that Joe doesn't know how to clean toilets.

4. Why does the woman ask the man when he was born?

   (A) to emphasize how old-fashioned she thinks the man is

   (B) to find out if he was born in the Dark Ages

   (C) to find out how old the man is

   (D) to begin a conversation about the history of women's rights

5. Listen again to part of the conversation.

   Which of the following best expresses the man's attitude toward the woman?

   (A) He doesn't like her.

   (B) He likes her a lot.

   (C) He doesn't understand her point of view.

   (D) He is worried that she will get his job.

6. Why does the man talk about the way he was brought up?

   (A) to let the woman know that he comes from an educated family

   (B) to let the woman know that he thinks even women who are doctors should do all of the household chores

   (C) to explain to the woman that his mother was happy doing all the chores

   (D) to explain that he was brought up to think about things in a particular way, but that he is beginning to see things differently

Self-Assessment Log

Check (✓) the words in this chapter you have acquired and can use in your daily life.

Nouns	Verbs	Adjectives	Expression
▦ highlights	▦ hold to a standard	▦ envious	▦ in its entirety
▦ meat	▦ launch into	▦ nurturing	
▦ parody	▦ refresh	▦ sympathetic	
▦ perspective	▦ run into		
▦ rebuttal			

Check (✓) your level of accomplishment for the skills introduced in this chapter. How comfortable do you feel using these skills in real situations?

	Very comfortable	Somewhat comfortable	Not at all comfortable
Taking notes using abbreviations and symbols	☐	☐	☐
Distinguishing between sincere and insincere congratulations and condolences	☐	☐	☐
Understanding expressions such as *It couldn't have happened to a better person* and *All the best in the years to come* when used to express congratulations	☐	☐	☐
Understanding expressions such as *My thoughts are with you* when used to express condolences	☐	☐	☐
Using expressions such as *It couldn't have happened to a better person* and *All the best in the years to come* to express congratulations	☐	☐	☐
Using expressions such as *My thoughts are with you* and *If there's anything I can do to help, please don't hesitate to ask* to express condolences	☐	☐	☐

Think about the topics and activities in this chapter and complete the statements.

In this chapter, I learned something new about _____

_____

_____

I especially liked (topic or activity) _____

_____

_____

I would like to know more about _____

_____

_____

4 Aesthetics and Beauty

"I go to a restaurant for the food,
not the visual stimulation, but
I sure like a table with a view if
I can get it... If the aesthetics
are just frosting on the cake...
well, I prefer my cake with
frosting."

Greg Barnett
Director of Operations, College of Imaging
Arts and Sciences at Rochester Institute
of Technology

Lecture Looking Good Matters—Aesthetics as a Pillar
of Industrial Design

Learning Strategy Using Reference to Create Cohesion

Language Function Admitting a Lack of Knowledge

Connecting to the Topic

1. What does the quote on the opposite page mean to you? Share
some examples from your own life.

2. How might it relate to the work of the industrial designers who
designed the look, shape, and feel of the train in the photo?

Did You Know?

- Today we are accustomed to talking about beautiful machines—from automobiles to computers—but it was not until 150 years ago that we began to develop an aesthetic concern for the need of beauty in industrial design.

- Many industrial designers are concerned not only with the function of a product, but also with the form, how it appears to the eye and feels to the touch. Others, however, think that beauty is, in many cases, beside the point. They suggest that a thirsty man rushes to drink at the spring and does not consider its appearance; it's only after he is no longer thirsty that he can step back and say, "Hey, that's a lovely spring, isn't it?"

- The International Council of Societies of Industrial Design (ICSID) facilitates cooperation and interaction among more than 150 Member Societies in over 50 countries. Its first international conference took place in 1957.

1 **What Do You Think?** Discuss the following questions in pairs.

1. What do you think is something that was considered beautiful in another era but is considered ugly now? Conversely, can you think of something that was considered ugly in the past but is seen as beautiful today?

2. Why do you think standards of beauty change from one generation to the next?

3. What is it about some machines that almost makes us whistle out loud at their beauty?

4. What do you think is meant by "A thirsty man rushes to drink at the spring and does not consider its appearance"? Do you agree with this statement? Why or why not?

5. Why do you think that the International Council of Societies of Industrial Design might be concerned with notions of beauty and aesthetics?

2 **Discussing Elements of Aesthetics** Share your answers to the following questions in small groups.

1. Do you think cultural values or style can influence our aesthetic choices, choices we make about what is pleasing to us? Share some examples from your own experience.

2. Think of something that you have chosen to buy and use (other than clothing) mainly because you like the way it looks or feels. Are you satisfied with the way this product works? If you could buy a similar product that worked better, but didn't look or feel as good to you, would you do so? Why or why not?

3. Consider the following list of adjectives. Rank them in order of importance to you when you are purchasing a product. Explain why you ranked the words in this particular order.

_____ bold; sassy	_____ seductive; sexy
_____ colorful	_____ sleek; streamlined
_____ contemporary; modern	_____ solid; sturdy
_____ cutting-edge	_____ soothing
_____ delicate	_____ sophisticated
_____ elegant	_____ sporty
_____ exciting; stimulating	_____ timeless; classic
_____ feminine	_____ trendy
_____ masculine	_____ unique
_____ natural; earthy	_____ well-crafted; well-made

▲ This couple is shopping for a sofa that is streamlined, yet also elegant and well-crafted.

3 Determining Meaning from Context The following words are used in the conference presentation in this chapter. Read the definitions and complete the sentences that follow with the correct forms of the words.

Words	Definitions
by and large	*for the most part; generally*
catch your eye	*to get/capture your attention*
consumer	*a user or buyer of a product*
create a stir	*to create a controversy or create excitement*
crux	*the main point or factor of an issue*
eye opener	*a surprising fact that leads to a new realization*
hammer a point home	*to strongly emphasize a point*
illustrious	*famous for positive qualities*
infamous	*famous for negative reasons; ill-famed*
insinuate	*to suggest indirectly; to imply*
ploy	*a trick*
reside (in)	*to live or exist in*
shamelessly	*without embarrassment or shame*
split second	*an instant; a tiny fraction of a second*
subliminal	*subconscious; below the level of awareness*
widget	*a nickname used for any small invention or product*

1. The _____ of the matter is whether or not the consumer thinks the product is beautiful.

2. Do you mean to _____ that some advertising on TV contains _____ messages? That would be a terrible _____, don't you think?

3. It doesn't matter how useful the _____ is that your factory produces. If you want it to sell, it still has to be beautiful.

4. The speaker is well-known, but controversial; he is regarded as _____ in some circles and _____ in others.

5. _____, it only takes a _____ for a beautiful product to _____.

6. Sometimes, the designer Brooks Stevens _____ promoted his ideas by _____ until everyone was convinced of his point of view.

7. Brooks Stevens _____ in the field of industrial design with his notions of the relationship of beauty and marketing.

8. This may be an _____ for you, but I do not think that product beauty _____ only in the eye of the _____.

Strategy

Using Reference to Create Cohesion

For a paragraph to make sense, the individual sentences must fit together. Likewise, for a series of paragraphs to make sense, they must also be connected in a logical manner. When sentences or paragraphs are well connected, we say that they *cohere*, or that they are *cohesive*. This literally means that they stick together.

co = together   here = to stick

One of the ways to maintain cohesion in both spoken and written language is called *reference*. Reference is the use of nonspecific words to refer back to a specific noun or idea which is called the *referent*.

Using Personal Pronouns to Create Referential Cohesion

Consider the following sentences:

1. In 1954, Brooks Stevens, one of the founders of the American Society for Industrial Design, introduced a controversial idea into the field of industrial design.
2. Brooks Stevens introduced the term *planned obsolescence* to describe the mission of industrial designers.

The meanings of these sentences are *independent* of each other. They seem to be related to the same topic, but they are not clearly connected. The meaning of one sentence does not depend on the meaning of the other.

To make more connection or cohesion between sentences, you can use personal pronouns to create a *dependent* relationship between them. Personal pronouns can connect sentences in such a way that together they have meaning, but alone, one of them is ambiguous. For example:

3. In 1954, Brooks Stevens introduced the term *planned obsolescence* to describe the mission of industrial designers.
4. He was not fully prepared for the controversy that followed.

Sentence 3 establishes that we are talking about a man named Brooks Stevens. In Sentence 4, the word *he* refers to Brooks Stevens, but this would not be clear without Sentence 3. The meaning of Sentence 4 is dependent on Sentence 3, and this dependence, or referential relationship, makes them more clearly connected or cohesive. Using the pronoun *he* in Sentence 4 also helps to avoid repetition or redundancy.

Using the Pronoun *It* to Refer to a Comprehensive Idea or Concept

In contrast to *he* and *she, it* is often used to refer to an entire idea or concept that is comprehensive and complex. For example:

5. In 1954, Brooks Stevens impulsively introduced the term *planned obsolescence* to describe the mission of the industrial designer to instill in a product buyer the desire to own something a little newer, a little better, a little more beautiful, and to own it sooner than is truly necessary—thus, angering many in the field by reducing industrial design to little more than a marketing ploy.

6. It may or may not have been a smart move on his part.

In Sentence 6, *it* refers to the actions and ideas of Brooks Stevens described by all of Sentence 5.

Personal Pronouns: A Review

Subject pronouns	Object pronouns	Possessive pronouns	Possessive adjectives
I	me	mine	my
you	you	yours	your
we	us	ours	our
he	him	his	his
she	her	hers	her
they	them	theirs	their
it	it	its (rarely used)	its

Using Demonstrative Pronouns to Create Referential Cohesion

Similar to personal pronouns, the demonstrative pronouns *this, that, these*, and *those* can be used referentially to create cohesion between sentences. Consider the following sentences where *that* and *it* are used effectively in the second sentence to refer back to the first sentence:

7. Brooks Stevens created an uproar in the field of industrial design when he introduced the notion of *planned obsolescence*; enemies were instantly created who challenged his ideas, supporters who never quite understood what he meant constantly misinterpreted him, and the media mobbed him wherever he went.

8. That was the way it went some days in the life of someone as outspoken as Brooks Stevens.

Notice that the word *that* in Sentence 8 refers to a particular circumstance described and feeling conveyed by Sentence 7. However, the word *it* in Sentence 8 refers to daily life in general.

Sometimes a demonstrative pronoun can be used *before* rather than after its referent. When a speaker or writer does this, it is usually to grab the attention of the listener or reader by creating expectation, curiosity, or suspense. Consider the following example where the demonstrative pronoun in the first sentence refers to an idea in the second sentence:

9. This was going to be difficult.
10. Stevens never enjoyed telling a friend that he was wrong, but this was a question and answer session, after all.

In this case, the word *this* in Sentence 9 does not refer back to something already mentioned. Instead, *this* refers ahead to "telling a friend that he was wrong," which is mentioned in Sentence 10.

Strategy

Avoiding Ambiguity and Confusion When Using Reference Words

Instead of bringing clarity and cohesion to your speaking and writing, reference words, if not used properly, can merely bring ambiguity and confusion. Consider the following sentence:

11. The friend smiled at Stevens as he raised his hand.

Whose hand is it? In the context of Sentences 9 and 10 above, most likely it is the friend who raised his hand in order to ask a question. However, what if Sentence 9 had been this?:

12. This was going to be difficult; Stevens, weary from so many misguided questions, raised his hand to signal that he was through.

In that case, Sentence 11 would be confusing and ambiguous because we could not be certain whose hand is being referred to—Stevens' or his friend's.

Ways to Avoid Ambiguous or Confusing References

When speaking or writing:

- Do not overuse reference words.
- Restate exactly who or what you are talking about periodically.

When listening or reading:

- For all reference words, ask yourself: Who? Whose? What? When? Where? Immediately try to connect the reference word with its referent.
- If you do become confused, stop the speaker at an appropriate time and ask for clarification, or put a question mark in the margin of your book or notes and ask for clarification from an instructor or friend later.

1 Considering the Topic Discuss the following questions in small groups.

1. Earlier in this chapter, you learned that industrial designers are the people who design the look, the shape, and the feel of products. How many products can you think of that you use or see every day where you notice the influence of an industrial designer? Make a list. Now think about what you've learned in this chapter about industrial design and try to extend the list by adding names of products where the influence of an industrial designer is not so obvious.

2. What is the main function of a bathroom or kitchen faucet? Why do you think there is such great variety in appearance for a product that has virtually only one function?

3. Why might a beautiful medical device be more effective than an ugly one?

Listen

2 Listening for the Gist and Most Important Points Listen to the lecture once all the way through to get the main topic and the gist of the main points. Take notes below.

Main Topic: What the lecture is mainly about

_____

_____

_____

Most Important Points:

_____

_____

_____

_____

_____

_____

_____

_____

_____

_____

3 Listening for Reference Words that Create Cohesion In the following exercise, you will see excerpts from the lecture that contain reference words. Listen to the lecture again and fill in the blanks in each of the items with the appropriate information. Note that:

- In items 1–5, the "clue" question has been provided, and you simply answer it.
- In items 6–18, you must write both the "clue" question and the answer.
- In items 1–10, the reference words are italicized.
- In items 11–18, you must first find the reference words before completing the rest of the items.

Example Good evening and thank you for inviting me speak to you…

Question: _____ *Speak to whom?* _____

Answer: _____ *to the audience* _____

1. Now some of you may think I'm exaggerating just a bit, but certainly all of *us*, being industrial designers, will agree that design is the single most important way a business connects with its customers.

   Question: All of whom?

   Answer: _____

2. *They* see *it* first, before they use *it*.

   Question: Who are *they*?

   Answer: _____

   Question: What is *it*?

   Answer: _____

3. And *he*, of course, coined that famous, or infamous, term "planned obsolescence"…

   Question: Who coined the term?

   Answer: _____

4. *He* created quite a stir when he first introduced *that controversial concept*…

   Question: Who created quite a stir?

   Answer: _____

   Question: What controversial concept?

   Answer: _____

5. OK, I can tell that most of you are with me, but just in case we still have any doubters out there… think about *this*.

   Question: Think about what?

   Answer: _____

▲ Why are there so many different designs for an essentially one-function device?

6. OK, now that makes a total of six designs in all, correct?

   Question: _____

   Answer: _____

7. *They* were all manner of shapes and sizes and finishes…

   Question: _____

   Answer: _____

8. Beneath *their* outward appearance…

   Question: _____

   Answer: _____

9. By and large, *they* all perform excellently, and will last for a good number of years.

   Question: _____

   Answer: _____

10. Anyone who has ever watched a nature program about monkeys or chimpanzees using branches as a device to grab or dig for food can see that *this* is not the case.

    Question: _____

    Answer: _____

11. And this one might very well be an eye opener for some of you.

    Question: _____

    Answer: _____

12. Now one would think that the only important features of a medical device are safety, durability, and whether or not it performs its intended function well…

    Question: _____

    Answer: _____

13. Now this is the interesting thing.

Question: _____

Answer: _____

14. My friend informs me that looking good matters in this area of industrial design as well as in any other.

Question: _____

Answer: _____

15. If the device has a high "wow" factor for the user, it will be used more often and more appropriately than if it doesn't.

Question: _____

Answer: _____

16. This is true for both patients and doctors.

Question: _____

Answer: _____

17. This is especially true for children.

Question: _____

Answer: _____

18. So… now we can get back to the crux of it.

Question: _____

Answer: _____

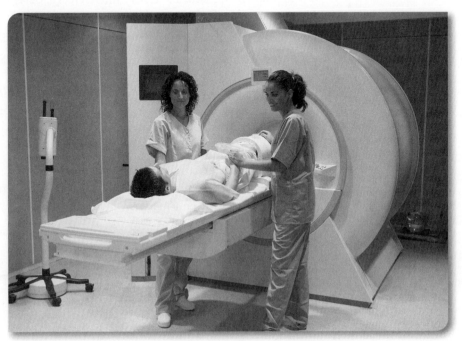

▲ Why is a beautiful medical device often more effective than an ugly one?

4 Discussing the Lecture In small groups, discuss the following questions that the speaker raises at the end of the lecture. As you discuss, listen for reference words. Ask for clarification of references as necessary. Share the highlights of your discussion with the rest of the class.

1. What makes a product more beautiful or more attractive to the consumer than another product?
2. Is the perceived beauty of a product merely what's "in" or trendy in a particular culture at a particular time? Or is the true beauty of a product something more permanent?
3. Does the beauty of a product reside in its genius or usefulness?
4. What makes us say a product has "timeless beauty"?
5. Is there a type of beauty in a product that could be considered universal?

Talk It Over

5 Understanding and Using Reference Words Find a short article or ad in a magazine or newspaper that deals with aesthetics or beauty and bring it to class. Skim quickly through your article to make sure it includes two or more reference words. In small groups, use the following steps to guide your discussion of these articles.

1. Take turns reading your articles aloud.
2. Whenever those who are listening hear a reference word, they should call out the appropriate questions to clarify the reference. Several people may call out similar questions at the same time.
3. Someone in the group who did not ask the question should answer it.
4. Continue in this way until you have read the whole article.

6 Identifying Reference Words Find on the Internet (or in a magazine or newspaper) an article related to an industrial designer. If possible, find something about an industrial designer from your native country. Try to pick out and circle:

- examples of reference words
- examples of ambiguous references
- examples of extended references in which the thing referred to is described in a whole sentence or paragraph, not just one word

Bring your written examples to class and discuss them with your classmates. Consider the following questions:

1. What did most of the reference words refer to? Things? People? Ideas?
2. Were the examples of extended reference hard to find? Why or why not?
3. How or why was a reference ambiguous?
4. How could the ambiguity have been avoided? What happened because of the ambiguity? Was there a misunderstanding?

Strategy

Admitting a Lack of Knowledge in Formal and Informal Situations

In the United States and Canada, a person's ability to admit a lack of knowledge is valued. In fact, students will often criticize an instructor who is unwilling to admit ignorance and will often praise an instructor who is willing to admit ignorance. The same is true for how students view each other. Therefore, it is important to know a variety of ways to admit a lack of knowledge.

Formal Ways to Admit a Lack of Knowledge

One of these:	Followed by one of these:
I'm afraid…	I can't remember.
I'm sorry, but…	I can't/couldn't tell you.
	I don't know.
	I don't remember.
	I forget.
	I have no idea.
	I'll have to get back to you on that.
	I just don't know.
	It's slipped my mind.
	I'm not sure.

Note: In addition to using the expressions above, if you add a reason for your lack of knowledge, you will seem even more polite. For example:

A: Can you tell me where the post office is?
B: No. I'm afraid I couldn't tell you. I'm new here myself.

Informal Ways to Admit a Lack of Knowledge

The following expressions are used frequently among friends, but may sound rude in other contexts. As with other expressions in English, if your tone reflects anger or irritation, these expressions will not sound polite, even with friends.

Beats me.	I have no idea.
(I) Can't/couldn't even begin…	I give up!
Don't ask me.	I sure don't know.
(I) Haven't (got) a clue.	It's beyond me.
(I) Haven't the foggiest (idea).	You('ve) got me!
How do/should I know?	

1 Listening for Formal and Informal Admissions of a Lack of Knowledge Listen to the following conversations in which one person admits a lack of knowledge. In some conversations, the second speaker is more formal, and in others, he or she is more informal.

- Circle the word that best describes the *second speaker*.
- When you are finished, compare your answers in small groups and discuss the conversations. Do you think that any of the second speakers sounded rude? Why?

Conversation 1

formal   informal

Conversation 2

formal   informal

Conversation 3

formal   informal

Conversation 4

formal   informal

Conversation 5

formal   informal

Talk It Over

2 Using Formal Expressions to Admit a Lack of Knowledge Listen to the lecture on industrial design again with a partner.

- As you listen, stop the recording frequently so that one partner can ask a question. It can be about anything that occurs to you as you listen to the lecture, but it should be a complex, difficult question to answer.
- The other partner should practice responding using a variety of formal expressions (found on page 73) to admit a lack of knowledge.
- When the lecture is over, change roles and do the activity again.

3 Using Informal Expressions to Admit a Lack of Knowledge In small groups, brainstorm a list of products that you use every day. You could also cut out photos of products from magazines to enhance your list.

- Take turns asking questions that require specific knowledge of facts about the design of these products.
- Take turns responding to these questions using informal expressions to admit a lack of knowledge.

List of products

_____

_____

_____

_____

_____

_____

_____

_____

_____

_____

▲ Why is it that some designs seem timeless and never go out of style?

4 **Designing a More Appealing Product** In small groups, brainstorm a list of products that you think are particularly unattractive, or that you even consider to be downright ugly. Imagine that your group is an industrial design team and that you have been given the job of enhancing the marketability of the ugliest product on this list by making it more beautiful.

1. Write a description of the new design and draw simple sketches of various aspects of your design to accompany it.

2. Do the following as you work together to accomplish this task and reach agreement on what the new design should be.

   - Make sure that all members of your group contribute and are heard.
   - Ask questions about various design elements and rationales for these elements.
   - If there is any question you cannot answer, be sure to admit your lack of knowledge by using an appropriate expression.

▲ "We know the product does the job, so why isn't it selling?"

3. Share your new designs with the rest of the class.

   - Imagine that your design team is making a presentation to the board of directors of the company.
   - Use your sketches to enhance your oral presentation.
   - Make sure that all members of your team contribute to the oral presentation.

TOEFL iBT

F⊙CUS

Comprehension Questions with Multiple Answers

Many standardized tests, such as the TOEFL® iBT, include comprehension questions that require you to choose two correct answers instead of just one. To prepare to answer these types of questions, it is important, as always, to take notes to help you remember main ideas and details and to pay special attention to negative words such as *no, not,* and *never.* It is also important to read all of the answer choices carefully, as some choices may seem very similar at first and it is only after reading more closely that you notice the subtle differences between the choices. Finally, it is important to notice that while some answers may very well be true, they may not be correct according to the listening passage. You must choose answers that are specifically stated in the passage. Answers that are true according to your own feelings or information other than what is provided in the passage, don't count.

1 Answering Comprehension Questions with Multiple Answers Listen to the lecture about a controversy in the field of website design. Close your books and take notes as you listen. After the speaker finishes talking, you will hear a series of questions. Open your books and fill in the bubble of the best answer to each question.

1. Which of the following websites might appeal to a user or a designer that is primarily concerned with form rather than function? Choose two answers.

   (A) a website with lots of lovely colors and which is tricky to manipulate

   (B) a website that is very plain and gets you the information you need quickly

   (C) a website that has a beautiful typeface and striking pictures and does not link up easily with other sites

   (D) a website that uses simple text and very few colors and is easy to use

   (E) a website that is not very attractive and is easy to use

   (F) a website that is ugly and is easy to use

2. Which of the following would *not* be a concern of the designer or user who is more concerned with function than form? Choose two answers.

   (A) bells and whistles

   (B) easy-to-read text

   (C) accessible information

   (D) simple, straightforward menus

   (E) fun pop-ups

   (F) great links

3. According to the speaker, what is the current controversy in the field of website design about? Choose two answers.

   (A) chasms and divides

   (B) cultural tastes and preferences

   (C) bells and whistles

   (D) form and function

   (E) look and feel

   (F) what works and what doesn't

4. Why do you think the speaker is interested in this topic? Choose two answers.

   (A) People love to have fun on websites.

   (B) The controversy is still not settled.

   (C) People don't like to have difficulty using anything.

   (D) Japanese and Saudi website users are interested in this topic.

   (E) People need to understand that everyone is different.

   (F) Sharing ideas on this topic is stimulating.

5. What might the speaker talk about next time? Choose two answers.

   (A) bells and whistles

   (B) standards of beauty across cultures

   (C) settling the debate

   (D) cultural factors in website design

   (E) form versus function

   (F) questions and answers

Self-Assessment Log

Check (✓) the words in this chapter you have acquired and can use in your daily life.

Nouns	Verbs	Adjectives	Idioms and Expressions
▧ consumer	▧ catch your eye	▧ illustrious	▧ by and large
▧ crux	▧ create a stir	▧ infamous	▧ eye opener
▧ ploy	▧ hammer a point home	▧ subliminal	▧ split second
▧ widget	▧ insinuate	**Adverb**	
	▧ reside (in)	▧ shamelessly	

Check (✓) your level of accomplishment for the skills introduced in this chapter. How comfortable do you feel using these skills?

	Very comfortable	Somewhat comfortable	Not at all comfortable
Understanding reference words and their referents	☐	☐	☐
Using reference words to be a more cohesive speaker	☐	☐	☐
Understanding formal expressions such as *I'm afraid I couldn't tell you* used to express a lack of knowledge	☐	☐	☐
Using formal expressions such as *I'm afraid I couldn't tell you* to express a lack of knowledge	☐	☐	☐
Understanding informal expressions such as *Beats me* used to express a lack of knowledge	☐	☐	☐
Using informal expressions such as *Beats me* to express a lack of knowledge	☐	☐	☐

Think about the topics and activities in this chapter and complete the statements.

In this chapter, I learned something new about _____

_____

_____

I especially liked (topic or activity) _____

_____

_____

I would like to know more about _____

_____

_____

5 Transitions

"The four stages of man are infancy, childhood, adolescence, and obsolescence."

Art Linkletter
U.S. TV-show host
and author

In this
CHAPTER

Radio Program The Stages of Life—A View from Shakespeare

Learning Strategy Understanding and Using Figurative
Language

Language Function "Telling It Like It Is"

Connecting to the Topic

1. Which stage of life (infancy, childhood, adolescence, young
adulthood, middle age, old age) do you think is the easiest? Why?

2. Which stage of your future life are you looking forward to the
most? Why?

3. Which stage of your life up to this point would you like to do over,
either to repeat exactly or to make some changes? Why?

Did You Know?

Some people like change and some don't. Everett Rogers (1931–2004), a well-known sociologist, communications scholar, and teacher, divided people facing life changes into five basic categories.

- "Innovators" are adventurous and eager to try new things right away. They are usually young and don't care too much what others think. (2.5% of the population)

- "Early Adopters" enjoy change and are willing to take some risks to make it happen if it will be the best thing for a lot of people. They are often respected leaders within the established social system. People ask for their opinions before adopting new ideas. (13.5%)

- "Early Majority" people are followers rather than leaders. They make changes only after a lot of their friends do. (34%)

- "Late Majority" people are doubtful of change and cautious about adopting new ideas. They have little influence on the actions of others. (34%)

- "Resisters" are very suspicious of new ideas and generally think things were better in the past. They are not curious and do not take risks. (16%)

1 **What Do You Think?** Discuss the following questions in pairs. Then share the highlights of your discussion with the rest of the class.

1. Why do you think that "Innovators" are usually young and only represent about 2.5% of the population?

2. Why do you suppose that "Early Adopters" are often respected community leaders?

3. Why do you think "Late Majority" people have little influence on the actions of others?

4. Why do you think that "Resisters" are the way they are (not curious and do not take risks)? Does it have to do with age, gender, or culture, for example?

5. Which of the five personality types best describes you? Why?

6. Which of the five personality types best describes your parents or grandparents? Why?

2 Recalling Transitions Everyone experiences transitions in life. These might include changing schools, getting married, or just getting older and facing new responsibilities and privileges. In small groups, discuss two transitions that you've faced.

1. Why were these transitions important in your life?

2. When you were going through these transitions, did you feel in control or did you feel caught by the circumstances and events surrounding these times?

3. As a result of these transitions, how do you feel you changed physically, emotionally, mentally, spiritually, or otherwise?

▲ Moving away from home for the first time is a major transition for a young adult.

3 **Vocabulary in Context** The underlined words and expressions in the following sentences are used in the lecture. Match the definitions on the right to the underlined words in the sentences on the left. Then share your answers with your classmates.

Sentences

1. _____ We shouldn't be surprised that it is difficult to figure out other people's motives for the things they do when we can't even figure out our own.

2. _____ People who believe that we are like puppets and have little control over our lives may feel that our efforts in life will produce only "sound and fury" and in the end will not mean anything.

3. _____ Some children will whine on and on until their parents finally can't stand it anymore and give them whatever they want.

4. _____ Some people believe that passion is the cause of much suffering in life, while others believe that passion is the only thing that makes life worth living.

5. _____ Extremely confident and strong-willed people can easily intimidate others who are shy and less confident.

6. _____ The man was so driven by ambition that he rarely went home from work until 10 or 11 at night.

7. _____ He beat around the bush for 15 minutes before he finally directly said, "Due to changes in the company, you're fired."

Definitions

a. forced or compelled by one's own choices or desires

b. reasons for doing something

c. to say something indirectly

d. to frighten by showing power or making threats

e. to complain, often by making a soft but irritatingly high-pitched noise through the nose

f. intense emotion

g. words and anger that have no power to change anything

4 Using Vocabulary The italicized expressions in the following sentences are used in the lecture. Discuss the following questions in small groups.

1. Have you ever felt as if you were *in a rut* doing the same things over and over and wanted to make a major change in your life? If so, when? Why?

2. Do you think it's important to become well known for something, *to make a name for yourself* in life? Why or why not?

3. What are some of the things you would do *at the drop of a hat*, without thinking very long about it? (For example: Help a friend in trouble? Eat a piece of chocolate cake? Go for a swim in the ocean?)

▲ Would you do this *at the drop of a hat*?

4. There's a fine line between honesty and rudeness. But sometimes you have to speak out and say something in a straightforward manner, in other words, *put it bluntly*. When was the last time you had to do this? What were the circumstances? What did you say?

5. Sometimes it seems that there are *laws of irony* operating in the universe. For example, Jeremy called Susan to invite her to a party and left a message about the party with her roommate. When Susan called back two hours later, Jeremy rushed to answer the phone and fell and broke his arm. It was bad enough that he had broken his arm, but *to add insult to injury*, to make the situation even worse or more ironic, it turned out that Susan was planning to go to the party with someone else instead. What have been some of the ironies in your life, or situations that added insult to injury?

Strategy

Understanding and Using Figurative Language

Figurative language is language used to create images and is not meant to be taken literally. Analogies and metaphors are two types of figurative language. They make language more interesting and vivid, and are powerful ways to make your ideas understandable. Analogies and metaphors do not have to be complex; in fact, they can be quite simple. It is common for people to use analogies and metaphors to help others understand what they are trying to say. Therefore, it is important for you to be able to recognize them and to know the difference between literal and figurative language as you develop your listening skills.

An analogy is a comparison that shows the logical relationship between two things. If the analogy uses the words *like* or *as*, it is called a simile. For example:

> Life is like a river—always changing, yet ever the same.

Metaphors are similar to analogies and similes because they show the relationship between two things, but metaphors differ from analogies and similes in that they say that one thing "is" another thing and not just similar to it. Some examples of metaphors are:

1. Good ideas are seeds; some will grow into strong plants and others will never mature.
2. History is merely gossip. *—Oscar Wilde*
3. Love is food for the soul, but jealousy is poison.
4. Life is a disease. The only difference between one man and another is the stage of the disease. *—George Bernard Shaw*

Analogies and metaphors can be paraphrased as equations. For example, the four previous examples can be represented by the following equations:

1. idea = seed
2. history = gossip
3. love = food for the soul; jealousy = poison
4. life = disease

Expressions Often Used in Making Analogies

about the size of a	mean(s)	similar to
almost like	seem(s) like	the same as
as… as		

1 Considering the Topic Discuss the following questions in small groups.

1. Do you think people have much influence over their own growth and development (physical, mental, and emotional)? Or do you think that "free will" does not exist and that human beings are like puppets whose strings are pulled by forces beyond their control? Why?

▲ The puppet master controls the life and actions of the lady puppet by pulling her strings.

2. Assume for the moment that you *do* direct your own life, or "pull your own strings" as the expression goes. What do you personally want to achieve to feel successful? (Give at least one example.) What are the steps you plan to take to make this happen?

3. Consider the following quotations about time. What do you think they mean? Does any one of them hold particular significance for you? Why? If you can, tell about an event or time in your life when one of these quotations might have been significant. Let your classmates guess which quotation best applies to the situation you describe.

- Time wasted is existence, used [it] is life. —*Henry Wadsworth Longfellow*
- I recommend you take care of the minutes, for the hours will take care of themselves. —*Lord Chesterfield*
- Unhappy is he who trusts only to time for his happiness. —*Voltaire*

Public Radio Newsletter

Transitions in Literature Series
Program 6

Jacques' Speech from *As You Like It*

All the world's a stage,
And all the men and women merely players.
They have their exits and their entrances,
And one man in his time plays many parts,
His acts being seven ages. At first the infant,
Mewling and puking in the nurse's arms,
Then whining schoolboy, with his satchel
And shining morning face, creeping like a snail
Unwillingly to school. And then the lover,
Sighing like a furnace, with a woeful ballad
Made to his mistress' eyebrow. Then a soldier,
Full of strange oaths, and bearded like a pard,
Jealous in honor, sudden and quick in quarrel,
Seeking the bubble reputation
Even in the cannon's mouth. And then the justice,
In fair round belly with good capon lined,
With eyes severe, and beard of formal cut,
Full of wise saws and modern instances,
And so he plays his part. The sixth age shifts
Into the lean and slippered Pantaloon,
With spectacles on nose and pouch on side,
His youthful hose, well saved, a world too wide
For his shrunk shank, and his big manly voice,
Turning again toward childish treble, pipes
And whistles in his sound. Last scene of all,
That ends this strange eventful history,
Is second childishness and mere oblivion,
Sans teeth, sans eyes, sans taste, sans everything.

▲ Jacques from Shakespeare's play *As You Like It*

2 **Listening for Figurative Language** Listen to the lecture once all the way through and note the main ideas. Then play it again and make a mark in the box each time you hear an analogy or a metaphor. Share your answers with your classmates.

List the main ideas in the lecture	Count the analogies and metaphors

3 **Completing Analogies and Metaphors** Listen to the lecture a third time. As you listen, complete the following analogies and metaphors. Use the lecturer's words if you can. Otherwise, complete them in your own words. When you are finished, share your answers with your classmates.

Examples

Life is like a giant _puzzle_   .

A Buddhist would probably see transformation or change as _____

_____ _an opportunity for spirtual growth_ _____.

1. We seem to be afraid that all our planning and struggling for success are simply

   _____

   _____.

2. One of the most disturbing visions is the idea that we are just _____

   _____.

3. Or even worse, what if we are just _____
_____ ?

4. The seven stages of life are _____
_____ .

5. The schoolboy creeps to school like _____
_____ .

6. When the lecturer says "the hero burns with desire," he means that desire is like _____
_____ .

7. The young hero thinks that becoming a man means _____
_____ .

8. The young soldier grows a beard so he will look as fierce as _____
_____ .

9. As the man grows older, he loses the clear voice of youth. Now his voice _____
_____ .

10. Reaching old age, the man has almost come full circle. He is now like _____
_____ again.

After You Listen

4 Deciphering the Meaning of Analogies and Metaphors In small groups, discuss the meaning of each analogy and metaphor in Activity 3 on pages 89–90. Whenever possible, share examples from your own experience that these analogies and metaphors might describe.

Talk It Over

5 Making Analogies In small groups, think of as many analogies as you can for each of the items in the chart on page 91. One way to do this is to "free associate"—to just see what pops into your head when you read each item—and then make an analogy comparing the item with the idea that just came to you. Or you may prefer to be more deliberate and analytical in devising your analogies.

- While brainstorming, have one person in the group record all of the analogies for each item on a separate piece of paper.
- After brainstorming, choose your favorite analogies to fill in the chart on page 91.

1. time	*time = flowing river*	*Time is like a flowing river, constantly changing, yet always the same.*
2. love		
3. infatuation		
4. passion		
5. life		
6. death		
7. a man		
8. a woman		
9. youth		
10. old age		
11. a realist		
12. a dreamer		
13. a friend		
14. ambition		

6 **Determining the Subjects of Analogies** In the same small groups, share your group's most interesting, most profound, and most amusing analogies with the rest of the class by playing the following guessing game. Consider all the analogies your group created and select a few favorites. Then, substitute the pronoun *it* for the subject of each of these analogies and see if the rest of the class can guess which item you are talking about.

Example

It is like a flowing river, constantly changing, yet always the same.
Question: What is *it*?
Answer: Time.

Strategy

"Telling It Like It Is" Politely

"Telling it like it is" means being honest, telling the truth with no extra words to soften it, being blunt, and speaking directly to the point. This can be a good thing. Speakers who "tell it like it is" are usually not long-winded, and their honesty can be very refreshing and helpful in a world where people are often afraid to reveal their opinions and true feelings. It is a true friend that "tells it like it is" when we are about to make a big mistake by buying an expensive item that is not very well made and that we cannot afford, or "tells it like it is" when we hurt someone's feelings and should do something to make up for it.

However, even though people who "tell it like it is" may be trying to be helpful, we also need to keep in mind that their opinions and feelings may only represent one point of view. Sometimes, people may even hide behind the shield of honesty of "telling it like it is" in order to say something that is very negative or critical. The negative comment may be based on accepted fact, or it may be just a personal opinion, in which case the thin line between blunt honesty and rudeness becomes even thinner.

Whether you are trying to truly be helpful or trying to make a constructive criticism without being rude, you should use one of the following expressions with a sympathetic tone of voice.

Expressions for "Telling It Like It Is"

Actually,…	I'm sorry to tell you…
Frankly,…	It could be said that…
Quite frankly,…	Let's face it:…
To be frank,…	Let's not beat around the bush.
Honestly,…	Not to beat around the bush,…
To be honest,…	The truth is,…
To be honest with you,…	This is difficult/hard to say, but…
I don't like saying this, but…	To put it bluntly,…
I hate to say this, but…	To tell the truth,…
I'm afraid…	To tell you the truth,…
I'm sorry to say…	

Combining Expressions: Most of the expressions for "telling it like it is" can be combined for emphasis. For example:

Actually, it could be said that…
Frankly, I'm sorry to tell you…
Honestly, I'm afraid….
I don't like saying this, but let's face it…

1 Listening for Tone of Voice You will hear three pairs of conversations. Each pair of conversations uses exactly the same words, but the two versions of the conversation in each pair differ in meaning according to the tone of voice used by one of the speakers. Listen to each conversation and answer the questions. When you are finished with each pair of conversations, share your responses with your classmates.

Conversation 1A

1. Is Gloria really concerned about Ted?

_____

Is Mickey? _____

_____

2. How do you know? _____

_____

_____

▲ What's up with Ted?

3. How do you think Ted would feel if he overheard this conversation?

_____

Why? _____

_____

Conversation 1B

1. Is Gloria really concerned about Ted now?

_____

Is Mickey? _____

2. How do you know? _____

_____

3. How do you think Ted would feel if he overheard this conversation?

_____

Why? _____

_____

Conversation 2A

1. How does the father feel about not going to his daughter's wedding?

_____

_____

2. How do you know? _____

_____

3. What reason might he have for not going? _____

_____

Conversation 2B

1. How does the father feel about not going to his daughter's wedding?

_____

2. How do you know? _____

_____

3. What reason might he have for not going? _____

_____

Conversation 3A

1. Does Jane like Paul's artwork? _____

2. How can you tell? _____

_____

3. Does Jane like Paul? _____

4. How can you tell? _____

_____

Conversation 3B

1. Does Jane like Paul's artwork? _____

2. How can you tell? _____

_____

3. Does Jane like Paul? _____

4. How can you tell? _____

_____

2 Listening for Expressions that "Tell It Like It Is" In the lecture, the instructor uses various expressions to "tell it like it is"—to introduce his "honest," "true" comments. Listen to the lecture one or more times. As you listen, write down as many of the expressions as you can and the "truth" that the lecturer reveals. What can you tell about the lecturer's attitudes from the tone of voice used with each one? Share your responses with the class.

▲ Enjoying life's stages

Expression for "telling it like it is"	The "truth" that is revealed	Lecturer's attitude revealed by tone
Let's face it ...	We also see time and change as negative because they always bring our decline and eventual death.	Sincere and sympathetic; he gently points out a "truth" about our fear of time related to our fear of death.

3 **Role-Playing "Telling It Like It Is"** Choose a partner and together select one of the situations below as the basis for a role-play, and do the following:

1. Invent two characters who might find themselves in this situation and decide which of you will play each one.

2. Select an attitude and tone of voice for each character from the list on page 97. The characters can use the same tones of voice or different tones of voice.

3. Role-play a dialogue in which the characters talk about the situation they find themselves in. Practice "telling it like it is" using the expressions on page 92. (See the sample dialogue on page 97.)

4. If time permits, choose another situation, another set of characters, and new tones of voice and do a new role-play.

Situations

1. the birth of a baby
2. a child's first day at school
3. a child skipping class
4. a child pretending to be sick so he or she won't have to go to school
5. graduating from school
6. cheating on an exam
7. being interviewed for a job
8. getting offered a job you don't want
9. getting fired
10. retiring
11. falling in love with someone who doesn't love you
12. getting divorced
13. getting married
14. changing careers
15. becoming a widow or widower
16. a situation of your choice

Tones of voice

1. sad	11. sarcastic
2. angry	12. guilty
3. depressed	13. powerless
4. delighted	14. powerful
5. excited	15. nervous
6. frightened	16. passionate
7. loving	17. confused
8. hurt	18. envious
9. vengeful	19. mean
10. shy	20. amused

Sample dialogue

Situation: Birth of a baby.

Terry speaks in a *depressed* tone and Francis is *amused*.

Terry: Did you hear what happened after Jennifer's baby was born?

Francis: No! What happened?

Terry: Well, after seeing the baby, Jennifer's husband went home and cried.

Francis: You're kidding! Why?

Terry: Well, to put it bluntly, their baby is really ugly. Isn't that depressing?

Francis: No, not particularly. Let's face it: All newborn babies are ugly.

Terry: To tell the truth, I agree with you. It's a wonder more fathers don't go home and cry after they see their babies for the first time.

Francis: Well, why waste tears so soon? By the time they're teenagers, the parents will really have reasons to cry!

 4 Guessing Situations and Emotions With your partner, present a dialogue to the rest of the class, but do not tell your classmates which situation or emotions you have selected. After you've finished, let them guess the situation and emotions.

F🔍CUS

Classification Questions

Some listening questions on the TOEFL® iBT are not multiple choice. Instead of choosing one or two options from a list, classification questions ask you to click on certain boxes to categorize ideas from the passage. This shows that you are able to sort and classify the information that you are given.

1 Sorting and Classifying Information Listen to the lecture about stage-of-life topologies. While you listen, close your book and take notes. After the lecture, you will hear some instructions. Open your book and use your notes to complete the table below.

For each item, mark an X in the appropriate box to indicate which of the four topologies each statement goes with best, according to the lecture. To simulate a real test, give yourself only five minutes to complete the table.

	Functional	Maturational	Ritual	Bureaucratic
1. "rites of passage"				
2. the Hindu system of four life stages				
3. the riddle of the Sphinx				
4. Confucian-based practices marking birth, maturity, marriage, and death				
5. ages at which the law permits marriage, voting, etc.				
6. a system involving "sucking," "braces," and "gumming" stages				
7. a system that contrasts sharply with some almost poetic topologies				
8. baptism, confirmation, etc. in European societies				

Self-Assessment Log

Check (✓) the words in this chapter you have acquired and can use in your daily life.

Nouns	**Verbs**	**Adjective**	**Idioms and Expressions**
▦ motives	▦ intimidate	▦ driven	▦ add insult to injury
▦ passion	▦ whine		▦ at the drop of a hat
			▦ beat around the bush
			▦ in a rut
			▦ laws of irony
			▦ make a name for yourself
			▦ put it bluntly
			▦ sound and fury

Check (✓) your level of accomplishment for the skills introduced in this chapter. How comfortable do you feel using these skills?

	Very comfortable	Somewhat comfortable	Not at all comfortable
Understanding analogies and metaphors	☐	☐	☐
Using expressions such as *about the size of* a and *as… as* to make analogies	☐	☐	☐
Listening for expressions such as *let's face it* and *to put it bluntly* that can signal a speaker is "telling it like it is"	☐	☐	☐
Using expressions such as *let's face it* and *to put it bluntly* to "tell it like it is"	☐	☐	☐

Think about the topics and activities in this chapter and complete the statements.

In this chapter, I learned something new about _____

_____

_____

I especially liked (topic or activity) _____

_____

_____

I would like to know more about _____

_____

_____

6 The Mind

"When you dream, you dialogue with aspects of yourself that normally are not with you in the daytime and you discover that you know a great deal more than you thought you did."

Toni Cade Bambara
African-American writer,
documentary filmmaker, and
social activist

Lecture Dreams and Reality

Learning Strategy Understanding and Using Comparison
and Contrast

Language Function "Looking at the Bright Side"

Connecting to the Topic

1. What is happening in the photo?
2. What are the advantages of having an experience like this?
3. What are the disadvantages?

Did You Know?

- We begin dreaming about 90 minutes after we fall asleep and continue to do so about every 90 minutes. With approximately five dreams a night, we will have about 136,000 dreams in a lifetime, spending a total of six years in a dream state. Scientists do not yet know exactly what purpose all of this time in the dream state serves; they only know that people deprived of dreamtime can suffer severe mental breakdowns.

- The dream state is called REM (rapid eye movement) sleep because when most people dream, their eyes move rapidly as if they were watching an exciting movie. The person in a REM state is aware of light and noises in the room, but is not able to move any part of the body at all. Scientists think that this "paralysis" occurs during REM sleep so that we will not sleepwalk and act out our dreams.

- If you "imprint" the mind with an image, it doesn't matter if it comes in through the reality you experienced while awake, through dreams, or through intense imagining; it still has the same effect. That's why, for example, athletes mentally rehearse over and over the night before an event. That's also why students who imagine doing well rather than poorly on a test actually do score higher.

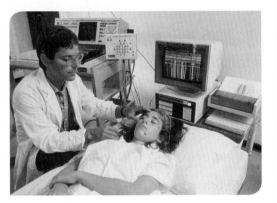

▲ Scientists examine eye movement and brainwaves in a dream research lab.

1 **What Do You Think?** Discuss the following questions in pairs.

1. Why do you think we spend so much of our lives dreaming?

2. Why do you think the images we have when dreaming are often so fanciful, or even bizarre?

3. Do you believe dreams can help people deal better with daily life? If so, how?

4. Do you think you can actually improve physical performance of a task by rehearsing it only in your mind? Give examples.

5. Why do you think we are so fascinated by virtual reality games (computer simulations that use 3-D graphics and allow the user to interact with the screen)?

6. What do you think will be the next logical advancement in the science of virtual reality?

2 Talking About Dreams Answer the following questions in small groups.

1. How often do you remember your dreams? Every night? Once in a while?

2. Some people say that what you do just before you go to bed can affect your dreams and your ability to remember them. When are you most likely to remember your dreams? After you've eaten a large meal? After seeing an exciting movie? At the end of a stressful day? Or is it a day or so later, when an experience during the day somehow triggers, quickly causes, a recollection of the dream that occurred in deep, seemingly unconscious, REM sleep?

3. What is the most fanciful or bizarre dream you've ever had? Tell about it.

4. Have you ever had the same dream repeatedly? If so, tell about it. Why do you think you have had this recurring dream?

▲ *What daytime activities do you think might have triggered this dream?*

3 Sharing Definitions The following words are used in the lecture. You may already know the meanings of some of them. However, the words you know may be different from the ones your classmates know. In small groups, match the definitions on the right with the words on the left, sharing the definitions you know with your classmates.

Words

1. _____ chaotic
2. _____ conceptualize
3. _____ the downside
4. _____ fleeting
5. _____ flexibility
6. _____ in tune with
7. _____ manipulate
8. _____ perception
9. _____ trivial
10. _____ the upside
11. _____ visualize

Definitions

a. unimportant; ordinary

b. to form mental images

c. the ability to bend; the ability to adjust to new situations

d. the positive side; the good part

e. disorganized; in a state of confusion

f. lasting only a short time; vanishing quickly

g. insight gained through the senses; observation

h. to manage (people, numbers, stocks, and so forth) skillfully for one's own profit

i. in harmony with; in agreement with

j. to form theories, ideas, or concepts

k. the negative side; the bad part

4 Vocabulary in Context With a partner, choose roles in the following telephone conversation and read it out loud. Then read it out loud a second time, pausing to replace the underlined words with the correct forms of the expressions introduced in Activity 3. Note: not all of the words in the list are used.

Telephone Conversation

Stacy: Hi, Hank. What's up? How's the psych course going? Is it good?

Hank: Yeah. The chapter this week is pretty interesting.

Stacy: Oh yeah? What's the topic?

Hank: It's about dreams.

Stacy: What's so interesting about dreams?

Hank: Well, for one thing, it's been hard for scientists to agree on only one theory about why we dream and how dreams affect us, so they have formed ideas about several theories.

Stacy: Like what?

Hank: Well, let's see. There's the theory that dreams are not just unimportant images that have no real effect on our lives. This theory says that dreams can actually change our reality.

Stacy: What do you mean by that?

Hank: Some philosophers say that those quickly disappearing images we have in our sleep may be an extension of this crazy, unorganized world we live in. And they say that our <u>view</u> of the world, which we get through sight, sound, touch, taste, and smell when we are awake, may actually be changed through dreams.

Stacy: Wow! That's certainly not <u>unimportant</u>. What else did you learn?

Hank: Well, that in some cultures, the <u>images of things</u> that come in dreams are considered to be no different than reality. And people in those cultures hold on so strongly to this belief that they act in waking life as though the dreams were true. They seem to have no <u>willingness to adjust or change their minds</u> on this matter. For example, a Zulu man reportedly broke off a friendship after he dreamt that his friend intended to harm him. And the Aborigines in Australia believe that dreaming is just a continuation of the reality of being awake.

Stacy: I wonder how that would work in our culture. People would try to <u>control and guide</u> their dreams, don't you think?

Hank: Sure. I know I would. Wouldn't *you* want to be <u>in harmony with</u> your dreams like that, and have a chance to make things better during the day by controlling your dreams?

Stacy: Yeah, I guess I would.

Hank: Hey, listen. Enough about school. You want to catch a movie Thursday night?

Stacy: Sure. What did you have in mind?

Hank: Renoir's *The Grand Illusion* is playing at the Fine Arts. Want to see it?

Stacy: Sure, come by for me at 6:00.

Hank: OK, see you then. Bye.

Stacy: Bye.

PART 2   Comparison and Contrast

Strategy

Understanding and Using Comparison and Contrast

In Chapter 5, you learned about using analogies for comparison—that is, looking at the similarities between two things. English speakers commonly use analogies both in formal and informal situations. For example, in a lecture on the nature of dreams, you might hear:

> Dreams are like smoke. You can't quite hang on to them, and they disappear so quickly that you can barely remember them.

In a casual conversation, a friend might say:

> In my dream last night, the clouds were like human heads, each one smiling and wearing a funny hat. I woke up laughing.

Another way of looking at the relationship between two things is to point out the differences between them, that is, to contrast them.

Comparisons and contrasts are indicated in three main ways:

1. through expressions that signal comparison or contrast
2. through pairs of antonyms within a single statement
3. through stress on particular words

Expressions that Signal Comparison

again	just as/like
also	likewise
and so does	similarly
equally important	the same way (as)
in a similar way	

Expressions that Signal Contrast

although/though/even though	meanwhile
but	nevertheless
by/in contrast	on the contrary
conversely	on the other hand
however	whereas
instead	yet

Antonyms Used to Signal Contrast

Antonyms can show contrast within a single topic or idea when used in pairs.

> **Examples**
> Fortunately…/Unfortunately…
> The advantages are…/The disadvantages are…
> The best part is…/The worst part is…
> The good news is…/The bad news is…
> The positive features are…/The negative features are…
> The upside is…/The downside is…

Word Stress

Word stress can also indicate comparison and contrast. In the following sentences, comparison is indicated by stressing the words *mind* and *body*.

> The *mind* repairs itself during sleep.
> The *body* repairs itself during sleep.

In the following sentences, contrast is indicated by stressing the words *mind*, *body*, and *can*.

> The *mind* creates things that we cannot touch.
> The *body* creates things that we *can* touch.

1 Listening for Comparison and Contrast in Informal Conversations The following conversations contain examples of each type of indicator of comparison or contrast. Listen to each conversation once and then discuss the gist of it with a partner. Then listen a second time, and together list which indicators of comparison and contrast were used by the speakers. When you are finished, compare your answers with another pair.

1. Otto and Henry _____

_____

_____

2. Judy and Paula _____

_____

_____

3. A teaching assistant and students _____

_____

_____

Before You Listen

2 Considering the Topic In small groups, discuss the following questions.

1. Have you ever dreamed about something that had actually happened earlier? How did the dream differ from reality?

2. Have you ever dreamed about something that actually happened later? For example, you might have dreamed about receiving a gift or seeing a car accident and then had the exact same thing happen in real life. How did the experience make you feel?

3 **Listening for Comparison and Contrast** Listen to the lecture to get the main ideas and write them in the first column of the chart below. In the other two columns, write down any words or phrases that might signal a comparison or a contrast.

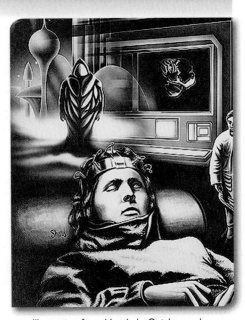

▲ Illustration from Ursula LeGuin's novel *The Lathe of Heaven*

Main ideas	Expressions signaling a comparison	Expressions signaling a contrast

Listen to the lecture again. Fill in the following chart with details about the comparisons and contrasts in the lecture as you listen.

Dreams versus Reality		
	Comparison	Contrast
1. Dreams while we are sleeping and dreams after waking		
2. Two types of dreams		
3. Dr. Haber's reaction to George and other people's reaction to George		
4. George and Dr. Haber		
5. The lathe of heaven and a child playing with a recording		
6. Our concept of time and LeGuin's concept of time		

4 Comparing Responses In small groups, share your answers to Activity 3 and answer the following questions. Listen to the lecture again if necessary.

1. Are there any places in the lecture that comparisons and contrasts are not introduced by the usual signal words? Where?

2. Which comparisons are marked by stress?

Talk It Over

5 Comparing and Contrasting Dreams Some dreams are symbolic; others are more straightforward representations of actual events. In this activity, you will be comparing and contrasting two dreams stimulated by the same event. In small groups, do the following steps.

1. Read Situation 1 and the two dreams aloud.

2. Discuss these questions.
   - How are the dreams similar?
   - How are the dreams different?
   - Which one is more symbolic and which is more related to actual events? Why do you feel this way?

3. Do the same for Situations 2–5, stopping to discuss each one in turn. Try comparing and contrasting, using the indicators that you learned on pages 105–106.

Situation 1

You and a friend read the following story in a newspaper: The Hotel Ritz in Dallas has been robbed. Three gunmen, posing as doctors, entered the hotel about 10:00 A.M. Because there was a medical convention in the hotel at the time, the gunmen made a "clean getaway," leaving after the robbery without being caught.

Dream 1: A doctor is examining you, but instead of being in an office, you are in your car. All of a sudden, the doctor pulls out a gun.

Dream 2: You have invited a few friends for dinner. You are making the final preparations in the kitchen. As you reach for the butter, it turns into a pistol.

Situation 2

The atmosphere at school has been chaotic because final examinations will be given next week. Of course, students are studying intensely. You're especially worried about your economics final because your instructor is hard to understand. Besides that, the way he moves reminds you of a rhinoceros.

Dream 1: While you are in the library with your economics book, you notice a rhinoceros chewing a textbook on the table next to yours. Nobody but you seems to notice.

Dream 2: You are reading a paperback in bed with music playing very loudly in the background. Everything is fine. All at once, your normally well-behaved dog jumps on the bed and begins charging at you like a rhinoceros and will not stop.

Situation 3

Two men in the office are arguing about administrative policies. Jim, who has worked there longer, wants the promotion, but the offer was made to Michael, a newer employee who has been working for Jim. No seniority system exists at the company.

Jim's dream: A rock band is playing in the cafeteria, and everyone is eating pink and green food with stars on it. Jim asks the band to play some folk music, but the band members ignore him. He tries to buy some of the pink and green food with stars on it, but the young man at the cash register says he's too old to eat this food and asks him to leave.

Michael's dream: Michael has a conversation with Jim and apologizes for the argument. Jim forgives him and announces that he has a new job at twice the salary at a Japanese company just opening down the street.

Situation 4

You have read in the newspaper about a group of skiers who have been missing for two weeks. Rescue teams fear the worst, that the skiers are dead, because avalanches have been occurring almost daily this winter.

Dream 1: You are jogging in shorts and a T-shirt. The weather changes drastically, and it begins to rain. To make matters worse, you are eight miles from home.

Dream 2: You are walking in the snow thinking about how fresh and clear the air is. Your warm clothing feels too heavy and tight all of a sudden. Soon you are having trouble breathing. Your hat keeps falling down over your eyes, and your collar creeps up over your mouth. You wake up gasping for air.

Situation 5

Tom reads in the paper that since it is the first Sunday in November, he must set his clock back one hour.

Dream 1: He dreams that he wakes up in the morning and everything is backward. He walks backward to the bathroom to brush his teeth and sees the back of his head in the mirror. He feels like he is putting on his clothing correctly, but when he looks down, it is all backward. The car goes in reverse to work, and at the end of the day when he climbs into bed, he finds his head where his feet usually rest.

Dream 2: Tom dreams that he is an hour early for a major appointment with a man named Mr. Timekeeper. Mr. Timekeeper is very impressed that Tom is so early and gives Tom four million dollars' worth of business.

6 **Analyzing Dreams** In this activity, you will be doing some more dream analysis, this time as part of a team of "psychoanalysts" analyzing patients' dreams.

1. Work in groups of three or four to analyze each patient. Use the following questions to guide your analyses.

   - How are each patient's three dreams alike, and how are they different?
   - Which dreams represent a single major issue and which deal with several different issues in the person's life?
   - What does each dream mean?

2. Discuss your findings with the other groups.

Patient 1

Peter is a 38-year-old used-car salesman who has recently filed for bankruptcy. His wife has threatened to leave him unless he gets out of debt.

Dream 1: He jumps off the Eiffel Tower but is picked up by a stork and carried to the Caribbean.

Dream 2: He is at his bank making a night deposit when two female outlaws hold up the bank and leave him tied up and gagged with a scarf so that he cannot talk.

Dream 3: He flies to Italy to order lasagna, but can find only pizza. As he enjoys the pizza, a helicopter lands across the street and two men get out and offer him $77,000.

Patient 2

Martin, from Denver, Colorado, marries Sulin from France and they live and work in Paris for three years. Then they move back to Denver.

Dream 1: Martin is back in Paris at their apartment talking to the neighbors.

Dream 2: Martin is alone in an airplane, and all the signs and control indicators are labeled in French. He picks up an equipment manual, which is written in French, and realizes he can't read it.

Dream 3: Martin goes to the office in Denver and finds that all the people there are his coworkers from France. None of them speaks English, and all of them need his help. He speaks French perfectly and easily arranges housing for his coworkers. When he finishes, everyone cheers and they pick him up on their shoulders and carry him around the office.

Patient 3

Mr. Hill, an elderly man, describes these dreams.

Dream 1: Mr. Hill is in college taking courses and living in the dorms. Although he does very well, no one notices or sees him.

Dream 2: Mr. Hill is a young man working on his father's ranch. Everyone is looking at the blue sky and hoping for rain.

Dream 3: Mr. Hill meets his first grandchildren. They are twins, a boy and a girl. The boy looks like him and the girl looks like his deceased wife.

Patient 4

Tina is a freshman at Santa Barbara City College, majoring in computer science.

Dream 1: Tina is in a computer store selecting a laptop. As she walks up to look at one, it changes into an ice cream sundae. The second one changes into a bicycle, the third into a small swimming pool, the fourth into a refrigerator, and the fifth into a sculpture of a dancer. She leaves the store feeling worried that she'll never find a computer that will stick around.

Dream 2: Tina walks into class feeling confident about the exam she is about to take. She sits down and the instructor passes out the exam. She takes one look at it and can't remember anything.

Dream 3: Tina is at a party and three men come up to her and ask her to dance. She can't decide what to do.

7 Interviewing People about Dreams If possible, ask a native speaker of English about a dream he or she remembers. Or ask someone to tell you in English about a dream he or she has had.

- Find out as much as you can about the dream. Then share your findings with your classmates.
- Discuss whether anyone could have had this dream or only a native speaker of English? Why?

Strategy

"Looking at the Bright Side"

People often need others to listen to their complaints. It is quite common, for example, to find ourselves listening to the complaints of family, friends, or colleagues about something that has gone wrong at home, at school, at work, or at a shop.

To console or cheer up the unhappy person, we can suggest ways to look at the problem as though it were "all for the best." This ability to look at the positive, or bright side, of an issue is useful in both informal conversations and formal discussions.

Statements that demonstrate a positive view, or a "look at the bright side," are often introduced in one of three ways:

1. by expressions that signal contrast (see page 106)
2. by expressions that present a positive view
3. by comparing this situation with one that is even worse

The following are some examples of two ways (numbers 2 and 3 above) to indicate the positive view.

Expressions that Present a Positive View

But, on the bright side…
But at least…
It's all for the best, because…
It's just as well, because…
The good news is…
The upside (of this) is…
Well, look at the bright side.
Well, try to look at it this way.
Yes, that's true, but just think…

Expressions that Compare a Situation with One that Is Worse

Just imagine if…
On the other hand,…
Yes, but it/things could be worse! What if…
Yes, but look at it this way. You could have/be…
You think that's bad? I heard about a person who…

1 Listening for the Positive View Listen to the following conversations and answer the questions that follow each one.

- Share your answers to the questions in small groups.
- Can you imagine yourself responding similarly to any of the speakers? Share why or why not with your classmates.

Conversation 1

Gary and Julius

1. What expression does Gary use to help Julius "look at the bright side"?

   _____

2. Is Gary's suggestion amusing? _____

   Why or why not? _____

   _____

Conversation 2

Christine and Eric

1. What does Eric suggest doing instead of going to the picnic?

   _____

2. What expression does he use to introduce this suggestion?

   _____

3. Do you think Eric was glad the picnic was rained out? _____

   Why or why not? _____

   _____

Conversation 3

Clara and Joyce

1. What is Joyce's complaint? _____

   _____

2. What does Clara suggest? _____

   _____

3. What expression does Clara use to introduce her suggestion about the course?

   _____

4. Was Clara able to convince Joyce to see the bright side? _____

   How do you know this? _____

   _____

2 Summarizing the Positive View Listen to the lecture again as you complete this exercise.

- Before you listen, read through the five statements. They are paraphrases of parts of the lecture.
- Listen specifically for situations that might be considered negative or unpleasant.
- As you listen, write a summary of the positive response to the situation given in the lecture. Be sure to include the optimistic expression that the speaker uses in your response.

Example Often our dreams seem trivial and useless.

On the other hand, many breakthroughs in science and inspirations in the

arts have originated in dreams.

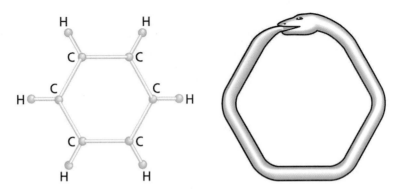

▲ It was a visionary dream that helped F.A. Kekulé von Stradonitz visualize the structure of the Benzene molecule.

1. After Coleridge's writing was interrupted by a visitor, he could not remember the rest of the poem he had created in a dream.

_____

_____

_____

2. And one night last week, I dreamed about hot dogs piled up on a bridge—no useful images for scientific discoveries or artistic creations there that I can figure out.

_____

_____

_____

3. Every time George dreams a new reality, each person has a new set of memories to fit this new reality. They remember nothing of the old reality.

_____

_____

_____

4. Dr. Haber has been trying to use George's dreams to change the world.

_____

_____

_____

5. When Dr. Haber wakes up from his dreams, everything is gray—the people, the buildings, the animals, and the plants.

_____

_____

_____

3 **Comparing Answers** Share your answers to Activity 2 in small groups. Then discuss the following question.

Is it easier to understand a lecture that presents contrasting points of view or a lecture that presents only one point of view? Why?

Talk It Over

4 **Debating as Optimists and Pessimists** In this activity, you will have a chance to become an extreme optimist, looking only at the bright side, or an extreme pessimist, who can see only the dark side. Follow the guidelines below to form teams and debate the positive and negative sides of the topic you choose. Your instructor or a neutral classmate can serve as moderator. Each team gets a point for each good argument it presents "for" or "against" a particular point of view.

1. Form teams of three or four. Then find another team to be your opponents in a debate.

2. Work with the other team to choose one of the topics from the list to debate. Decide which team will take the positive point of view and which will take the negative.

3. Spend ten minutes preparing for the debate. Imagine what the other team's position will be and come up with arguments against their point of view.

4. During the debate, take turns with the other team in presenting and then defending your point of view. (Those presenting the positive side can use expressions from page 114. Those presenting the negative side can use the expressions from Part 3 of Chapter 5 "Telling It Like It Is" on page 92.)

5. If time permits, stay on the same teams and choose a new topic, but take the opposite point of view. This time around, pessimists become optimists and optimists become pessimists.

Topics

1. hypnosis

2. telepathy

3. memorization as a primary method of study

4. many years of intense study on a particular subject, excluding all other areas of study

5. controlling anger at all times

6. being totally honest at all times

7. daydreaming

8. treatment of mental illness with drugs that may have terrible side effects

9. experimenting with mind-altering situations such as sleep deprivation or total sensory deprivation

(5) **Responding to Complaints Positively** Sometimes people complain or gripe too much, and an optimist who can see the bright side needs to come to the rescue. Follow these steps to practice positive ways to respond to complaints.

1. With a partner, choose a topic from the following list. One of you should complain all you want and say all the negative things you can about the topic. The other should offer a more optimistic view of the situation, using some of the expressions from page 114.

2. Choose another topic and begin again. This time switch roles.

3. Cover as many different topics as time permits, alternating roles with each new topic.

FYI

A conversation that is just one complaint after another is sometimes called a "gripe session." A gripe session can be a good thing because it helps to get feelings out into the open. Participants may also feel better because of the support and sympathy they receive. Sometimes, however, a gripe session may go on for a long time without producing positive results. At times like this, we welcome the optimist who helps everyone see the bright side and get back on a positive track.

Topics

1. dormitory or cafeteria food

2. bureaucracies/red tape

3. politicians/politics

4. traffic/parking

5. roommates

6. single life/married life

7. final exams/writing papers

8. going to the dentist

9. music/art

10. people who…

11. the high cost of…

12. the quality of…

13. the university system in my country

14. selfish people

15. staying up late at night to party

16. drivers who…

FOCUS

Varying of Question Types on Real Tests

In Chapters 1–5, you practiced answering basic-information questions, pragmatic-information questions, and classification questions. Of course, on real standardized tests, such as the TOEFL® iBT, these question types will not be grouped together but will be varied throughout the test. When you take notes to prepare to answer test questions, you must try to take the kind of notes that will help you with all types of questions. You must note main ideas and details, attitudes, feelings and intentions of the speakers, and categories into which information can be classified.

1 **Answering a Realistic Mix of Question Types** Listen to the conversation about dreams between a man and a woman. Close your books while you listen and take notes. After the speaker finishes talking, you will hear a series of questions. Open your books and fill in the bubble of the best answers to the following questions.

1. What was Brian doing when Angie arrived?
   - (A) dreaming
   - (B) studying
   - (C) eating
   - (D) reading

2. Why is Brian so tired?
   - (A) He's been reading a boring book.
   - (B) He's been losing touch with reality.
   - (C) He's been up late partying.
   - (D) He's been up late studying.

3. Listen again to part of the conversation.
   Why does Brian say to Angie, "It's you"?
   - (A) He's accusing Angie of waking him up.
   - (B) He was expecting someone else.
   - (C) He's accusing Angie of startling him.
   - (D) He was dreaming about someone else.

4. Listen again to part of the conversation.
   Why does Brian say, "anyway"?
   - (A) because staying up all night is the best way to study
   - (B) because it doesn't matter how he manages to get the good grade
   - (C) because he's getting to his main point
   - (D) because he thinks Angie is going to interrupt him

5. Fill in the following chart by putting the number of each statement below the chart in the correct category. Two of the statements will not be used.

Things that happened only in the dream:	• •
Things that really happened (but were not in the dream):	• •
Things that both happened in the dream and really happened:	• •

1. Someone eats a cookie.
2. Brian loses touch with reality.
3. Brian is studying in his room.
4. Someone talks to Brian about dreams.
5. Someone brings Brian some cookies.
6. Someone brings Brian some tea.
7. Someone tells Brian to relax.
8. Brian talks with his mouth full.

6. What didn't the girl in the dream do?

   Ⓐ She didn't tell Brian to relax.

   Ⓑ She didn't give Brian a pink rose.

   Ⓒ She didn't bring Brian some refreshments.

   Ⓓ She didn't hold Brian's hand.

7. Why was Brian surprised and a little anxious about the cookies?

   Ⓐ because he didn't like cookies

   Ⓑ because he wasn't sure who brought the cookies

   Ⓒ because he was losing touch with reality

   Ⓓ because the girl in the dream brought the cookies

8. Listen again to part of the conversation.

   What does Brian want to do?

   Ⓐ to share refreshments with the girl in the dream

   Ⓑ to share refreshments with his girlfriend, Angie

   Ⓒ to share refreshments with the famous Dr. Freud

   Ⓓ to share refreshments with some lovely young lady

Self-Assessment Log

Check (✓) the words in this chapter you have acquired and can use in your daily life.

Nouns	Verbs	Adjectives	Idioms and Expressions
▣ flexibility	▣ conceptualize	▣ chaotic	▣ in tune with
▣ perception	▣ manipulate	▣ fleeting	▣ the downside
	▣ visualize	▣ trivial	▣ the upside

Check (✓) your level of accomplishment for the skills introduced in this chapter. How comfortable do you feel using these skills?

	Very comfortable	Somewhat comfortable	Not at all comfortable
Understanding comparison and contrast in lectures and informal conversations	☐	☐	☐
Using expressions such as *likewise* and *equally important* to express comparison	☐	☐	☐
Using expressions such as *nevertheless* and *the upside is/the downside is* to express contrast	☐	☐	☐
Understanding expressions such as *It's all just as well because* and *Yes, but look at it this way* when used to express a positive view	☐	☐	☐
Using expressions such as *It's all just as well because* and *Yes, but look at it this way* to express a positive view	☐	☐	☐

Think about the topics and activities in this chapter and complete the statements.

In this chapter, I learned something new about _____

_____

_____

I especially liked (topic or activity) _____

_____

_____

I would like to know more about _____

_____

_____

7 Working

> "Work is either fun or drudgery. It depends on your attitude. I like fun."
>
> Colleen C. Barrett
> President Emeritus of
> Southwest Airlines Co.

In this
CHAPTER

Webcast Japanese and American Business Management

Learning Strategy Listening For and Noting Causes and Effects

Language Function Persuading and Giving In

Connecting to the Topic

1. What images does the term *work* bring immediately to mind?

2. Have you ever had a job that you thought was wonderful? What made it so good? Have you ever had a terrible job? What made it so bad?

3. What do you think the perfect job would be? Create a fantasy job in your mind and share it with your group. What is it? Where is it? What are the hours? How much do you earn? Who are your coworkers?

Did You Know?

An American business consultant, W. Edwards Deming, played an extremely important role in the economic growth of Japan after World War II. His principles, which American businesses were slower to adopt, are as follows:

- Quality is defined by the customer.

- Quality comes from improving the production process, not by sorting out and eliminating defective products.

- Long-lasting quality improvement comes from working "smarter" rather than from working longer, harder, or faster.

- Change and improvement must involve *everyone* in the organization.

- Ongoing training of all employees is the key to continuous improvement of processes and products.

- Education and self-improvement programs for employees lead to greater productivity than warnings (threats) and slogans (short phrases used repeatedly with the intent to increase motivation).

1 **What Do You Think?** Discuss the following questions about W. Edwards Deming's principles in pairs.

1. In what ways do you think quality is defined by the customer?

2. Why do you think improving the quality of the production process is ultimately more important than pulling defective products off of the production line and throwing them away?

◀ What might Deming say are the benefits of the cooperative team approach at this company?

3. Why do you think it's better to work "smarter" rather than harder or longer? Give an example.

4. Why do you think that Deming says that change and improvement *must* involve everyone in the organization? How is this different from saying that everyone *must* make whatever changes the boss requires?

5. Do you agree that ongoing training is the most important factor in the continuous improvement of processes and products? Give an example.

6. Why do you think that threats and motivational slogans might not work very well to improve productivity?

Sharing Your Experience

2 **Ranking Criteria for Job Satisfaction** Each person has a slightly different idea of what makes a job satisfying. Read the following list and rank the items from 1 (for most important) to 10 (for least important) according to your criteria for job satisfaction. Add some new criteria if you wish.

Discuss your answers with a partner, then with the rest of the class. Consider the following questions in your class discussion.

- Which criteria did students add to the list?
- Which criteria did most people rank first? Last?

_____ mental challenge	_____ flexible working hours
_____ good pay	_____ cooperative decision-making
_____ health and hospital care	involving both workers and
_____ long paid vacations	management
_____ friendly coworkers	_____ opportunities for advancement
_____ work that is socially	_____ individual recognition
responsible	_____ other _____

▲ Having friendly coworkers is the number one priority for these coworkers.

3 **Checking Assumptions About Job-Related Priorities** When it comes to job satisfaction, do you think that people from the United States have the same priorities as you do?

1. Discuss with a partner how you think most people from the U.S. would rank the categories in Activity 2.

2. To check your assumptions, interview three to five people from the U.S. who work in a variety of situations. If this is not possible, or if you need to get additional information, research this topic on the Internet. Try these keywords in various combinations to see what you can find: *job, satisfaction, benefits, priorities, working conditions, unions, employees, United States, values, criteria.*

3. Discuss the results of your interviews and/or Internet search with your classmates. Which criteria did most people rank first? Last?

Vocabulary Preview

4 **Sharing Definitions** The following words are used in the lecture. You probably already know the meanings of several of them. However, the words you know may be different from the ones your classmates know. In small groups, pool your knowledge to match the definitions on the right with the words on the left.

Words

1. _____ assemble
2. _____ consensus
3. _____ consultant
4. _____ dispute
5. _____ individualism
6. _____ initiative
7. _____ innovation
8. _____ interdependence
9. _____ quota
10. _____ top dollar

Definitions

a. the belief that the interests of the individual are more important than those of the group

b. to put together

c. the highest price

d. new idea, method, or device

e. unanimous agreement (everyone agrees)

f. person who gives expert advice

g. maximum number allowed

h. mutual reliance or support

i. ability and willingness to start things

j. disagreement

5 **Vocabulary in Context** Fill in the blanks with the appropriate forms of the words from the list in Activity 4 on page 126. Note: You will not use every word in the list.

When a U.S. company finds itself in economic trouble, its stockholders become uneasy, and quick action is essential. It is common practice for specialists to be called in to help find a solution for the company's problem. In fact, this situation has just occurred at a major corporation. A _____ has been hired by XYZ to find out why sales have
    1
declined in recent months. In order to learn more about the company's problems, the consultant has arranged a meeting with company managers. This consultant wants to be sure that she understands the existing philosophy before she introduces any _____ or makes any changes.
                                                          2

According to the company philosophy, each worker is expected to take the _____ in presenting new ideas; workers are not led by the
          3
hand. However, once the individual devises the idea, a _____,
                                                                    4
or collective agreement, is needed before the idea can be carried out. Once there is agreement about an idea, costs are carefully analyzed to judge whether the idea fits with the general plan. Then if the project is determined to be worthy of company effort, a team is _____. If the team
                                                          5
works well together, dividing up the responsibilities and parts of the project, this type of cooperation and _____ among workers makes the
                                        6
company's managers proud. The company's cooperative policies have been working well up until the past few months; workers have been content, and few _____ have occurred among the workers. Because the
      7
working conditions are so favorable, the sales slump must be caused by other factors. At least that is the assumption the consultant will start with.

Strategy

Listening for Causes and Effects

When businesspeople and researchers look at a successful company, they often ask themselves: What factors make the company successful? To answer this question, they examine various factors to decide which ones seem to be related. Then they determine if the relationship is one of cause and effect or just chance.

For example, one automobile dealership sells more cars than any other dealer. The other dealers wonder why. They look at many factors: location of the showroom, business hours, prices of the cars, and the amount of money paid to salespeople. When the dealers discover that the showroom location of each dealership is similar, the business hours are similar, and the prices of the cars are similar, but that the amount of money paid to the salespeople is greater at the most successful dealership, they suspect a cause-and-effect relationship.

Seeing cause-and-effect relationships can help us find solutions to problems in all aspects of life. Therefore, it's no surprise that instructors present causes and effects as they lecture. In explaining cause-and-effect relationships, lecturers generally use two approaches: straightforward and indirect.

Sometimes, a lecturer clearly lists the causes and the effects that are involved in a situation and uses specific expressions to introduce causes, effects, and cause-and-effect relationships. If a lecturer uses this straightforward approach, listening for these expressions will alert you to take notes on this important information.

Some lecturers will present causes and effects as a series of facts with implied connections rather than clearly listed ones. It is then the student's job to recognize the implications and make the connections. If a lecturer uses this more subtle, indirect approach, being familiar with cause-and-effect expressions can help alert you to the connections the speaker is implying, because you will be aware of where the speaker might have used one of these expressions.

Expressions Signaling Causes

because	for	since

Expressions Signaling Effects

as a consequence	hence	thus
as a result	so	
consequently	therefore	

Expressions Signaling a Cause-and-Effect Relationship

as a consequence of...	due to the fact that...	due to this fact	if... then
as a result of...	due to this	for this reason	when... then

Strategy

Noting Causes and Effects

Whether a lecturer uses a straightforward or indirect approach, an effective note-taking system is to put all of the causes on one side of the page and the effects on the other. If you can't sort out everything in this way during the lecture, just continue to take notes on important information and organize your notes to show cause-and-effect relationships later. The notes below on the garbage collectors' strike in New York City from a lecture on labor unions and management are an example of this type of note organization.

▲ One of the effects of a New York City garbage collectors' strike.

Labor Unions and Management: NYC Garbage Collectors' Strike

Causes	Effects
1a. low wages	1. workers strike
1b. long hours	
1c. dirty working conditions	
2. strike	2a. city looks ugly
	2b. areas smell bad
	2c. tourist business is lost
	2d. disease breaks out
3. picketers throw rocks at scab workers	3a. 25 people are arrested
	3b. bad feelings increase between management and employees

1 **Considering the Issue** Discuss the following questions in small groups.

1. Do you think it is always important for workers to cooperate and rely on each other?

2. Under what conditions is an interdependent work situation better than one in which each person does a separate task?

2 **How Would *You* Run a Doorbell Company?** Take the following audience survey. It will be referred to during the distance learning webcast "Japanese and American Business Management." Circle the description (a or b) that most closely mirrors how *you* would organize a company for each of the items listed.

Audience Survey

How Would *You* Run a Doorbell Company?

For each item circle either a or b.

1. Supervision of production; wages

   a. Use a supervisor. Have a supervisor record the number of doorbells each worker assembles; pay each person according to how many he or she produces.

   b. Don't use a supervisor. Have production teams of three to four workers each assemble the doorbells and record the number of doorbells assembled by the team. Provide equal bonuses for each member of the teams producing a specified number of doorbells.

2. Raises and promotions

   a. Give frequent raises and promotions to workers who work fastest. Give frequent raises and promotions to workers who work hardest. Give fewer rewards to the others.

   b. Give few but regular promotions and raises to everyone on the basis of age and number of years with the company.

3. Slow work periods

   a. Hire many workers during periods when the demand for doorbells is heavy; fire unnecessary workers when business slows down. Don't reduce pay of those who remain employed.

   b. Give all employees lifelong employment guarantees. Reduce pay and hours for both labor and management, but fire no one when business slows down.

4. Quality control

   a. Have an outside inspector responsible for quality control. The outside inspector is someone who is not involved in the production process.

   b. Make the work team responsible for quality control. Give extra money or time off for excellent records. Encourage team cooperation by giving awards and public praise.

5. Changes and improvements in the system

   a. Use outside consultants to get new ideas for improving electronic doorbells. Reward individual workers who make usable suggestions. To avoid disagreements among workers, let management decide on all changes.

   b. Use work teams to get new ideas for improving electronic doorbells. Have regular discussion meetings of the work team. Make changes slowly, only after workers and management agree.

Listen

3 **Listening for Expressions Signaling Causes and Effects** Listen to the lecture once all the way through to get the gist of what is being said. As you listen, try to write all of the expressions for introducing causes, effects, and cause-and-effect relationships in the chart on page 132. If you can't write the expressions, just put a check mark (✓) in the appropriate column on the chart.

Expressions signaling a cause	Expressions signaling an effect	Expressions signaling a cause-and-effect relationship

4 Taking Notes on Causes and Effects Read through the partial outline (pages 133–135) of causes and effects discussed in the webcast. Then listen to the webcast and take notes by completing the outline. Remember that not all of the causes, effects, and cause-and-effect relationships will be signaled with the expressions in the chart. Some of them will be implied in the speakers' statements of facts.

▲ These Japanese workers take advantage of time allowed for exercise during their work day.

▲ These Japanese auto workers are likely to have worked as a team to improve the quality of this product.

Causes	Effects
1a. Japanese products are easy to get.	1. Americans buy many Japanese products.
1b. Japanese products are _____ _____.	
1c. Japanese products are _____ _____.	
2. _____ _____	2. American companies are losing business.
3. _____ _____ _____ _____ _____ _____ _____	3a. Some leaders in business, labor, and government want protective taxes and _____ _____ _____.
	3b. Other leaders say the United States should _____ _____ _____.
4. U.S. manager encourages individual initiative.	4a. Separate people moving up from _____ _____.
	4b. Keep clear division between _____ _____ _____.
5. Japanese manager encourages group efforts.	5a. _____ _____
	5b. _____ _____
	5c. _____ _____
6a. Japan is a small country.	6. _____ _____ _____ _____ _____
6b. Japan is isolated.	
6c. Japan is _____ _____ _____.	

7a. The United States is _____

_____

_____.

7b. The United States has _____

_____

_____.

7c. The United States has _____

_____

_____.

7d. The people in the United States like

_____

_____.

7. Business practices that are competitive and free from rules may not be as good for modern industrial production as Japanese practices are.

8a. William Ouchi says the United States should strengthen the bond between workers and their companies by providing _____

_____

_____,

8b. _____

_____,

8c. _____

_____,

8d. and _____

_____.

_____,

8a. Then United States productivity will _____

_____

_____.

8b. And in the long run, these reforms will lead to _____

_____,

8c. _____

_____,

8d. _____

_____,

8e. and _____.

9a. IBM, Intel, Procter and Gamble, and Hewlett-Packard have _____

_____

_____.

9a. Decrease in _____

_____

_____,

9b. _____   9b. and _____

_____ ,

9c. and _____   9c. Increase in _____

_____ .

_____ ,

9d. and _____ .

After You Listen

 5 Comparing Notes Compare your outline notes with a few of your classmates, just as you would with a study group preparing for a test.

Talk It Over

 6 Discussing the Effects of Technology on Work and Society Browse the Internet, current magazines, mail-order catalogs, newspapers, business journals, or scientific journals. Print, cut out, or copy a few pictures and descriptions of very high-tech, new, "cutting edge" products. Bring these pictures to class and use them to do the following activity.

1. In small groups, read the descriptions of each item aloud and discuss the possible personal or workplace benefits of using this device.

2. Decide whether or not this device could have (or has already had) a major effect on your personal life. If so, would it be (or has it been) a positive or a negative effect?

3. Decide which of these devices might have (or has already had) the most dramatic effect on society as a whole. Why do you think so?

7 Describing Innovations In small groups, share your answers to the following questions. Then share a few of your group's most beneficial or most imaginative ideas with the whole class.

1. If you could design something to make your work (at school, at home, or on the job) easier, what would it be? Have some fun with this. What you design does not have to be something that can realistically be developed and manufactured right now.

2. Describe what your innovation would do and the effect it would have on your work. How would it affect society as a whole?

Strategy

Presenting Persuasive Arguments

The most effective way to persuade someone to agree with you is to present a strong argument. A persuasive argument may be purely logical and reasonable, or it may be based on feelings and emotions. In either case, you will need to give reasons why this particular argument or point of view is a good one.

To be persuasive, you can start off with a strong cause-and-effect statement. This can then be followed by additional support for your point of view to strengthen your argument. Consider the following example. Notice the expressions used to introduce the additional supporting information.

> **A Persuasive Statement of Cause and Effect:**
> More companies in this country should adopt Japanese-style management practices; a company in my town did this and doubled both productivity and sales.

> **Followed by Additional Points to Strengthen the Argument:**
> *Not only that, but* the employees are much happier, so they are generally healthier and don't have to take so many days off because of illness. *What's more*, the food in the employee cafeteria is really terrific, so the employees don't have to eat in expensive restaurants or take time to make their own lunches.

Expressions Used to Strengthen Arguments with Additional Information
Along with that...
And another thing...
And I might add...
Besides...
Furthermore...
In addition to that...
Moreover...
Not only that, but...
Not to mention the fact that...
Plus the fact that...
What's more...

Strategy

Giving In to Persuasive Arguments

When someone has managed to persuade you to agree with his or her point of view by presenting a convincing argument, you can "give in" by saying *OK* plus one of the following expressions.

Expressions Used When Giving In

Formal	Informal
I guess you're right (after all).	I give up.
If you really insist.	I'll buy that.
I'll go along with that.	I'm sold.
Maybe you are right.	OK, you've got me.
Perhaps in this case (you're right).	You win.
You may have a point there.	You're right.
(I guess) You've convinced me.	You've sold me.

Strategy

Giving In and Accepting an Enticing Offer

Persuading and *giving in* can occur in any situation, not just during formal discussions or debates. For example, someone may try to persuade you to actually do something for them, not just to agree with their point of view. They may even offer something very appealing to entice you to go along with their request. In the following example, Person A makes an enticing offer to Person B, a coworker, and Person B is persuaded to accept it.

A: Could you help me out? I'd really like to go to San Francisco for the weekend, but I've been scheduled to work on Saturday. Will you fill in for me on Saturday?

B: Well... I'm not sure if that's convenient.

A: How about if I work for you on a day you want to take off to visit your mother?

B: OK. You've talked me into it. What time should I show up on Saturday?

Expressions Used When Giving In and Accepting an Enticing Offer

Come to think of it...	On second thought...
If you insist...	That's an offer I can't refuse!
I'm sold!	When you put it that way...
In that case...	You've sold me!
Now that you mention it...	You've talked me into it.

Strategy

Giving In Reluctantly to an Unappealing Request

Sometimes people will try to persuade you to do something for them by presenting the negative consequences that will result if you do not do what they are asking. In the following example, Person A describes what will happen if Person B, a fellow employee, doesn't go along with a request and Person B reluctantly gives in.

A: Do you think you could work on Saturday?

B: Well... I have plans this Saturday.

A: We all have to put in some extra time this week. If we don't, the project won't be finished on time and the company could lose the contract. Plus the fact that if the company loses this contract, we might all get laid off.

B: Given that there seems to be no other choice... what time should I come in on Saturday?

Expressions Used When Giving In to an Unappealing Request

Given that there seems to be no other choice...

If I absolutely have to...

If that's the only alternative...

If that's the only way...

If that's the way it's got to be...

If there's no other alternative...

If there's no other way...

If you insist...

OK, just this once.

That's an offer I guess I'd better not refuse!

Well, under those circumstances...

When you put it that way...

1 **Listening for People Persuading and Giving In** Listen to the conversation and answer the following questions.

1. Where is the company executive from?

   _____

2. What does he want to do?

   _____

3. Who is he trying to persuade?

   _____

4. Who will work for the company?

   _____

5. Who will manage the company? _____

6. What does the company executive say about pollution problems? _____

_____

7. What is the mayor concerned about? _____

8. What enticing offer does the executive make? _____

9. Is the mayor persuaded? _____

2 **Listening for Expressions for Persuading and Giving In** Listen to the conversation a second time, and write down all the expressions you hear for persuading and giving in. When you are finished, compare your answers in small groups.

Persuading	Giving in
_____	_____
_____	_____
_____	_____
_____	_____
_____	_____

3 **Listening for Expressions Introducing Persuasive Arguments** Listen again to the webcast comparing Japanese and U.S. business customs and do the following in small groups.

1. As you listen, make a list of the expressions the speaker uses to introduce persuasive arguments.

_____

_____

_____

_____

_____

_____

2. The two speakers in the discussion share a particular point of view. In one or two sentences, state their point of view. Did the speakers persuade you to agree with them? Why or why not? Share your answers with your classmates.

_____

_____

4 Persuading in Informal Situations As a class, have fun discovering your classmates' "prices" for various actions.

1. Ask another student in the class (or your instructor) to do something unusual or something to which they would usually say no. For example:

> Will you pay for my trip to Paris next week?
>
> Will you marry my brother tomorrow?

2. When the student responds negatively (see page 32 for ways to say no), try to persuade your classmate by presenting various positive or negative consequences. For example:

> Well, would you pay for my trip if I gave you a 1% share of my company?
>
> If you don't marry my brother, he will be heartbroken.

3. If your classmate still refuses to do what you've asked, you must continue to present consequences that are more and more positive or negative until your classmate finally gives in. For example:

> If you don't pay for my trip, I will probably lose my entire business because I can't get to Paris to negotiate a big contract.
>
> If you marry my brother, you will be married to the richest, kindest, and most handsome man in my country. He will be devoted to you all your life.

4. After your classmate gives in, it is his/her turn to make an unusual request of someone else in the class and to keep rephrasing the request until that person finally gives in. Continue on until everyone in the class has had at least one turn.

5 Debating Work-Related Issues Form teams to represent opposite sides in debates on work-related issues. Choose from the following topics or create your own topics for debate. As you debate, use persuasive expressions to convince your opponents to accept your point of view. Give in each time your opponents present a convincing argument.

Debate Topics

1. Selecting children at a young age and training them for certain professions (is/is not) best for these individuals and for society as a whole.
2. Management (should/should not) involve itself in the personal life and well-being of its employees.
3. Industrial spying (is/is not) justifiable.
4. White-collar jobs (should/should not) have more prestige than blue-collar jobs.
5. Women (should/should not) be allowed to do any job they choose if they meet the basic qualifications.
6. Robots in the workplace are a (help/hindrance) to the welfare of workers.
7. Trade unions (are/are not) the best means of solving problems in the workplace.
8. Companies (should/should not) be responsible for the costs of continuing education for employees.

▲ An electrician installs wiring in new construction.

6 **Role-Playing Persuading and Giving In** In pairs, choose one of the following situations to role-play. Use the expressions for persuading and giving in as your characters express their views.

- If time permits, change partners one or more times and do the activity again.
- Present one of the role-plays to the class.

Situations

1. You love to ski and try to go to the mountains on the weekends as often as possible. Therefore, you support the idea of a four-day, ten-hour workweek. A coworker, on the other hand, likes to play tennis every afternoon after work and wants to continue working five days a week for eight hours a day. The matter will be voted on by the employees tomorrow. Try to persuade your coworker to vote for the four-day workweek.

2. You are waiting for a plane at the airport. You start a conversation with a friendly Japanese woman sitting next to you. She works for an American computer company, perhaps Apple, in Japan. You work for a Japanese computer company, perhaps Fujitsu, in Chicago. Each of you is happy with your work situation and tries to convince the other person that your company is the best.

3. You have recently begun a new job with an American company and the boss has asked to meet with you to hear your opinions on several issues. There have been problems between workers and management at the company in recent years. When you start to suggest some changes based on Japanese management style, the boss says he doesn't think the company needs to change so much. Try to convince him that the company really does need to make some changes.

FOCUS

TOEFL® iBT

Integrated Speaking Tasks

Unlike earlier versions of the test, the TOEFL® iBT contains a speaking section. You will be asked to give very short responses (45 or 60 seconds each) to *six prompts*, or sets of directions. Four of these prompts are for "integrated" tasks involving at least two language skills. You will always hear a short listening passage before you give your spoken response. In some integrated tasks, you must also read a short passage on the same topic as the listening passage. Your response should be based on the information you read and/or hear.

To be able to respond well to an integrated prompt, you must take notes on the main ideas and supporting details in the listening passage as you have been doing in previous chapters. It will also help if you look for patterns of information, that is, information that can be sorted and classified or grouped together. This will help you to organize your spoken response to the integrated prompt.

1 Responding to an Integrated-Speaking Prompt Give yourself 90 seconds to read the short passage below. Then listen to a segment from a lecture about a step-by-step problem-solving system. As you listen, close your books and take notes. When you are finished listening, open your books and follow the prompt for the integrated-speaking task. If possible, say your response to another student, who can give you feedback. If this is not possible, try recording your response so you can listen to it and evaluate it yourself.

Reading Passage

Step-by-step systems for solving problems are popular because they help simplify confusing, complicated situations. Five-step, seven-step, or twelve-step programs are relatively easy to remember and to follow. When facing the shapelessness and uncertainty of a real-life problem, a person welcomes the comfort of a well-defined system. Such approaches also encourage problem-solvers to slow down and analyze situations. This analysis often leads to a surprising redefinition of the problem, as previously unnoticed aspects become apparent.

These types of programs are very helpful when the problem must be solved by several people, not just one. The steps of the system function as a set of rules for the problem-solving team. Thus, disagreements about various aspects of the problem can be settled before the team moves from one step to another. This creates a sense of solidarity and team accomplishment—especially if a satisfactory solution is reached.

Integrated-Speaking Prompt

How does information from the lecture illustrate principles described in the reading? Your response should include specific examples from both the reading and the lecture. You have 30 seconds to prepare your response and 60 seconds to speak.

Self-Assessment Log

Check (✓) the words in this chapter you have acquired and can use in your daily life.

Nouns

- consensus
- consultant
- dispute
- individualism
- initiative
- innovation
- interdependence
- quota

Verb

- assemble

Idiom

- top dollar

Check (✓) your level of accomplishment for the skills introduced in this chapter. How comfortable do you feel using these skills?

	Very comfortable	Somewhat comfortable	Not at all comfortable
Understanding expressions such as *since, consequently,* and *due to the fact that* when used to introduce causes, effects, and cause-and-effect relationships	☐	☐	☐
Using expressions such as *since, consequently,* and *due to the fact that* to introduce causes, effects, and cause-and-effect relationships	☐	☐	☐
Understanding and using expressions such as *not to mention the fact that* for making arguments more persuasive	☐	☐	☐
Understanding and using expressions such as *You've sold me* for giving in to persuasive arguments	☐	☐	☐
Understanding and using expressions such as *Well, under those circumstances* for giving in to an unappealing request	☐	☐	☐

Think about the topics and activities in this chapter and complete the statements.

In this chapter, I learned something new about _____

_____

_____

I especially liked (topic or activity) _____

_____

_____

I would like to know more about _____

_____

_____

8 Breakthroughs

"The most exciting breakthroughs of the 21st century will not occur because of technology but because of an expanding concept of what it means to be human."

John Naisbitt
U.S. author

Lecture Discovering the Laws of Nature

Learning Strategy What to Do When You Don't Understand Complex Concepts

Language Function Giving and Receiving Compliments

Connecting to the Topic

1. What is the scientific breakthrough shown in the photo?

2. What other innovations did this breakthrough make possible?

3. Breakthroughs or discoveries can happen in all areas of life, not just in science. Can you think of an ideological breakthrough in this century that has changed life for society?

Did You Know?

- The word *physics* comes from the Greek word *physis*, which means, "that which shows itself and becomes observable." So physics is the study of the observable world and what makes it work. It is the science of matter and energy.

- After Relativity Theory, Quantum Mechanics, and Fiber Optics, some scientists say that the next most important breakthrough in 21st-century physics is Chaos Theory. Ian Stewart, a British mathematician, said that chaos is "lawless behavior governed entirely by law."

- Edward Lorenz, a meteorologist, proposed Chaos Theory in 1960 to explain the difficulty in making accurate weather predictions. Chaos Theory says that a small event can produce big results. The most common example is the "butterfly effect." This is the idea, for example, that a butterfly in China could influence weather patterns in New York City.

- Scientists interested in the motion of fluids, especially the complicated, irregular motion called turbulence, have used the principles of Chaos Theory to develop products to benefit the average consumer. For example, the Daewoo Company of Korea claims to have created the first washing machine based on Chaos Theory in 1990. It was supposed to produce cleaner, less tangled clothes.

▲ Chaos theory helps explain the effects of turbulence.

1 What Do You Think? Discuss the following questions in pairs.

1. If physics is the study of the physical world, what do you think metaphysics might be?

2. What do you think Ian Stewart was trying to do when he described chaos paradoxically as "lawless behavior governed entirely by law"?

3. What could be the possible effects of a tiny butterfly beating its wings in China on the weather in New York?

4. Were you surprised that Chaos Theory was used to develop a better washing machine? What do you think are some other things involving turbulence that might be improved by the application of the principles of Chaos Theory?

2 **Discussing Learning about Physics and Personal Breakthroughs**
Discuss the following questions in small groups.

1. In what ways did you learn in school about the laws of physics? For example, did you learn about these laws through textbooks? Lectures? Class discussions? Laboratory experiments? Which way worked best for you?

2. In your everyday life, what have you learned about the physical laws of nature? Share what you have learned and how you learned it.

3. Breakthroughs in your personal life are usually moments of realization, or a sudden jump in proficiency at a task after a long struggle of trying to improve. Just as with a scientific breakthrough, many things after a personal breakthrough change in significant ways. Share a nonscientific breakthrough that you have made in your life or that someone you know has made in his/her life. What were the consequences?

Vocabulary Preview

3 **Choosing from Multiple Meanings** Many English words have more than one meaning. Sometimes the meanings are quite similar, but often they are very different. The words in the list below are defined as they are used in the lecture. In the following exercise, choose the sentences that use the words as they are defined in the vocabulary list and then compare your answers in small groups.

Words	Definitions
bleed	*to cut and let blood flow out from a patient as part of a cure*
cosmos	*the universe considered as an orderly system*
matter	*that which is material, physical; not mental or spiritual*
relative	*not absolute; dependent on something else*

1. to bleed

   (A) He was very lucky. After the accident he was only bleeding from the nose.

   (B) Modern doctors have recently experimented with bleeding patients as a cure for certain ailments.

   (C) Don't put your new black T-shirt in the wash with your white clothes because it might bleed.

2. matter

   (A) The brain has both gray and white matter.

   (B) It doesn't matter to me.

   (C) It's only a matter of time.

3. cosmos

    (A) My uncle, Cosmos, is a world-famous physicist.

    (B) The cosmos she planted in the garden came up late this year.

    (C) He often looked up and wondered about the nature of the cosmos.

4. relative

    (A) My cousin Pete is my favorite relative.

    (B) Time and space are relative to each other.

    (C) He finished the exam with relative ease.

④ Vocabulary in Context The following words used in the lecture do not have multiple meanings. Choose the sentences in the exercise that use the words correctly and then compare your answers in small groups.

Words	Definitions
metaphysical	*having to do with the branch of philosophy that deals with the nature of truth and knowledge in the universe*
paradigm	*a unifying idea or set of principles*
such and such	*referring to a condition, person, place, thing, or time not specifically mentioned*
wild goose chase	*a task that cannot be completed because of lack of information or being given incorrect information*

1. metaphysical

    (A) He had a metaphysical at the doctor's office.

    (B) She metaphysicals on her way to work.

    (C) They were both interested in metaphysical ideas.

2. paradigm

    (A) She met a paradigm at the party.

    (B) Her paradigm was the model for all the research that followed.

    (C) The paradigm, an early model of the parachute, had many faults.

3. such and such

    (A) The instructor gave this example to illustrate the theory: If you were going at such and such a speed for such and such an amount of time through space, the amount of time that seemed to pass on Earth might be quite different.

    (B) He was such and such a difficult instructor that the student wondered if she should wait until someone else taught the physics course.

    (C) They were not interested in metaphysical ideas such and such as these.

4. wild goose chase

    (A) During the mating season for geese, we often see one wild goose chase another goose.

    (B) The quest for a unified field theory encompassing all the laws of nature may turn out to be a wild goose chase.

    (C) It was their first wild goose chase, and they were proud of their success.

PART 2   When You Don't Understand the Concepts

Strategy

What to Do When You Don't Understand Complex Concepts

Anyone who is trying to understand a complex subject or concept may have a problem understanding it even when every word is familiar. For example, when you listen to the lecture in this chapter, "Discovering the Laws of Nature," you may find that some of the concepts are difficult to comprehend, even though the words are not. In this case, the following strategies will be very helpful.

Seven Ways to Approach Complex Concepts

1. **Don't panic.** Remember that you're not alone. Your classmates are probably having difficulty, too.

2. **Don't give up.** Continue to concentrate on the topic. Try not to let your mind wander. Thinking about something you *do* understand about the topic usually helps.

3. When you feel lost, **listen for key nouns and verbs** in the next few sentences. These words carry most of the meaning.

4. **Continue to take notes** even though they may not be perfect. Any nouns and verbs you manage to write down will be useful later when you start asking questions to determine exactly what you missed.

5. **Write down any negative terms** such as *never* and *not*. Without these words, your notes may appear to say the opposite of what the speaker intended.

6. **Try repeating to yourself** the sentence or sentences you can't seem to understand. If this does not help, try punctuating the sentence differently or changing the rhythm, stress, or intonation patterns as you repeat it to yourself. Sometimes a small change is all it takes to jump from the muddle of incomprehension to the "Aha!" of understanding.

7. **Familiarize yourself with the speaker's topic ahead of time.** If you are in an academic class, complete the assigned readings before the lecture. If there are no assigned readings, or if the readings are very difficult, try to find some general information on the topic from an encyclopedia, a magazine, or a textbook from a lower-level course.

FYI

Have you shopped for a computer, a smartphone, or some other high-tech device lately? If so, you may have found it difficult to follow exactly what the salesperson was saying. Maybe you thought you should understand because you knew all the words the salesperson used, but you still "just didn't get it." If this has happened to you, don't worry. This happens to everyone, even native speakers.

1 Pooling Knowledge about Scientific Concepts Pooling knowledge of difficult concepts with classmates can considerably expand your understanding. In small groups, briefly share your understanding of the following concepts.

energy	light	matter	space
gravity	magnetism	motion	time

As a group, select the concept that you understand best and discuss the following.

1. Do you think that your understanding of this concept is more correct than the understanding of a student five years ago? 15 years ago? 50 years ago? 250 years ago? 2,500 years ago?

2. Why do you feel this way?

Listen

2 Practicing Seven Ways to Approach Difficult Concepts Some of the concepts in the lecture on "Discovering the Laws of Nature" may be familiar to you and some may not. Some may be easy for you to understand and some may be quite difficult. Practice using the seven helpful strategies for when you don't understand from page 149 by doing the following.

1. Listen to the lecture once all the way through and take notes as best as you can. If you get lost and don't understand a concept, try to use at least three of the strategies in the box on page 149 to get you back on track.

2. Listen to the lecture again. Fill in any gaps in your notes as necessary. Use the strategies in the box as needed.

▲ Physicist and Nobel laureate Albert Einstein's breakthrough in physics profoundly changed our world and inspired many young scientists to follow in his footsteps.

3 **Paraphrasing and Summarizing Notes** Look over your notes and paraphrase and/or summarize each of the major ideas to make sure that you really understand everything you wrote down.

4 **Comparing Notes** In small groups, compare your summaries. If your summaries are not similar, look at areas in your notes that may be incomplete or inaccurate and ask your classmates in your group if they can help you to fill in the missing information.

Talk It Over

5 **Comparing Strategies** In small groups, discuss which of the strategies from page 149 work best to help a listener get back on track and to clarify concepts when he or she doesn't understand what's being said. Use the following questions to guide your discussion.

1. Are the strategies that worked best for you when you were listening to the lecture the same ones that worked best for your classmates?

2. Earlier in this chapter, in the FYI box on page 149, the example of the computer salesperson was given to represent ordinary situations in which you may understand the individual words someone uses, but still not get the whole idea. Think of a similar situation in your own life. Did you use any of the strategies in the list? Did you use any other useful strategies? Share them with your classmates.

3. What strategies do your instructors use to help you to understand? Do they, for example, use study guides, charts, diagrams, or outlines?

4. What strategies do you routinely use during conversations to explain difficult concepts? For example, do you gesture with your hands? Do you draw diagrams? Which of the strategies to use when you don't understand might be useful to add to what you already do to help your listeners understand?

6 **Describing Scientific Processes** In small groups, take turns describing what happens to energy and matter in the following everyday situations. Most of the vocabulary should be familiar, but the concepts may be a bit tricky. Use a basic physics book or the Internet as a reference, if you wish, but don't make your explanations too technical.

1. blowing out a candle
2. riding a bicycle
3. grinding food in the garbage disposal
4. reflecting sunlight with a mirror onto a piece of paper
5. starting a car engine
6. planting a seed in a sunny garden
7. baking a cake
8. slipping on ice
9. rowing a boat
10. shooting an arrow
11. the turning of a windmill
12. the rising tides during a full moon

Strategy

Giving Sincere Compliments

People are often suspicious of flattery. Therefore, giving genuine compliments can be tricky. The keys to offering compliments appropriately are timing, number, and phrasing.

Timing

The person receiving the compliment will be more likely to feel it is sincere if it's deserved. Compliments are generally deserved when:

- a person has accomplished something special
- a person is discouraged and you are reminding them of their good efforts and steady progress

Number

How many compliments can you give at one time without overdoing it?

> One's OK, and two are fine;
> But stop at three, and draw the line.

Exception: If you give more than one compliment at a time to a superior at work or someone else in a position of authority, it may look like you are flattering them to gain favor or approval.

Phrasing

Take care to use adjectives and analogies that the person is pleased to identify with.

Example

Hank, you're really a *special* person. You have a *heart as big as the ocean*. Even though you're trying hard to complete your research, you still made time to raise money for the Homeless Children's Fund.

In addition to mastering timing, number, and phrasing, using the following expressions to introduce compliments will ensure that they sound sincere.

Expressions Used to Introduce Compliments

I don't mind saying…
I don't mind telling you…
I'd like to compliment you on…
If you ask me…
If you don't mind my saying…
I've been meaning to tell you…
Just between you and me…

Strategy

Receiving Compliments Graciously

A simple "thank you" is always an appropriate and gracious response to a compliment. If you feel this is not enough, add one of the following expressions.

Expressions Used to Receive Compliments Graciously

Coming from you, that means a lot.

Coming from you, that's a real compliment.

Do you really think so? How nice/sweet/kind of you to say that.

I appreciate your saying that.

I'm really glad/pleased you feel that way.

I'm really glad/pleased you think so.

I'm very flattered. (Note: Used in this way, *flattered* is positive, not negative.)

Thanks, I needed that!

That/Your opinion means a lot to me.

That's nice to hear.

That's very kind/nice/sweet of you.

What a nice/lovely/sweet thing to say!

You've made my day!

Note: To show modesty you can say:

> Oh, I can't take all the credit for that.
>
> (Name) deserves as much credit as I do.

Strategy

Dealing with Undeserved or Inappropriate Compliments

Undeserved Compliments

Sometimes, you may receive a compliment that you feel is undeserved. In this case, you may wish to be humble and say that the compliment is not true. However, do not deny or protest the compliment more than once or twice before you give in and accept the compliment graciously. Otherwise:

- People might think you are protesting too much and just "fishing for compliments," or really just looking for even more compliments.
- It might seem like you think the compliment is worthless, which could insult the speaker.

Inappropriate Compliments

Occasionally, you may receive a compliment that you feel is inappropriate.

- If the compliment is not offensive, you may either say a polite "thank you" or simply ignore it.
- If the compliment is offensive, you should consider telling the person so and/or reporting the incident to a friend or superior.

1 Listening for Appropriate and Inappropriate Compliments You will hear four conversations. The first two involve an instructor and some students, and the last two include several senior citizens. These conversations contain examples of both appropriate and inappropriate ways of giving compliments.

- Listen to each conversation, and answer the questions following it.
- Then compare answers with your classmates.

Conversation 1

Ron and Mr. McGovern are in the hall after class.

1. Ron's compliments to Mr. McGovern are inappropriate. What's wrong with Ron's timing? _____

_____

2. What's wrong with the number of compliments? _____

_____

3. What's wrong with the phrasing? _____

_____

Conversation 2

Sandra and Mr. McGovern are in the professor's office during office hours.

1. Are Sandra's compliments to Mr. McGovern appropriate? _____

2. Why or why not? Consider location of the interaction, number of

   compliments, and phrasing in your answer. _____

   _____

   _____

Conversation 3

Helen, Larry, and Martin are chatting at a retirement home.

1. How does Larry first compliment Helen? _____

   _____

2. What is Helen's response? _____

   _____

3. Why do you think she says this? _____

   _____

4. How does Martin compliment Helen? _____

   _____

5. How does Helen respond this time? _____

   _____

6. What do Helen and Larry tell Martin about his dancing? _____

   _____

   _____

▲ "If you don't mind my saying, you're a terrific dancer."

7. Who looked beautiful on the dance floor? _____

_____

_____

8. How does Martin feel about the compliments from Helen? _____

_____

_____

Conversation 4

Later in the day at the retirement home, Helen, Martin, and Larry continue chatting.

1. What's wrong with Martin?

_____

_____

2. Is the compliment Martin gives Helen appropriate?

_____

_____

3. How does Helen accept this compliment?

_____

_____

4. How does Larry try to cheer Martin up? _____

_____

_____

5. What does Helen say to encourage Martin? _____

_____

6. Does it work? _____

7. How does Martin respond? _____

_____

8. What does he mean by this? _____

_____

_____

2 **Giving and Receiving Compliments** Choose a partner for this activity. Listen to the lecture again. This time stop the recording each time you hear the speaker mention a breakthrough or other accomplishment, and do the following.

1. Pretend that your partner is the person the speaker is talking about. Imagine that you now have the opportunity to compliment this person on his or her achievements. Take this opportunity to really flatter him or her.

2. Let your partner respond to your compliments. Then continue listening to the recording.

3. When you stop the recording next time, change roles with your partner. This time, *you* will pretend to be the person who made the breakthrough and your partner will compliment *you*.

▲ Einstein's Theory of Relativity proposed that time and space were not independent principles of nature.

4. Continue taking turns in this way as you listen to the rest of the lecture.

5. When the lecture is finished, discuss which terms you used to give compliments, and how you felt as you were giving and receiving compliments in English.

▲ Newton demonstrated that the sun is the center of our solar system.

3 **Listening for and Discussing Compliments in Context** Watch a TV soap opera or comedy. Each time you hear a compliment, jot it down in the chart below. Also note the location, the situation or context, and the response. Listen until you hear at least three compliments.

Bring your notes to class. In small groups, describe the compliments, situations, and responses you noted. Did you or your classmates hear any inappropriate compliments? If so, list them underneath the chart. What made them inappropriate?

The Compliment	The Location	The Situation or Context	The Response

Inappropriate Compliments

_____

_____

_____

_____

4 **Discussing Inappropriate Compliments** Have you ever received an inappropriate compliment? If so, share the following information with your classmates.

1. What was the situation?
2. What was the compliment?
3. How did you respond?
4. If you could do it all over again, would you respond differently?

5 **Researching the Language Around You** For the next day or two, pay particular attention to any compliments that you give, receive, or overhear. Answer the following questions (answer questions 1–4 for each compliment). Then share the results of your research with your classmates.

1. What were the relationships of the people involved in each situation?
2. What were their attitudes toward each other?
3. What expressions did they use to give or receive compliments?
4. Were any expressions used that were new to you? If so, what were they?
5. How many compliments did you give in one day?
6. How many compliments did you receive?
7. Describe any situations in which you thought the compliments were inappropriate or insincere flattery.
8. Describe any situations in which you thought someone refused a compliment and protested too much, sounding as if he or she was "fishing for compliments."
9. Do you think that consciously observing the behavior of giving and receiving compliments caused you to give more compliments than usual, fewer compliments than usual, or had no effect on the number of compliments you usually give? Why?

Talk It Over

6 **Complimenting Colleagues** Be part of a "cutting edge" team on the verge of a real breakthrough. Then present your breakthrough invention to the world!

1. In small groups, imagine that you are a team of scientists living in the year 2200. You have recently made some important discoveries about the relationship of energy and matter. It is now your team's task to put these theories to practical use. You must design a device that converts energy into matter. As you brainstorm your ideas, make whatever drawings or diagrams you need to illustrate your ideas to your teammates.

2. As you work together, there should be opportunities to compliment your teammates on their ideas and to receive a few compliments yourself. When your team has finished the task, make a drawing or diagram of the device.

3. Imagine that your research team is at an international conference. As a group, present your device to the other "scientists" (your classmates) assembled in the main conference hall. Use the diagram your team developed to help explain the principles of the device. After each group has presented its work, be sure to compliment them on their presentation.

7 **Giving Insincere Compliments** Try this activity for fun! Take turns "buttering each other up"; that is, giving an excessive number of compliments because you want something very much and don't want to be refused. You may want to role-play one or more of the following small-group situations, or you may choose just to be yourselves.

Situations

1. a Hollywood party with producers, directors, and actors
2. a company holiday party
3. a reception for a famous visiting physicist
4. a reception for the president
5. a dinner party with your future in-laws

▲ What do you think the man might be saying to "butter up" his friend at the Hollywood party?

FOCUS

Biographical Narratives

Some of the lectures in the listening section of the TOEFL® iBT are biographical narratives. These tell about important events surrounding the accomplishments (or failures) of a certain person. The basic-comprehension questions about these narratives are likely to be about the timing and significance of the events.

When taking notes about such lectures, you should be aware that the basic structure of any narrative is chronological—related to time. Earlier events are likely to be described before later events. Also, each event in a biographical narrative is chosen because it says something about a person's character, social conditions, or notable contributions. Try to understand the reason for each stage of the narrative, paying special attention to the chronological sequence of events as you take notes.

1 **Basic Comprehension: Biographical Narratives** Listen to the biographical narrative about Albert Einstein. As you listen, close your books and take notes. After the speaker finishes talking, you will hear a series of questions. Open your books and fill in the bubble of the best answer to each of the questions that follow.

1. When was Einstein born?
   - Ⓐ in the 1850s
   - Ⓑ in the 1870s
   - Ⓒ in the 1930s
   - Ⓓ in the 1950s

2. Why did the Einstein family move to Italy?
   - Ⓐ because Albert had finished his schooling in Germany
   - Ⓑ because the family could not afford Albert's secondary school
   - Ⓒ because the father had failed an electrical engineering exam
   - Ⓓ because the family's electrical-supply business had failed

3. Which of the following is a likely source of the rumor that Einstein was a bad student, according to the professor?
   - Ⓐ He wasn't always interested in school.
   - Ⓑ He never graduated from high school.
   - Ⓒ He failed an exam.
   - Ⓓ He quit high school.

4. Which of the following is *not* a job that Einstein held, according to the lecture?

   (A) electrical engineer

   (B) patent-office clerk

   (C) school teacher

   (D) professor

5. What did Einstein do in his spare time during his two years as a patent-office clerk?

   (A) wrote scientific papers

   (B) read a lot of books on physics

   (C) talked to other physicists

   (D) taught mathematics and physics

6. Which institution gave Einstein a Ph.D. degree?

   (A) the Kaiser-Wilhelm Gesellschaft in Berlin

   (B) the German University of Prague

   (C) the University of Zurich

   (D) the University of Bern

7. Why, according to the lecture, is the year 1905 greatly significant in Einstein's life?

   (A) He got a job in the patent office.

   (B) He got a job as a university professor.

   (C) He published four brilliant scientific papers.

   (D) He was able to move back to Germany.

8. Which of the following best states why, according to the professor, Einstein left Germany in the 1930s?

   (A) German political leaders considered him an obstacle.

   (B) He believed war was not a good way to solve problems.

   (C) He had divorced Mileva Maric and wanted to remarry.

   (D) German physicists were jealous of his great fame.

Self-Assessment Log

Check (✓) the words in this chapter you have acquired and can use in your daily life.

Nouns	Verb	Adjectives	Idioms and Expressions
▪ cosmos	▪ bleed	▪ metaphysical	▪ such and such
▪ matter		▪ relative	▪ wild goose chase
▪ paradigm			

Check (✓) your level of accomplishment for the skills introduced in this chapter. How comfortable do you feel using these skills?

	Very comfortable	Somewhat comfortable	Not at all comfortable
Using strategies such as listening for key nouns and verbs, noting negative terms, and repeating things to yourself when you don't understand	☐	☐	☐
Recognizing when someone is giving you a compliment using expressions such as *I don't mind saying*	☐	☐	☐
Using expressions such as *I don't mind saying* to introduce compliments	☐	☐	☐
Understanding expressions such as *Coming from you that means a lot* and *What a lovely thing to say* when used to receive compliments	☐	☐	☐
Using expressions such as *Coming from you that means a lot* and *What a lovely thing to say* to receive compliments	☐	☐	☐
Understanding when flattery is used inappropriately	☐	☐	☐
Using flattery appropriately	☐	☐	☐

Think about the topics and activities in this chapter and complete the statements.

In this chapter, I learned something new about _____

_____

_____

I especially liked (topic or activity) _____

_____

_____

I would like to know more about _____

_____

Art and Entertainment

> "The battle for the mind of North America will be fought in the video arena: the Videodrome. The television screen is the retina of the mind's eye. Therefore, the television screen is part of the physical structure of the brain. Therefore, whatever appears on the television screen emerges as the raw experience for those who watch it. Therefore, television is reality, and reality *is* less than television."

Professor Brian O'Blivion
A character in the classic 1983 sci-fi film *Videodrome*

Radio Program Reality TV: Really Good or Really Bad?

Learning Strategy Distinguishing Between Fact and Opinion

Language Function Expressing Doubt or Disbelief

Connecting to the Topic

1. Do you enjoy watching movies like the sci-fi film *Videodrome*, which characterize TV as an evil force that can invade your mind? Why or why not?

2. Do you know what the retina of the eye does? If not, do an Internet search on the anatomy of the eye and then talk about what Professor O'Blivion means when he says, "The television screen is the retina of the mind's eye."

3. Do you enjoy watching reality TV shows or movies, such as *The Hunger Games* or *The Truman Show*, that use reality TV as a major part of the story? Why or why not?

Did You Know?

- Reality shows represent about 60 percent of all current television programming on both traditional and cable television channels.

- Americans spend about one-third of their free time watching television and about 60–70 percent of the shows they choose to watch are reality shows. In other parts of the world the percentages are even higher.

- Of the approximately 250,000 entertainment jobs in Los Angeles, about 20 percent of them are tied to reality shows and that percentage is increasing year by year.

- A reality show typically costs considerably less than what a prime-time dramatic show costs to produce, particularly because there are few, if any, paid professional actors on these programs.

- Reality shows are so popular that even national newscasts are using reality show techniques, such as following someone around over a period of time, using furniture and other props that may not really belong to the person in order to suggest a particular mood or idea, and even giving the person a "makeover" with specific clothes and makeup in order to look better (or sometimes even worse) than they normally do to gain audience interest or sympathy.

▼ Reality Shows Past and Present: Which ones have you seen?

- 16 & Pregnant
- 19 Kids & Counting
- 50 Cent: The Money and the Power
- A Double Shot at Love
- A Model Life with Petra Nemcova
- Ace of Cakes
- Addicted
- Adventures in Hollyhood
- Age of Love
- All American Girl
- The Amazing Race
- America's Got Talent
- America's Next Great Restaurant
- America's Next Top Model
- America's Toughest Jobs
- American Chopper
- American Gladiators

- American Hot Rod
- American Idol
- American Inventor
- Anything For Love
- The Apprentice
- Around the World in 80 Plates
- The Assistant
- Average Joe
- The Bachelor
- The Bachelorette
- Basketball Wives
- Battleground Earth
- Beauty And The Geek
- Being Bobby Brown
- Big Brother
- The Biggest Loser
- Big Man on Campus
- Brat Camp
- Breaking Bonaduce

- Bret Michaels: Life As I Know It
- Bridal Bootcamp
- Bridezillas
- Britney And Kevin: Chaotic
- Cake Boss
- Carnie Wilson: Unstapled
- Cash Cab
- The Celebrity Apprentice
- Celebrity Fit Club
- Celebrity Mole
- Celebrity Rehab with Dr. Drew
- Change of Heart
- Chasing Farrah
- Chef Academy
- Chopped
- College Life
- College Hill
- Combat Missions

- The Complex
- Confessions of a Matchmaker
- Confessions of a Teen Idol
- The Contender
- Cops
- Criss Angel Mindfreak
- The Crocodile Hunter
- Crowned: The Mother of All Pageants
- Cupcake Dreams
- Cupid
- Dance Machine
- Dance Moms
- Dancing with the Stars
- Date My Ex: Jo & Slade
- Date My House
- Dating in the Dark
- Deadliest Catch
- Denise Richards: It's Complicated
- DietTribe
- Dirty Jobs
- Dog The Bounty Hunter
- Dog Whisperer
- Dog Eat Dog
- Dream Job
- Driving Force
- Eco-Challenge
- Engaged and Underage
- Estate of Panic
- Ex-Wives Club
- Extreme Makeover
- Face Off
- The Family
- Fantasia For Real
- Farmer Wants a Wife
- Fashion Star
- Fear Factor
- Find My Family
- Flip This House
- Flipping Out
- Food Network Star
- Football Wives
- For Love Or Money
- Ghost Hunters
- The Glee Project
- Gone Country
- Great American Road Trip
- Hair Battle Spectacular
- Hard Knocks
- HGTV Design Star
- The Hills
- Hoarders
- Holmes on Homes
- Homeland Security USA
- House Rules
- I Love New York
- I Wanna Be a Soap Star
- I'm a Celebrity... Get Me Out of Here!
- Ice Road Truckers
- Intervention
- Iron Chef America
- The Jacksons: A Family Dynasty
- Jamie Oliver's Food Revolution
- The Janice Dickinson Modeling Agency
- Jersey Couture
- Jersey Shore
- Joe Millionaire
- Jon & Kate Plus 8
- Kathy Griffin: My Life on the D-List
- Keeping Up with the Kardashians
- Kitchen Nightmares
- Kourtney and Khloe Take Miami
- Kourtney and Kim Take New York
- LA Ink
- Last Comic Standing
- The Locator
- Love in the Wild
- Man vs. Wild
- MasterChef
- Maui Fever
- Meet My Folks
- The Millionaire Matchmaker
- The Moment of Truth
- My Super Sweet 16
- Mythbusters
- Nanny 911
- Nashville Star
- Newlyweds: Nick & Jessica
- Next Action Star
- The Osbournes
- Paranormal Investigators
- Paris Hilton's My New BFF
- Parking Wars
- The People's Court
- Project Runway
- Punk'd
- The Rachel Zoe Project
- The Real Housewives of Atlanta
- The Real Housewives of Beverly Hills
- The Real Housewives of D.C.
- The Real Housewives of Miami
- The Real Housewives of New Jersey
- The Real Housewives of New York City
- The Real Housewives of Orange County
- The Real Wedding Crashers
- The Real World
- Renovate My Family
- The Restaurant
- Rich Guy, Poor Guy
- Road Rules
- Scare Tactics
- Secret Millionaire
- The Simple Life
- The Sing-Off
- Skating with the Stars
- So You Think You Can Dance
- Storm Chasers
- Supernanny
- The Surreal Life
- Survivor
- Tabatha's Salon Takeover
- Toddlers and Tiaras
- Top Chef
- Tough Love
- Trading Spaces
- Treasure Hunters
- UFO Hunters
- Ultimate Cake Off
- Ultimate Recipe Showdown
- Undercover Boss
- The Voice
- The Weakest Link
- Whale Wars
- What Not To Wear

1 What Do You Think? Look over the representative list of reality TV shows on pages 166–167. Discuss the following questions in pairs. Then share your responses with your classmates.

1. Why do you think reality shows are so popular?

2. Do you think that reality shows really tell the truth about the people on them? Why or why not?

3. What do you think are the reasons that reality shows are so much cheaper to produce than other sorts of shows?

4. Why do you think that people want to be on reality shows?

5. Would you like to be on reality TV? Why or why not?

Sharing Your Experience

2 Discussing Reality TV Show Preferences Look over the representative list of reality shows on pages 166–167 again. In small groups, discuss the following questions.

1. Would you be surprised to know that the number of shows listed represents only about 20 percent of all reality shows that have been and are currently being produced? Why or why not?

2. What types of reality shows are the most popular in your native country? Singing contests? Game shows? Renovation and design shows? Cooking shows? Celebrities-at-home shows? Talk/interview shows? Hidden-camera shows? Dating shows? Makeover shows? Nature or animal shows? Crime shows? Medical shows? Other shows?

3. Do you watch reality TV shows? If yes, what is your favorite one? Why? Do you usually watch reality TV shows by yourself or with friends? Does it depend on the type of show? Why? If not, what types of shows do you prefer to watch? Do you usually watch these shows by yourself or with friends? Does it depend on the type of show? Why?

◀ On reality TV, cameras follow you everywhere.

3 **Crossword Puzzle** You will hear the following vocabulary words in the radio program in this chapter. Complete the crossword puzzle with the correct forms of the words on the list. Check your answers in the Appendix on page 251.

appalled	fired up	revenue	snag
aspirations	genre	ring true	soap opera
contrived	precursor	sensationalism	trend
exotic	pundit	sitcom	wacky

Across Clues

3. daytime TV serials that continue for many years and used to be sponsored by soap companies

6. attempts to be shocking or scandalous

7. authority or expert

8. disgusted; horrified

10. mysterious and glamorous; out of the ordinary

13. artificial; manufactured

14. something that comes before; forerunner

15. very excited

Down Clues

1. hopes; ambitions

2. sound real

4. crazy; wild

5. abbreviation for situation comedy, a type of TV show

6. grab

9. income

11. the latest fashion or popular thing

12. type or class

Strategy

How to Distinguish Between Fact and Opinion

Imagine this: A friend of yours made $50,000 on a reality game show answering general-knowledge culture questions. You think that you know as much about the culture as your friend, and you decide to try to make some money, too. You go to the tryouts for the game show and do pretty well during the first few rounds. One of the producers pulls you aside and tells you that you seem very smart, are good-looking, have a charming personality, and that this combination is certain to make you a very popular contestant. She encourages you to sign a contract to be on the game show. The contract says that you will give back all of the money you win on the show to the producers to pay for the cost of the transportation, hotel, and the makeover they will give you to make you look really good. She explains that you are sure to get a lot of other TV work after this show is over. She says that if you're *really* smart and want to become famous and rich, you'll sign the contract. Is this a fact or only the producer's opinion? How do you know?

Some statements about the future are facts. For example:

> The sun will rise in the east tomorrow.

On the other hand, some statements about the future are merely opinions. For example:

> You are sure to be a very popular contestant and get a lot of other TV work after this show is over.

In everyday life and in academic life, it is important to distinguish fact from opinion. Sometimes people will make statements in a strong, assertive way because they believe they are facts, they would like them to be facts, or they would just like them to sound like facts. But just because a statement is presented as fact, it doesn't mean it is. For example, people sometimes express their opinions as if they were facts. Because an opinion is someone's belief or judgment about someone or something, personal feelings, biases, and attitudes influence opinions. For example, if someone said with great confidence, "Elvis Presley was on a reality TV show in the 1950s," that would sound like a fact. It sounds like a fact because it has a date and the speaker confidently said *was*, but this statement is not true. If you doubt the information someone gives you, it would be wise to check its accuracy with a reliable source such as a reference librarian or a known scholar of the subject. The following are five ways to help distinguish fact and opinion.

Five Ways to Distinguish Opinions from Facts

1. Look/listen for words and phrases that may signal an opinion. For example:

I believe	It seems to me	probably
I bet	occasionally	sometimes
I feel	often	to my mind
In my opinion	personally	usually
I think	personally speaking	

2. Look/listen for adjectives that express value judgments. For example:

good	pretty	safe	ordinary
bad	ugly	dangerous	outrageous

3. Question the expertise of the speakers. Are they reliable sources? Are they well-known and well-respected authorities in their fields?

4. Question the sources the speakers use. How reliable are those sources?

5. Most important, try to form a contrasting point of view. Is this contrasting point of view as reasonable and acceptable as the speaker's? If so, the speaker may be presenting only opinions and not facts.

Before You Listen

1 Considering the Topic In small groups, answer the following questions based on the knowledge you already have. Then share your answers with the rest of the class to expand your shared knowledge of this topic.

1. What kinds of people appear on reality TV shows?
2. What might be some of the positive effects of watching reality TV?
3. What might be some of the negative effects of watching reality TV?
4. What are the ethical issues involved in producing a reality TV show?
5. Tell everything you know about the history of reality TV? For example, what were some of the earliest reality TV shows?

Listen

2 Listening to Get the Gist Listen to the radio program once all the way through to get the gist of what it is about. On a separate sheet of paper, take brief notes on the main ideas and a few supporting details. Use whatever techniques for note-taking, outlining, or diagramming that work best for you.

_____

_____

_____

_____

_____

3 **Listening for Facts and Opinions** Read the statements in this activity. Then listen to the radio program again and do the following:

1. Stop the recording after you hear the information contained in each statement.

2. For each item, mark whether the statement is a fact or an opinion and then explain why.

3. If you decide a statement is an opinion, indicate whether you agree or disagree with this opinion and explain why.

Example A "Media Watch" is a production of Wisconsin Radio.

___X___ Fact _____ Opinion Why? _____

Because it's the name of the show and the announcer would

not lie about this.

_____ Agree _____ Disagree Why? _____

_____

Example B In my opinion, soap operas belong in the sitcom or even comic satire category.

_____ Fact ___X___ Opinion Why? _____

Because the speaker said, "in my opinion."

___X___ Agree _____ Disagree Why? _____

Because I think the plots of soap operas are really silly, too.

1. Sociologists agree that reality TV is a phenomenon that can't be stopped.

_____ Fact _____ Opinion Why? _____

_____

_____

_____ Agree _____ Disagree Why? _____

_____

2. Reality shows now far outnumber all other types of shows on television and not only sociologists, but also doctors, are concerned about the influence these shows have on the viewing public.

_____ Fact _____ Opinion Why? _____

_____

_____ Fact _____ Opinion Why? _____

_____

3. It seems to me that someone should go online and edit this definition because we all know that professional actors, singers, models, athletes, and many other types of celebrities with aspirations to *be* professional actors have managed to

snag their own reality show either for the publicity or just to make a living when they can't get work elsewhere, right?

_____ Fact _____ Opinion Why? _____

_____

_____ Agree _____ Disagree Why? _____

_____

4. It is obvious that only a small portion of what is filmed ends up in the show, and the choices concerning which scenes to show and in what order can considerably change the reality presented to the viewers.

_____ Fact _____ Opinion Why? _____

_____

_____ Agree _____ Disagree Why? _____

_____

5. Most researchers agree that Allen Funt's show *Candid Camera*, *Ted Mack's Original Amateur Hour*, and *Arthur Godfrey's Talent Scouts* were the precursors, or shows that inspired the style and format, of shows like *Punk'd*, where hidden cameras capture the reactions of unsuspecting ordinary people to pranks or outrageous joke situations, and *American Idol* or *The Voice*, where supposedly amateur contestants compete for huge recording contracts based on both judges' and audience's votes.

_____ Fact _____ Opinion Why? _____

_____

_____ Agree _____ Disagree Why? _____

_____

6. Nowadays, we have shows such as *Survivor* or *The Amazing Race* where the prize can be a million dollars or more.

_____ Fact _____ Opinion Why? _____

_____

_____ Agree _____ Disagree Why? _____

_____

◄ Contestants on *The Amazing Race*, tell host Phil Keoghan about their incredible day.

7. Since the producers of *The Real World* deny that *Nummer 28* influenced them at all, I suppose we'll never know for sure, but I believe that either it truly did influence them or there was some sort of universal magic in the air that launched these groundbreaking reality TV techniques one right after the other merely by coincidence.

_____ Fact   _____ Opinion   Why? _____

_____

_____ Agree   _____ Disagree   Why? _____

_____

8. I bet that you can name just about any topic or any situation and there is a reality show about it.

_____ Fact   _____ Opinion   Why? _____

_____

_____ Agree   _____ Disagree   Why? _____

_____

9. There are shows about killing animals, eating animals, and stuffing animals as well as shows about saving the whales or raising pandas in captivity.

_____ Fact   _____ Opinion   Why? _____

_____

_____ Agree   _____ Disagree   Why? _____

_____

10. We tend to delight in, or are at least be entertained or fascinated by, the failings and problems of others.

_____ Fact   _____ Opinion   Why? _____

_____

_____ Agree   _____ Disagree   Why? _____

_____

11. But why do we watch when something painful is deliberately scripted and staged for our amusement? Can a steady diet of this type of reality TV be good for us? I think not.

_____ Fact   _____ Opinion   Why? _____

_____

_____ Agree   _____ Disagree   Why? _____

_____

12. Personally, I feel Cline is right since I, myself, have seen at least half a dozen reality shows that have this type of character.

_____ Fact _____ Opinion Why? _____

_____

_____ Agree _____ Disagree Why? _____

_____

13. Reality TV shows do get you to sit up and pay attention. As Poniewozik says, these shows may provoke us or even offend us, but at least they do something more than just help us get to sleep.

_____ Fact _____ Opinion Why? _____

_____

_____ Agree _____ Disagree Why? _____

_____

14. Probably, we love to laugh and judge and judge and laugh, and then gossip about it.

_____ Fact _____ Opinion Why? _____

_____

_____ Agree _____ Disagree Why? _____

_____

▲ Viewers seem to love watching the outrageous behavior of the *Real Housewives of Atlanta*.

4 Comparing Judgments In small groups, compare your answers from Activity 3 with your classmates and discuss the following questions.

1. Which strategies did you use to decide which items were facts and which were opinions?

2. Which strategy did you think was the most useful?

3. Did you all agree on which statements were facts and which were opinions? If yes, why? If not, why not?

Talk It Over

5 Role-Playing a Producer of a Reality TV Show The primary role of a television producer is to oversee all aspects of a show's production from developing an original idea for the show, to hiring the cast and director, to putting together the writing and design teams. Some producers write and direct the shows themselves, but others just oversee the daily business matters. However, it is generally the producer who is responsible for the overall quality and truthfulness of the show's content.

Follow these steps to role-play a team of producers who want to produce a very successful reality TV show.

1. Form small groups of 3–4 to role-play teams of producers.

2. In each group, brainstorm possible ideas for a successful reality TV show. Take some time to watch a few actual reality shows to get you started if necessary.

3. Then discuss the pros and cons of each idea until you come to a consensus on which idea you would like to "green light," to move forward to produce as a reality TV show.

4. Next, go into the planning stage for the show. Make the following decisions with your group: who will be on the show, who will direct it, and who will write it.

5. Prepare and present a "pitch," a brief talk to try to sell your idea to a TV network board of directors (the rest of your classmates). Each person on your team should speak for 1–2 minutes on a different reason why the network should buy your show. Try to include as many facts and opinions about your show as you can. Your classmates' job is to remember at least three facts and three opinions from your group's presentation.

6. After each group's presentation, discuss the various facts and opinions. Which do you and your classmates usually find most interesting, facts or opinions? Why?

7. Write a "check" for $100,000 and give it to the team of "producers" of the reality TV show idea you liked best. Add up the "checks" received by each team to see which show should be "green lighted."

PART 3 Expressing Doubt or Disbelief

Strategy

Expressing Doubt or Disbelief in Formal and Informal Situations

When people present information as facts that may be merely personal opinions or beliefs in unproven data, you may want to express doubt or disbelief. The formal expressions are appropriate in any situation. The informal expressions must be used with a warm, friendly tone to avoid sounding rude even with close friends and family.

Formal Expressions for Expressing Doubt or Disbelief

Are you sure that's/it's correct?   Do(es) he/she/they truly believe that?

Are you sure that's/it's OK?   Do you really believe that?

Are you sure that's/it's right?   I find that hard to believe.

Could he/she/they really do that?   Is that really true?

Could he/she/they really think that way?   Is that really possible?

Informal Expressions for Expressing Doubt or Disbelief

Are you serious?   Oh, come on!

Don't give me that!   Oh, sure!

Get out of here!   Really?

Get real!   Seriously?

I doubt it/that.   That can't be true!

I'll believe it/that when I see it.   You're kidding!

No way!   You've got to be kidding!

Note: You may wonder why *I don't believe it!* is not on this list. This is because when you use the expression *I don't believe it!* in this context, usually placing strong emphasis on the word *believe*, it shows surprise without disbelief. It really means "I believe you, but I'm very surprised."

1 **Listening for Expressions of Doubt and Disbelief** You will hear four conversations in which people's responses range from very formal to very informal. After listening to each one, answer the questions in the spaces provided. When you are finished, compare your answers in small groups.

Conversation 1

Emmett discusses a project with Professor Brandt.

1. What expression does Emmett use to express doubt? _____

2. Why do you think he uses that expression? _____

_____

_____

3. Professor Brandt expresses disbelief twice in this conversation. Is she polite to Emmett? _____ Why do you think so? _____

_____

4. The first time Professor Brandt expresses disbelief through intonation alone. What words does she use? _____

_____

5. What expression does she use the second time? _____

_____

Conversation 2

Amy chats with Jen about her daughter's TV show.

1. Is this conversation formal or informal? _____

2. When the second speaker says, "Get outta here," does she sound amused or angry? _____

3. How does the second speaker sound when she says, "Oh, sure!"?_____

_____

4. When the second speaker says, "Yeah, right, and I'm Mick Jagger," does she sound rude? _____

5. Why do you think the second speaker expresses disbelief this way? _____

_____

_____

Conversation 3

Thea and Nick talk about the TV show *Dancing with the Stars*.

1. Are Thea's expressions of disbelief formal or informal? _____

2. Is she polite or rude? _____

3. What are some expressions Thea uses?

_____

_____

_____

▲ Regardless of the hard work involved, female celebrities jump at the chance to dance in the arms of professional dancer Derek Hough on *Dancing with the Stars*.

Conversation 4

Rose attends Professor Pickering's music appreciation class.

1. Are Rose's expressions of disbelief formal or informal? _____

2. Is she polite or rude? _____

3. Does the professor seem impatient with Rose? _____

4. What are some expressions Rose uses? _____

_____

 2 Listening for Opinions When you listened to the radio program and did the activities in Part 2, you answered questions about some of the facts and opinions you heard. Listen to the radio program again. This time, listen for additional statements that you think are *not* proven facts.

a. When you hear something that sounds as if it has not yet been proven, ask the teacher to stop the recording and replay the statement.

b. Copy the statement onto the lines provided here.

c. After each statement, add a response that expresses your doubt or disbelief about it.

d. Share your responses with your classmates.

1. Statement: _____

_____

   Response: _____

_____

2. Statement: _____

_____

   Response: _____

_____

3. Statement: _____

_____

   Response: _____

_____

4. Statement: _____

_____

   Response: _____

_____

5. Statement: _____

_____

Response: _____

_____

6. Statement: _____

_____

Response: _____

_____

 ③ **Completing Conversations** Work with a partner to complete the following conversations using expressions of doubt or disbelief. A sample is provided for Conversation 1. If you wish, you can create some original conversations using the sample as a model. Choose one conversation (either one from the book or an original one) and present it to the rest of the class.

Conversation 1

A: I saw a terrific talent contest on TV last night.

B: Oh, which one?

A: It's called *Who's Got Talent?*, and a woman played the cello underwater.

B: *No way!*

A: *Not only that, but the piano player was underwater, too.*

B: *Get out of here!*

A: *Really! That show is famous for all kinds of weird talents.*

B: *Yeah, I know, but I'll believe it when I see it!*

Conversation 2

A: Do you remember the contemporary artist, Christo, who wrapped the coast of Australia in canvas and an entire island in pink plastic?

B: Yeah, why?

A: Because his latest project is wrapping the Eiffel Tower in blue silk.

B: _____

A: _____

B: _____

(Etc.)

▲ Christo wrapped up nature to create his art.

Conversation 3

A: What a disaster at the TV studio tonight!

B: Why? What happened?

A: We were trying to rehearse, and first the lights went out, then the scenery fell over, then the leading man was taken to the hospital, and as if that weren't enough, we put out a fire in a garbage can just in time! I think someone is trying to tell us something.

B: _____

A: _____

B: _____

(Etc.)

Conversation 4

A: Did you hear what your friend Terry did?

B: No, what?

A: He decided to try out for _American Idol_, but he knows that he can't carry a tune.

B: _____

A: _____

B: _____

(Etc.)

4 **Presenting Facts and Expressing Doubts** This is a game that you can win by fooling your friends.

1. Divide into two teams and share interesting or unusual facts about your life that have to do with the arts or entertainment. These events do not have to involve you directly, but you must be connected to them in some way. For example:

   - One of my drawings is on display in the city hall in my hometown.
   - My father-in-law is a famous actor.
   - I once got a standing ovation for my dancing at a folk dance festival.
   - When I was ten, I won third prize in a whistling contest.
   - My friend's aunt is a well-known pop artist.
   - My cousin once played the cello at a concert attended by the mayor.

2. Now make up some events that did not actually happen and share these with your teammates, too.

3. With your team, choose some of the real and imaginary events to tell the other team about. Each person can present facts about himself or herself, or about other team members.

4. Take turns presenting these "facts" to the other team. They can choose to believe what you say and respond, "OK, I believe that," or they can respond with expressions of doubt or disbelief.

5. Each time a team is correct in distinguishing factual from imaginary events, it gets a point. The team with the most points wins.

TOEFL® iBT

Narratives Containing Opinions or Analysis

Sometimes the narratives on tests such as the TOEFL® iBT, as well as the lectures you attend in your courses, contain opinions. Sometimes the opinions are very personal in nature and the speaker may or may not be saying that everyone else feels the same way or even *should* feel the same way. Sometimes the opinions are less personal and more universal and represent conclusions arrived at after a very thoughtful and formal analysis by a knowledgeable person on a particular subject. In this case, the speaker, feeling that he or she has been very objective in the analysis, states the opinions as if they were facts. These kinds of statements, while they are often reasonable and *feel* true, are merely *convincing* and are easy to confuse with statements of fact that contain data that can be verified.

On a test such as the TOEFL® iBT, there is an effort to distinguish both of these types of opinions from factual information. Any questions about information that can be interpreted as opinion will include phrases such as:

- according to the speaker
- according to the lecture
- as stated in the lecture

1 Answering Questions about Facts and Opinions Listen to the historical review of a music festival. While you listen, close your books and take notes. After the speaker finishes talking, you will hear a series of questions. Open your books and fill in the bubble of the best answer to each of the questions.

1. According to the speaker, which of the following statements describes the festival?

   (A) It was a large "happening."

   (B) It was an important sociological event.

   (C) It was an important political event.

   (D) All of the above.

2. What was the nickname for the festival?

   (A) Aquarian Exposition

   (B) Woodstock

   (C) Music and Art Fair

   (D) The Happening

3. Approximately how many people went to the festival?

   (A) as many as one million

   (B) between 16 and 30 thousand

   (C) more than 400,000

   (D) anyone who could walk there

4. According to the speaker, why did the promoters decide to let everyone in for free?

    (A) because the people stuck on the highway without tickets were becoming violent

    (B) because they were impressed with the people's need to learn a common language

    (C) because they didn't have enough employees to sell that many tickets

    (D) because they were impressed with the people's desire to gather together to share something they all loved

5. According to the speaker, what was the main reason people went to the festival?

    (A) because they happened to get stuck in a traffic jam in Bethel

    (B) because they wanted to go on a pilgrimage to Bethel

    (C) because they wanted to protest traditional values and goals

    (D) because they wanted to see the cast of top rock stars

6. Which of the following was *not* a problem at the festival?

    (A) an inadequate sound system

    (B) an inadequate sanitation system

    (C) an inadequate amount of food

    (D) an inadequate amount of dry ground

7. Listen to part of the music review again.

What does the speaker mean when he says that the power of Woodstock cannot be overestimated?

    (A) that any number you might guess for how many people attended would not be high enough.

    (B) that the craziness of the youth was more powerful than it seemed

    (C) that the power of the amplified music system cannot be determined

    (D) that the influence of people with a common purpose can change history

8. Listen to part of the music review again.

What is the speaker's opinion about Woodstock in relation to the Peace Movement?

    (A) It was a high point.

    (B) It was a low point.

    (C) It signaled the beginning of the Vietnam War.

    (D) It was not significant and should be forgotten.

Self-Assessment Log

Check (✓) the words in this chapter you have acquired and can use in your daily life.

Nouns

- aspirations
- genre
- precursor
- pundit
- revenue

- sensationalism
- sitcom
- snag
- soap opera
- trend

Adjective

- appalled
- contrived
- exotic
- wacky

Idioms

- ring true
- fired up

Check (✓) your level of accomplishment for the skills introduced in this chapter. How comfortable do you feel using these skills?

	Very comfortable	Somewhat comfortable	Not at all comfortable
Using strategies such as questioning the expertise and sources of speakers and trying to formulate a contrasting view, to distinguish between fact and opinion	☐	☐	☐
Understanding words and phrases such as *extraordinary* and *It seems to me* that express value judgments	☐	☐	☐
Understanding formal and informal expressions such as *I find that hard to believe* and *Don't give me that!* when used to express doubt	☐	☐	☐
Using formal and informal expressions such as *I find that hard to believe* and *Don't give me that!* to express doubt	☐	☐	☐

Think about the topics and activities in this chapter and complete the statements.

In this chapter, I learned something new about _____

_____

_____

I especially liked (topic or activity) _____

_____

_____

I would like to know more about _____

_____

_____

Conflict and Resolution

"You must be the
change you wish
to see in the world."

Mohandas Karamchand Gandhi
Indian political and spiritual
leader and non-violent activist

In this
CHAPTER

Resident Advisor Training Session Dealing with Conflicts

Learning Strategy Predicting Exam Questions

Language Function Acquiescing and Expressing Reservations

Connecting to the Topic

1. Who is the man in the photo?

2. Why is he famous?

3. He once said in regards to conflict and resolution, "If we keep following the idea of an eye for an eye and a tooth for a tooth, we will end up in an eyeless, toothless world." What does this mean?

Did You Know?

Conflict afflicts all nations and all cultures. There are innumerable sayings and advice from wise individuals about conflict and resolution. Consider the following examples.

- The second word makes the quarrel. — Japanese proverb
- There is no situation so bad that getting angry can't make it worse.
  — *Anonymous*
- You can't shake hands with a clenched fist. — *Indira Gandhi*
- He that cannot forgive others breaks the bridge over which he must pass himself, for every man has need to be forgiven. — *Lord George Herbert*
- American industrialist Henry Ford once stated, "Thinking is the hardest work there is, which is the probable reason so few people engage in it." Conflict resolution is probably the second-hardest work there is, and it requires thinking, which is the probable reason why so many conflicts remain unresolved. — *Bheki Sibiya, CEO of the Chamber of Mines of South Africa*
- When angry, count to ten before you speak; if very angry, count to a hundred.
  — *Thomas Jefferson*
- When angry, count to four; when very angry, swear. — *Mark Twain*
- Before I criticize someone, I like to walk a mile in their shoes. That way, if they get mad, they're barefoot and a long way away. — *Anonymous*

1 What Do You Think? Discuss the following questions in pairs. Then share your answers with another pair or with the rest of the class.

1. What do you think each of the quotes in the box means? Explain them in your own words. Give examples.
2. Which quotes do you think are funny? Why?
3. Which quotes "speak" to you, or have the greatest meaning for you? Why?

Sharing Your Experience

2 Resolving Conflicts in the Past In small groups, discuss the following questions.

1. What conflicts did you have as a child? How did you resolve them?
2. What conflicts did you have as an adolescent? How were they different from the ones you had as a child? How did you resolve them?

3 **Breaking a Secret Code** Follow these steps to discover the secret code!

1. With a partner, read the puzzle clues and the puzzle answers. Then match the definitions on the left to the appropriate expressions in the list on the right.

Definitions—Puzzle Clues	Word List—Puzzle Answers
a. extreme anger	_____ arousal state
b. to be calm; relax (slang)	_____ big picture
c. to calm down after being angry (slang)	_____ chill out
d. to cause, create, produce	_____ contingency
e. excited state	_____ cool off
f. the sharing of ideas when trying to solve a problem; compromise in negotiation	_____ generate
	_____ give-and-take
g. old information; something you already know	_____ honor
	_____ old hat
h. well-meaning; having the plan to help, not hurt	_____ rage
i. to respect	_____ trial balloon
j. a complete sense or view of a situation	_____ well-intentioned
k. a test case used to judge whether to continue with something or not	
l. unforeseen event; unexpected situation	

2. Use the clues (definitions a–l) to fill in the blanks with the correct forms of the vocabulary words. The first one has been completed for you.

a. <u>r</u> <u>a</u> <u>g</u> <u>e</u>
   1   2   3   4

b. __ __ __ __ __   __ __ __
   5 6 7 8 8   9 10 11

c. __ __ __ __   __ __ __
   5 9 9 8   9 12 12

d. __ __ __ __ __ __ __ __
   3 4 13 4 1 2 11 4

e. __ __ __ __ __ __ __   __ __ __ __ __
   2 1 9 10 14 2 8   14 11 2 11 4

f. __ __ __ __ - __ __ __ - __ __ __ __
   3 7 15 4   2 13 16   11 2 17 4

g. __ __ __   __ __ __
   9 8 16   6 2 11

h. $\underline{}\ \underline{}\ \underline{}\ \underline{}\quad\quad \underline{}\ \underline{}\ \underline{}\ \underline{}\ \underline{}\ \underline{}\ \underline{}\ \underline{}\ \underline{}\ \underline{}\ \underline{}$
   18 4 8 8   7 13 11 4 13 11 7 9 13 4 16

i. $\underline{}\ \underline{}\ \underline{}\ \underline{}\ \underline{}$
   6 9 13 9 1

j. $\underline{}\ \underline{}\ \underline{}\quad\quad \underline{}\ \underline{}\ \underline{}\ \underline{}\ \underline{}\ \underline{}\ \underline{}$
   19 7 3   20 7 5 11 10 1 4

k. $\underline{}\ \underline{}\ \underline{}\ \underline{}\ \underline{}\quad\quad \underline{}\ \underline{}\ \underline{}\ \underline{}\ \underline{}\ \underline{}\ \underline{}$
   11 1 7 2 8   19 2 8 8 9 9 13

l. $\underline{}\ \underline{}\ \underline{}\ \underline{}\ \underline{}\ \underline{}\ \underline{}\ \underline{}\ \underline{}\ \underline{}\ \underline{}$
   5 9 13 11 7 13 3 4 13 5 21

3. Now decode the secret phrases! To find and then fill in the letters of the secret phrases, match the number under each letter blank with the corresponding number under the blanks from Step 2. Note that not all of the letters from the vocabulary in Step 2 are used, and *m* and *q* are given. When you are finished, discuss the meanings of the quotes with your classmates.

A. $\underline{}\ \underline{}\quad \underline{}\ \underline{}\ \underline{}\ \underline{}\quad \overset{m}{\underline{}}\ \underline{}\ \underline{}\quad \underline{}\ \underline{}\ \underline{}$
   18 4   6 2 15 4   4 11   11 6 4

   $\underline{}\ \underline{}\ \underline{}\quad \overset{m}{\underline{}}\ \underline{}\quad \underline{}\ \underline{}\ \underline{}\quad \underline{}\ \underline{}\quad \underline{}\ \underline{}\quad \underline{}\ \underline{}.$
   4 13 4   21   2 13 16   6 4   7 14   10 14

   —*Walt Kelley*

B. $\underline{}\ \underline{}\ \underline{}\ \underline{}\quad \underline{}\ \underline{}\ \underline{}\ \underline{}\quad \underline{}\ \underline{}\ \underline{}\quad \underline{}\ \underline{}\ \underline{}$
   17 4 4 20   5 9 9 8   2 13 16   21 9 10

   $\underline{}\ \underline{}\quad \overset{m}{\underline{}}\ \overset{m}{\underline{}}\ \underline{}\ \underline{}\ \underline{}\quad \underline{}\ \underline{}\ \underline{}\ \underline{}\ \underline{}\ \underline{}\ \underline{}\ \underline{}.$
   5 9   2 13 16   4 15 4 1 21 19 9 16 21

   —*St. Just*

C. $\underline{}\ \underline{}\ \underline{}\ \underline{}\quad \underline{}\ \underline{}\ \underline{}\ \underline{}\ \underline{}\quad \underline{}\ \underline{}\ \underline{}\ \underline{}\ \underline{}\ \underline{}$
   18 6 4 13   2 13 3 4 1   2 1 7 14 4 14

   $\underline{}\ \underline{}\ \underline{}\ \underline{}\ \underline{}\quad \underline{}\ \underline{}\quad \underline{}\ \underline{}\ \underline{}$
   11 6 7 13 17   9 12   11 6 4

   $\underline{}\ \underline{}\ \underline{}\ \underline{}\ \underline{}\ \overset{q}{\underline{}}\quad \underline{}\ \underline{}\ \underline{}\ \underline{}\ \underline{}\ \underline{}.$
   5 9 13 14 4   10 4 13 5 4 14

   —*Confucius*

D. $\overset{}{\underline{}}\quad \underline{}\ \underline{}\ \underline{}\quad \underline{}\ \underline{}\ \underline{}\ \underline{}\ \underline{}\quad \underline{}\ \underline{}\ \underline{}\ \underline{}$
   7   18 2 14   2 13 3 1 21   18 7 11 6

   $\overset{m}{\underline{}}\ \underline{}\quad \underline{}\ \underline{}\ \underline{}\ \underline{}\ \underline{}\ \underline{}:$
   21   12 1 7 4 13 16

   $\underline{}\quad \underline{}\ \underline{}\ \underline{}\ \underline{}\quad \overset{m}{\underline{}}\ \underline{}\quad \underline{}\ \underline{}\ \underline{}\ \underline{}\ \underline{},$
   7   11 9 8 16   21   18 1 2 11 6

   $\overset{m}{\underline{}}\ \underline{}\quad \underline{}\ \underline{}\ \underline{}\ \underline{}\ \underline{}\quad \underline{}\ \underline{}\ \underline{}\quad \underline{}\ \underline{}\ \underline{}.$
   21   18 1 2 11 6   16 7 16   4 13 16

$$\overline{7} \quad \overline{18} \; \overline{2} \; \overline{14} \quad \overline{2} \; \overline{13} \; \overline{3} \; \overline{1} \; \overline{21} \quad \overline{18} \; \overline{7} \; \overline{11} \; \overline{6}$$

$$\overset{m}{\rule{0pt}{0pt}} \; \overline{21} \quad \overline{12} \; \overline{9} \; \overline{4}:$$

$$\overline{7} \quad \overline{11} \; \overline{9} \; \overline{8} \; \overline{16} \quad \overline{7} \; \overline{11} \quad \overline{13} \; \overline{9} \; \overline{11},$$

$$\overset{m}{\rule{0pt}{0pt}} \; \overline{21} \quad \overline{18} \; \overline{1} \; \overline{2} \; \overline{11} \; \overline{6} \quad \overline{16} \; \overline{7} \; \overline{16} \quad \overline{3} \; \overline{1} \; \overline{9} \; \overline{18}.$$

—*William Blake*

PART 2   Exam Questions

Strategy

Predicting Exam Questions

One important student goal is to do well on tests. One strategy for doing well is to predict the questions an instructor will ask on an exam.

Information Likely to Be on Exams

1. Any point the instructor explicitly tells you will be on the exam or anything the instructor directly states would make a good exam question.

2. Information that the instructor repeats from the textbook or class readings.

3. Things stated more slowly or more loudly than other things. (Instructors often slow down or speak louder when they want to point out something important.)

4. Key facts.

5. Information about recent research, especially the instructor's own research. (Instructors want to make sure their students are up to date. Also, asking questions about data that is not in the textbook is a good way to find out if students have been attending class.)

6. Information on handouts.

1 **Considering the Context** The lecture in this chapter comes from a training course for resident advisors (RAs). In small groups, discuss the following questions.

FYI

Resident advisors are students living in dormitories (dorms) who receive special training and then are paid to assist students. They answer questions new students may have about campus life and help resolve conflicts in the dorms.

1. Are you now living in a dorm? If yes, do you like it? Why or why not? If not, do you think you would like to live in a dorm? Why or why not?

2. What questions do you think a resident advisor needs to be able to answer?

3. What kinds of conflicts do you think people might have in dorms? How would you handle these conflicts?

▲ What kinds of conflicts might a first-year student encounter in the dorms?

Listen

2 **Listening to Predict Exam Questions** As you listen to the senior resident advisor's lecture, "Dealing with Conflicts," imagine that you are one of the new resident advisors.

- Use the handout on page 193 to take notes on the important points the senior resident advisor makes.

- Put an asterisk (*) next to any point on the handout that you think is likely to be an exam question.

Seven Strategies for Dealing with Conflicts

1. Cool off, chill out.

2. Talk and listen to each other.

3. Be clear about needs.

4. Brainstorm solutions.

5. Evaluate the solutions.

6. Choose one solution, or use a combination of solutions.

7. Agree on contingency, monitoring, and reevaluating strategies.

3 **Evaluating Possible Exam Questions** For each of the following questions, circle *Yes* or *No* to indicate whether you think the senior resident advisor would include this question on the exam, and write a reason why. Share your answers with your classmates.

Question	Good exam question?
Example	
Conflict resolution is an important skill for a resident advisor to have.	Yes (No) Reason: *too easy*
1. When did Dale Carnegie write *How to Win Friends and Influence People?*	Yes No Reason: _____
2. What are three ways to get angry people to cool down?	Yes No Reason: _____
3. What are some ways to restate what a speaker is saying?	Yes No Reason: _____
4. What did Jack Benny say to the thief?	Yes No Reason: _____
5. Why is it important to provide a contingency plan?	Yes No Reason: _____

4 Using Your Notes to Answer Questions With a partner, share the notes you made on the handout on page 193 while you were listening to the lecture and fill in any gaps. Listen to the lecture again if necessary. Then use your notes to fill in any gaps in your answers to the questions in Activity 3.

Talk It Over

5 Discussing Types of Exam Questions Discuss the following questions in small groups.

1. What are the different types of questions that might appear on tests? For example: multiple choice, essay, integrated reading/speaking, etc.

2. How does the subject matter of the course (math, literature, business, etc.) tend to influence the types of questions the instructor chooses? What kinds of questions, for example, might be asked in the following courses? Add to the list any additional courses that are of interest to you.

architecture	history	
biology	marketing	other _____
business	philosophy	_____
chemistry	public health	_____
computer science	sociology	_____
engineering	statistics	_____
English	urban planning	

3. Why or when might an instructor go against expectations for a particular course when designing test questions? For instance, when might a literature instructor choose to ask a true-false question? When might a mathematics instructor choose to ask an essay question?

What type of test do you think is ▶ the toughest, and would require every minute to finish?

6 Asking and Answering Exam Questions Use your lecture notes to complete the following with a partner.

1. Make a list of five to ten questions you think might appear on an exam that covers the lecture.

2. Ask a partner your exam questions.

3. After your partner has answered your questions, answer his or her questions.

4. Change partners and try the activity again. If time permits, do this once more.

5. Discuss with your classmates which questions seemed to be the best types of exam questions.

6. As a class, choose the best questions for a 30-minute exam. Write them on the board or on large pieces of paper that can be hung for all to see.

7. Take the exam. How did you do?

PART 3 Acquiescing and Expressing Reservations

 Strategy

Deciding Whether to Acquiesce or Express Reservations

Whether you are having an informal discussion with a friend or engaging in a formal business negotiation, if the person presents a logical, well-supported argument, you will probably be convinced of his or her point of view. In this case, it is appropriate to acquiesce, or agree.

On the other hand, there will be times when you will have doubts or reservations about what the other person is suggesting. If so, you should express them. If the person is very aggressive in expressing his or her opinions, you may be tempted to just "give in," or acquiesce, without expressing your reservations, even if the person does not make a convincing argument. Knowing some appropriate expressions for expressing reservations will certainly help you in such a situation.

The following expressions are the most common for acquiescing and for expressing reservations.

Expressions for Acquiescing and for Expressing Reservations

Acquiescing	Expressing reservations
Do whatever you think is best.	How long do I have to think it over?
If that's what you really want.	I'd like to get a second opinion.
If you think that's best.	I have some reservations about…
I'm putting myself completely in your hands.	I'm not sure.
	I'm not sure that will work for me.
I'm willing to go along with you just this once.	Let me think it over.
	One concern I have is…
I suppose you must know best.	One drawback is…
I trust you completely.	Possibly, but…
OK, I'll go along with you this time.	What bothers me is…
That sounds good/great/fine.	What I'm afraid of is…
Whatever you say.	Yes, but the question really is…

1 **Listening for Acquiescence and Reservations** Listen to the conversation between a resident advisor and students in her dorm, in which they acquiesce or express reservations. Then answer the questions. When you are finished, compare your answers in small groups.

1. Why does the resident advisor allow Mohammed to speak first?

_____

2. What expression does James use to acquiesce?

_____

3. What is the problem?

_____

4. What expression does James use to express reservations?

_____

5. What do James and Mohammed agree to try?

_____

6. What expressions do they use to show that they have acquiesced?

_____

2 **Listening for Suggestions about Conflict Resolution** In the lecture, the senior resident advisor suggests three ways to help people cool down when they are angry. Listen to that part of the lecture again.

- Write the suggestions and decide how you would react to each one. Would you acquiesce, or would you express reservations? Write the expression that feels most appropriate for conveying your feelings.
- Discuss your responses with your classmates.

Students ▶ always seem happy to learn about ways to relieve tensions and resolve conflict.

1. RA's suggestion:

   _____

   _____

   Your response:

   _____

   _____

2. RA's suggestion:

   _____

   _____

   Your response:

   _____

   _____

3. RA's suggestion:

   _____

   _____

   Your response:

   _____

   _____

3 Listening for Ways to Express Reservations In the lecture, the senior resident advisor suggests getting people to talk and listen to each other by restating the problem and expressing reservations.

- Listen to this part of the lecture again. Write down the suggested ways to express reservations.
- Discuss your answer with your classmates. Did you each write down the same information? Share your opinions about the various ways to express reservations.

_____

_____

_____

_____

_____

Talk It Over

4 Acquiescing and Expressing Reservations Follow these steps to role-play situations where you will acquiesce or express reservations.

1. Look over the five following situations. Divide into groups according to the number of characters for each situation. Each group will work on a different situation.

2. Role-play the conflict, using appropriate expressions to acquiesce or express reservations. Stay "in character" as you express the opinions of the character that you are role-playing.

3. Perform your role-play for the class.

4. Re-form groups and try role-playing a different situation or make up your own situation and perform this role-play for the class.

Situation 1

Tony, Ming, Ruth, Tareq, and Masa are sitting in a dorm room at 9:00 A.M. planning what to do on Sunday. They each want to do one of three things: have a picnic, rehearse for a play they are in, or study for an exam that will take place the next day.

Characters

- Tony, who lives to play sports and be outdoors
- Ming, who would like to be an actor after she graduates
- Ruth, who wants to get all "As" so she can get into graduate school
- Tareq, who hates to stay up late and doesn't want to "pull an all-nighter" studying for the exam
- Masa, who is enjoying college and just wants to reach a compromise that will work for everyone

Situation 2

The office workers in a computer company are planning an office party. They cannot agree on a theme, the kind of food, date, or a location.

Characters

- So Young, an administrative assistant in human resources
- Donald, a computer programmer
- Spencer, a young manager who hopes to date the administrative assistant in human resources
- Mohandas, a 40-year-old manager who is a single parent and hopes to bring his kids to the party
- Emma, a 35-year-old supervisor who is a single parent and hopes to leave her kids with a babysitter
- Monique, a young receptionist who is working and going to school and wants to make sure that the party doesn't conflict with final exams

Situation 3

Marcia, 20, is a pre-med student who has just gotten back her chemistry midterm exam with a grade of C$^+$ on it. She looks over the exam and realizes that the professor did not see page three of her six-page exam. This professor, however, had announced on the first day of class that he never changes a grade. Grades are important to Marcia, and she decides to speak to the professor about her exam anyway.

▲ Do you think the professor will acquiesce to Marcia's request to change her grade?

Characters

- Marcia
- Professor Thomas

Situation 4

Five students are looking for a house to rent. They know they would like to live together, but have different ideas about what constitutes a good living space.

Characters

- Daniel, who wants a house with a large living room for parties, and doesn't mind sharing a room
- Adama, who loves to cook and share meals together, and prefers cats to dogs
- Samuel, who wants a computer room so they don't have to keep the computers in their bedrooms
- Salim, who wants to make sure that no one has to share a bedroom
- Norm, who wants to have a backyard so he can keep his dog

Situation 5

Abdul and Simon are roommates in the dorm. They are having several problems. First, Abdul wants to keep the dorm room door open and Simon likes to play loud music, so other students complain. Second, Simon is an early riser and Abdul likes to sleep late. Third, Simon is very messy and Abdul is neat.

Characters

- Abdul
- Simon

 5 Discussing Conflicts and Resolutions Discuss the following questions in small groups.

1. Describe a conflict you've had with someone in the last six months. How did you resolve the conflict? Which of the steps for conflict resolution mentioned in the lecture did you use?

2. Describe a time when you helped someone resolve a conflict. What steps did you take? What expressions of acquiescing or expressing reservations did you use?

PART 4 Focus on Testing

FOCUS

TOEFL® iBT

Classroom Interactions in Listening Questions

Some of the listening passages on the TOEFL® iBT involve interactions between a teacher and several students. These interactions may be in the form of a lecture or in the form of a less-formal conversation. In both cases, the interactions may include questions.

In either case, part of your task is to follow the exchange as it moves from one speaker to another. You must find ways to recognize each of several voices and in your notes, associate each voice with certain information or points of view.

Begin by identifying the *main* speaker—almost always a teacher. This person will be the source of most information. Then as each student speaks, ask yourself: Why did the student speak? It might have been in response to a question from the teacher, to ask for clarification, or to challenge something the main speaker has said, for example. Prepare for the teacher's response to each of the speakers and jot notes about it when you hear it. Many listening questions focus on these responses.

 1 Listening for Information and Point of View in Classroom Interactions Listen to the following discussion about upcoming exams in a conflict-resolution class. As you listen, close your books and take notes. After the speaker finishes talking, you will hear a series of questions. Open your books and fill in the bubble of the best answer to each of the questions.

1. Which topic may or may not be on the final exam?

    (A) the conflicts in the Middle East

    (B) the conflicts in Northern Ireland

    (C) the conflicts in Africa

    (D) the conflicts in South Asia

2. Which of the following is *not* mentioned by the professor as a possible source for material on the exam?

    (A) a video shown in class

    (B) the discussion section

    (C) lectures

    (D) student presentations

3. Listen again to part of the exchange.

    What is the male student's concern about the essay?

    (A) what kinds of questions it has

    (B) how long it will be

    (C) how it will be graded

    (D) what it will cover

4. Listen again to part of the exchange.

    Which of the following best states the meaning of the professor's comment, "Life is cruel"?

    (A) There are worse things in life than exams.

    (B) The test will be hard, but that's the way life is.

    (C) The test will cover very bad incidents during conflicts.

    (D) Very few people will be able to pass the test.

5. Listen again to part of the exchange.

    Why does the professor ask the female student to wait?

    (A) She is speaking too fast.

    (B) The professor won't discuss material until the exam.

    (C) The question is not relevant to the discussion.

    (D) The professor wants to finish one thing before moving on to the next.

6. Listen again to part of the exchange.

    Which of the following best describes the situation?

    (A) The male student was correct and the female student was incorrect.

    (B) The female student was correct and the male student was incorrect.

    (C) Both students answered correctly.

    (D) Both students answered incorrectly.

Self-Assessment Log

Check (✓) the words in this chapter you have acquired and can use in your daily life.

Nouns	Verbs	Adjective	Idioms and Expressions
▮ arousal state	▮ chill out	▮ well intentioned	▮ big picture
▮ contingency	▮ cool off		▮ give-and-take
▮ rage	▮ generate		▮ old hat
▮ trial balloon	▮ honor		

Check (✓) your level of accomplishment for the skills introduced in this chapter. How comfortable do you feel using these skills?

	Very comfortable	Somewhat comfortable	Not at all comfortable
Predicting exam questions by recognizing things that are likely to be on exams	☐	☐	☐
Understanding expressions such as *Do whatever you think is best* and *I'm putting myself completely in your hands* when used to acquiesce	☐	☐	☐
Using expressions such as *Do whatever you think is best* and *I'm putting myself completely in your hands* to acquiesce	☐	☐	☐
Understanding expressions such as *I have some reservations about…* and *Yes, but the question really is…* when used to express reservations	☐	☐	☐
Using expressions such as *I have some reservations about…* and *Yes, but the question really is…* to express reservations	☐	☐	☐

Think about the topics and activities in this chapter and complete the statements.

In this chapter, I learned something new about _____

_____

_____

I especially liked (topic or activity) _____

_____

_____

I would like to know more about _____

_____

_____

Audioscript

PART 2 Understanding Main Ideas

2 Listening for Main Ideas page 8

3 Listening for Details page 9

Lecture: Why English? Henry Hitchings' Views on the Current Lingua Franca

Lecturer: Good afternoon everyone. How're y'all doin' today? OK?

Students: Fine. Yeah. Sure. Great.

Lecturer: That's good, 'cause we have a lot to cover before the midterm exam next week. Last week we introduced the idea of English as the global lingua franca, right? And some of you raised the question of "Why English?" Why is it English and not some other language that has become so widespread and commonly used as the lingua franca, hmm? So today I want to dig deeper into this question by sharing with you some of the thoughts of Henry Hitchings, one of my favorite writers on language issues. Some of you may have heard of him. He's written a couple of bestsellers. Let's see... there was *Doctor Johnson's Dictionary*... and then there was *The Secret Life of Words*... and his latest book, *The Language Wars*... Well, that's the one that I'll be referring to most today. So... let's get started, shall we?

In *The Language Wars* Hitchings says that, internationally, the desire to learn English seems insatiable. No language in history has ever spread as widely as English. But why should this be so? And the big question is: Will this romance with English last? Will English hold its place as the global lingua franca or will it be replaced by another language within our lifetimes? First off, Hitchings explains that the adoption of English as the lingua franca of business and popular culture is just a symptom of the world becoming more urban and more middle class.

While native languages may still be associated with tradition, home, religion, culture, early schooling, arts, and social sciences, English has become the language of higher education, commerce, economics, science and technology in many, many countries around the world. This may not surprise you, but think about it. English has become the dominant language in so many, many areas... you may be aware of its use in computing, education, medicine, and all the other sciences... but there's also shipping, transportation, diplomacy, online shopping, Facebook... I could go on and on.

Hitchings tells us that English has become so widespread because of a complex set of circumstances which includes British colonialism, of course. Then there were the advances of the Industrial Revolution, and the American economic and political dominance that followed, and then the further technological developments in the second half of the twentieth century that took place in America. And wherever English was used, it lasted. Why is this? We know that in the colonial period of Britain and then in the United States that the language of the settlers dominated the languages of the native peoples whose land was taken. But now, the fact that English has endured through the struggle to be free from British rule, for example, remains a mystery to some. Yet, even in India, where English is definitely associated with the negative aspects of colonialism, it is still the dominant language of the media, administration, education, and business, and the number of its uses and speakers continues to increase exponentially.

Having a global lingua franca to ease communication between peoples is not a new idea. And English is not the first language to be used for this purpose. In fact, as those of you who read the homework assignment may have discovered, the term *lingua franca* originally referred to the common language consisting of Italian mixed with French, Spanish, Greek, and Arabic that was used as the language of commerce in Mediterranean ports for centuries. Now, of course, it's come to mean any language that we have in common that helps us to communicate and understand each other.

In the early decades of the twentieth century, science fiction writer H. G. Wells imagined that English would become known as World English, the international language of communication. Not too long ago, Jean-Paul Nerrière conceived of a form of English that he called Globish. It consists of only 1,500 words and thus is intended to make it possible for everyone in the world to understand everyone else. Needless to say, it has not caught on yet. But perhaps we shouldn't laugh. Madhukar Gogate, a retired Indian engineer, has come up with a way to use only phonetic spellings in English and thereby make English much simpler to learn. And a German linguist named Joachim Grzega has invented something he calls Basic Global English which has only 20 grammatical rules, and 750 basic words.

Hitchings suggests that these new Englishes are trying to do more than just simplify the language to be learned. They are also trying to neutralize the language, that is, take away all of the negative aspects associated with colonialism, or military dominance, and at the same time to establish a *community*... and I quote... "without territorial boundaries," a community "of people who use English, to make its use seem not just normal, but also prestigious and to market it as a language of riches, opportunity, scholarship, democracy and moral right." Ah... but isn't this exactly what's happening with English as it is? Increasingly, English is not just a foreign or a second language. Instead, in many countries it is becoming something like a second first language. When education for life skills and careers, all modern technology, transportation, commerce, and negotiations are increasingly conducted in English, how could it be anything else?

Hitchings tells us that there were many invented languages proposed as lingua francas in the 19th and early 20th centuries. There was Volapük, devised by a Bavarian named Schleyer in 1879 that was popular for a couple of years. And, even earlier, in 1870, Ludwik Zamenhof began his work on Esperanto, his version of a universal language, and even though it is still spoken by a small number of devotees, it never did catch on. Indeed, all of you in this room are more likely to be familiar with Klingon, which was originated by Marc Okrand for the *Star Trek* films, or the wonderful language... oh, I've forgotten the name... but it was spoken by the blue-skinned Na'vi in the 2009 film *Avatar*. Remember?

Students: Right. So cute. Loved it. Sure. That was amazing.

Lecturer: But even though you loved Klingon and the Na'vi languages, I don't hear you speaking them, do I? So what's up with that? Why not? It's still English, English, English everywhere you go, right? Ah... but will it last?

Well, Hitchings says that even though some might resist the dominance of English around the world, there are still far more of the world's citizens eagerly jumping on board the English train rather than looking for alternatives. In fact, he says many speakers of English as a second language "perceive it as free from the limitations of their native languages." Even though their native languages are deeply connected to their cultural roots and the warmth and beauty that lie therein, they associate English with power and social status, and as a symbol of choice and liberty. On the other hand, there are still those who still perceive English as an instrument of oppression. So English has a kind of paradoxical status, which the Australian scholar Alastair Pennycook clearly explains. He says that English "is at the same time a language of threat, desire, destruction, and opportunity." It's no wonder then that there are mixed feelings about English, eh?

Robert McCrum, I think, has the coolest way of describing the World English paradox. He says that English has "the capacity to run with the hare and hunt with the hounds." What he means is that English is not only the language of the little people, the hares, but also the language of the people in power, the hunters. English can articulate both the ideas of government and its opposition; it can be the language of power and authority as well as the language of the people. He says... and you're gonna love this... "English is both the language of rock' n' roll and royal decree."

So... let's finish up today with the question of possible challengers in the language dominance game. There seem to be only two possible contenders... Spanish and Mandarin Chinese. Both have more first language users, or native speakers, than English. However, most Mandarin Chinese speakers, so far, live in one country. And with the exception of Spain, most Spanish speakers are in the Americas. It does not seem likely, although it is possible in a more distant future, that either of these languages will usurp the position of English anytime soon. Instead, Hitchings suggests, the main challenges to English may come from within. For instance, many writers whose first language is not English have managed to capture the flavor of their culture and native language in English, thus parading their heritage while still reaching the widest possible audience by writing in English. Almost all of the fiction or memoir writers who were born or grew up in the U. S. but whose parents came from other countries fall into this category as they write about their family cultural experience in English.

And then, of course, we cannot forget the challenges from without. As English is embraced in the world's two most populous countries, there are bound to be changes made to the language that will persist simply because of the sheer number of speakers. English is being diluted, changed, mixed with Hindi or Chinese, at this very moment, somewhere in India and China. And certainly it is being mixed with Arabic and Urdu and all of the African languages, and on and on. But yet... as long as it remains the language we hold in common I think it will maintain its status as a global lingua franca, don't you? And as I told you last week, while the number of languages in the world is diminishing overall, the number of different Englishes is increasing.

So... that's it for today. We'll pick up next time with the differences between the various Englishes. Have a great evening... and don't forget to answer the questions at the end of the chapter and put them in my box before our next class, OK?

PART 3 Requesting the Main Point

1 Listening for Appropriate Expressions and Tone of Voice
page 14

Conversation 1

Robert: Did you catch the late breaking news last night?

Elizabeth: No, what about it?

Robert: Well, they showed the "English only" law protest march that I participated in with my friends from my linguistics class. You know, the one where we went to the state capitol building and we protested, and there were some people dressed up as immigrants from the early 1900s and stuff, and anyway, I was really surprised at the way the newscaster handled it. Remember I told you about how it was raining really hard that day and some people were even throwing things at us and I forgot my umbrella—most people did—and we all got drenched, absolutely soaking wet. Well, the march was picked up by the major news networks, and boy, did their reports surprise me! I didn't think that the march was going to be so controversial. It didn't feel like a very daring thing to do at the time.

Elizabeth: Get to the point, would you? How did the networks handle it?

Conversation 2

Professor Robinette: Well, students, I want to reorganize our schedule and change the date of the midterm. You know, we had scheduled the readings of Hitchings and McCrum for the 16th. Then the midterm was going to be right after that on the 18th, and the readings by Pennycook and Gorham were due earlier on the 14th and those by McVey and Gill were on the 12th. Well, I want to move Hitchings and McCrum to the 14th, the midterm to the 12th, Pennycook and Gorham to the 16th, and McVey and Gill to the 18th.

Student: So what are you driving at? I don't get it. Are you trying to tell us that we only have two more days until the midterm? And what about all those readings? They're not going to be on the midterm, are they?

Conversation 3

Professor Salerno: OK, now students, let me explain how we'll organize this fact-finding expedition. You'll want to have a buddy of the opposite sex and to keep your buddy with you at all times. You are to knock on as many doors as possible during the afternoon, and get as many questions answered about the languages and dialects used in these households as possible, but remember... men... always wear your jackets, never offer your hand to a woman, and drink whatever beverage they offer you unless it's alcoholic... then you can say no thanks. And women... remember to keep your heads and your ankles covered, talk only to the women unless the men talk to you first, politely refuse anything to eat or drink... we might be able to accept their hospitality on a second visit, but not now. And all of you... be sure to make friends with the kids, because they might be the only ones who speak English.

Enrico: Excuse me, Professor Salerno? I don't quite understand what you're getting at. Could you explain, please?

Professor Salerno: Well, Enrico, I think my point is that these families have very specific cultural rules and if we're going to have good communication with them and get the information that we need to help them, we certainly don't want to offend them in any way, right?

2 **Requesting the Main Point** page 14

Lecture: Why English? Henry Hitchings' Views on the Current Lingua Franca

Lecturer: Good afternoon everyone. How're y'all doin' today? OK?

Students: Fine. Yeah. Sure. Great.

Lecturer: That's good, 'cause we have a lot to cover before the midterm exam next week. Last week we introduced the idea of English as the global lingua franca, right? And some of you raised the question of "Why English?" Why is it English and not some other language that has become so widespread and commonly used as the lingua franca, hmm? So today I want to dig deeper into this question by sharing with you some of the thoughts of Henry Hitchings, one of my favorite writers on language issues. Some of you may have heard of him. He's written a couple of bestsellers. Let's see... there was *Doctor Johnson's Dictionary*... and then there was *The Secret Life of Words*... and his latest book, *The Language Wars*...

Stop 1: Request the Main Point

Well, that's the one that I'll be referring to most today. So... let's get started shall we?

In *The Language Wars* Hitchings says that, internationally, the desire to learn English seems insatiable. No language in history has ever spread as widely as English. But why should this be so? And the big question is: Will this romance with English last? Will English hold its place as the global lingua franca or will it be replaced by another language within our lifetimes? First off, Hitchings explains that the adoption of English as the lingua franca of business and popular culture is just a symptom of the world becoming more urban and more middle class. While native languages may still be associated with tradition, home, religion, culture, early schooling, arts, and social sciences, English has become the language of higher education, commerce, economics, science and technology in many, many countries around the world. This may not surprise you, but think about it. English has become the dominant language in so many, many areas... you may be aware of its use in computing, education, medicine, and all the other sciences... but there's also shipping, transportation, diplomacy, online shopping, Facebook... I could go on and on.

Stop 2: Request the Main Point

Hitchings tells us that English has become so widespread because of a complex set of circumstances which includes British colonialism, of course. Then there were the advances of the Industrial Revolution, and the American economic and political dominance that followed, and then the further technological developments in the second half of the twentieth century that took place in America. And wherever English was used, it lasted. Why is this? We know that in the colonial period of Britain and then in the United States that the language of the settlers dominated the languages of the native peoples whose land was taken. But now, the fact that English has endured through the struggle to be free from British rule, for example, remains a mystery to some. Yet, even in India, where English is definitely associated with the negative aspects of colonialism, it is still the dominant language of the media, administration, education, and business, and the number of its uses and speakers continues to increase exponentially.

Stop 3: Request the Main Point

Having a global lingua franca to ease communication between peoples is not a new idea. And English is not the first language to be used for this purpose. In fact, as those of you who read the homework assignment may have discovered, the term *lingua franca* originally referred to the common language consisting of Italian mixed with French, Spanish, Greek, and Arabic that was used as the language of commerce in Mediterranean ports for centuries. Now, of course, it's come to mean any language that we have in common that helps us to communicate and understand each other.

In the early decades of the twentieth century, science fiction writer H. G. Wells imagined that English would become known as World English, the international language of communication. Not too long ago, Jean-Paul Nerrière conceived of a form of English that he called Globish. It consists of only 1,500 words and thus is intended to make it possible for everyone in the world to understand everyone else. Needless to say, it has not caught on yet. But perhaps we shouldn't laugh. Madhukar Gogate, a retired Indian engineer, has come up with a way to use only phonetic spellings in English and thereby make English much simpler to learn. And a German linguist named Joachim Grzega has invented something he calls Basic Global English which has only 20 grammatical rules, and 750 basic words.

Stop 4: Request the Main Point

Hitchings suggests that these new Englishes are trying to do more than just simplify the language to be learned. They are also trying to neutralize the language, that is, take away all of the negative aspects associated with colonialism, or military dominance, and at the same time to establish a *community*... and I quote... "without territorial boundaries," a community "of people who use English, to make its use seem not just normal, but also prestigious and to market it as a language of riches, opportunity, scholarship, democracy and moral right." Ah... but isn't this exactly what's happening with English as it is? Increasingly, English is not just a foreign or a second language. Instead, in many countries it is becoming something like a second first language. When education for life skills and careers, all modern technology, transportation, commerce, and negotiations are increasingly conducted in English, how could it be anything else?

Stop 5: Request the Main Point

Hitchings tells us that there were many invented languages proposed as lingua francas in the 19th and early 20th centuries. There was Volapük, devised by a Bavarian named Schleyer in 1879 that was popular for a couple of years. And, even earlier, in 1870, Ludwik Zamenh of began his work on Esperanto, his version of a universal language, and even though it is still spoken by a small number of devotees, it never did catch on. Indeed, all of you in this room are more likely to be familiar with Klingon, which was originated by Marc Okrand for the *Star Trek* films, or the wonderful language... oh, I've forgotten the name... but it was spoken by the blue-skinned Na'vi in the 2009 film *Avatar*. Remember?

Students: Right. So cute. Loved it. Sure. That was amazing.

Lecturer: But even though you loved Klingon and the Na'vi languages, I don't hear you speaking them, do I? So what's up with that? Why not? It's still English, English, English everywhere you go, right? Ah... but will it last?

Well, Hutchings says that even though some might resist the dominance of English around the world, there are still far more of the world's citizens eagerly jumping on board the English train rather than looking for alternatives. In fact, he says many speakers of English as a second language "perceive it as free from the limitations of their native languages." Even though their native languages are deeply connected to their cultural roots and the warmth and beauty that lie therein, they associate English with power and social status, and as a symbol of choice and liberty. On the other hand, there are still those who still perceive English as an instrument of oppression. So English has a kind of paradoxical status, which the Australian scholar Alastair Pennycook clearly explains. He says that English "is at the same time a language of threat, desire, destruction, and opportunity." It's no wonder then that there are mixed feelings about English, eh?

Stop 6: Request the Main Point

Robert McCrum, I think, has the coolest way of describing the World English paradox. He says that English has the "capacity to run with the hare and hunt with the hounds." What he means is that English is not only the language of the little people, the hares, but also the language of the people in power, the hunters. English can articulate both the ideas of government and its opposition; it can be the language of power and authority as well as the language of the people. He says... and you're gonna love this... "English is both the language of rock 'n' roll and royal decree."

Stop 7: Request the Main Point

So... let's finish up today with the question of possible challengers in the language dominance game. There seem to be only two possible contenders... Spanish and Mandarin Chinese. Both have more first language users, or native speakers, than English. However, most Mandarin Chinese speakers, so far, live in one country. And with the exception of Spain, most Spanish speakers are in the Americas. It does not seem likely, although it is possible in a more distant future, that either of these languages will usurp the position of English anytime soon. Instead, Hitchings suggests, the main challenges to English may come from within. For instance, many writers whose first language is not English have managed to capture the flavor of their culture and native language in English, thus parading their heritage while still reaching the widest possible audience by writing in English. Almost all of the fiction or memoir writers who were born or grew up in the U. S. but whose parents came from other countries fall into this category as they write about their family cultural experience in English.

Stop 8: Request the Main Point

And then, of course, we cannot forget the challenges from without. As English is embraced in the world's two most populous countries, there are bound to be changes made to the language that will persist simply because of the sheer number of speakers. English is being diluted, changed, mixed with Hindi or Chinese, at this very moment, somewhere in India and China. And certainly it is being mixed with Arabic and Urdu and all of the African languages, and on and on. But yet... as long as it remains the language we hold in common I think it will maintain its status as a global lingua franca, don't you? And as I told you last week, while the number of languages

in the world is diminishing overall, the number of different Englishes is increasing.

Stop 9: Request the Main Point

So... that's it for today. We'll pick up next time with the differences between the various Englishes. Have a great evening... and don't forget to answer the questions at the end of the chapter and put them in my box before our next class, OK?

PART 4 Focus on Testing

1 **Taking Notes to Answer Basic-Comprehension Questions** page 17

Lecturer: Increasing globalization has created a need for people in the workforce who can communicate in multiple languages. Areas of need include international business and trade, technology, media, and science as well as peace negotiations and diplomacy. Many countries such as Japan and China have instituted policies requiring students to study as least one foreign language at the primary and secondary school levels in order to fill this need. However, some countries such as India, Singapore, Malaysia, Pakistan, and the Philippines, who use a second official language in their government operations, must assume that a large portion of the population need to eventually become fully bilingual.

According to Wikipedia, although the need to learn foreign languages is almost as old as human history itself, the origins of modern-language education can be found in the teaching of Latin in the 17th century. Latin had for many centuries been the dominant language of education, commerce, religion, and government in much of the Western world, but it was displaced by French, Italian, and English by the end of the 16th century. With the rise of Italian and the like, the study of Latin diminished from the study of a living language to be used in the real world to merely a subject in the school curriculum. It was kept in the curriculum because proponents then claimed that the study of Latin developed intellectual abilities, and the study of Latin grammar became an end in and of itself. Thus, "Grammar schools" from the 16th to 18th centuries focused on teaching the grammatical aspects of Classical Latin.

John Comenius was one of many people who tried to reverse this trend. He composed a complete course for learning Latin, covering the entire school curriculum, culminating with his *Opera Didactica Omnia*, in 1657. In this book, in addition to a complete curriculum for learning Latin, Comenius also outlined his theory of language acquisition. He is one of the first theorists to write systematically about how languages are learned and about the appropriate methodologies that should be used to teach language. He believed that language acquisition must be allied with sensation and experience, that teaching must be oral and not just written and that the schoolroom should have real things or the models of things, and failing that, pictures of them. As a result, he also published the world's first illustrated children's book called *Orbis Sensualium Pictus*.

The study of modern languages did not become part of the European school curriculum until the 18th century. It seems that Comenius' theories were forgotten because just as with the curriculum for Latin in the traditional grammar schools, conversation practice was minimal, and students were instead required to memorize grammatical rules and apply these to translating texts in the target language. This method became known as the grammar-translation method.

There have been numerous innovations in language teaching over the last two hundred years, however, and the grammar-translation method has all but been discarded, or at least regarded as having very limited use if the goal of the study of a particular language is true fluency. These days the current methodology is focused on total immersion of the student studying a language in the listening, speaking, reading, and writing skills necessary to gain native-like fluency in that language. Less attention is paid to the study of grammar per se, and the main focus is on using the language in real-world contexts. The current methodologies, if applied appropriately, can certainly help to produce the multiple-language speakers so desperately needed in today's world.

Question 1: Which countries conduct much of their government business in English?

Question 2: When was Latin replaced as a spoken language by modern European languages?

Question 3: Why was Latin kept in the school curriculum until the 18th century?

Question 4: What did John Comenius include in his Opera Didactica Omnia in 1657?

Question 5: In the grammar-translation method, what are students required to do a lot of?

Question 6: What is the main focus of current language acquisition methodologies?

CHAPTER **2** **Danger and Daring**

PART 2 Noting Specific Details

2 Listening to Note Specific Details page 29

Lecture: Hooked on Thrills

Professor: Good morning.

Students: Good morning.

Professor: Niagara Falls, the three waterfalls that separate Canada from the state of New York, are famous for more than their spectacular beauty and as a destination for "honeymooners" from all over the world. Did you know that the two waterfalls at Niagara, New York, known as the American Falls and Bridal Veil Falls and the third waterfall, the Canadian Horseshoe Falls, have been a challenge to a variety of stuntmen and women since the early 1800s? In fact, these powerful waterfalls with an average height of 170 feet and a waterflow of 150,000 gallons per second are still irresistible to a variety of daredevils. Does anyone know what Annie Taylor did on her 63rd birthday in 1901?

Student A: I think she was mentioned in the article you gave us for homework. Wasn't she the first woman to go over the Falls in a wooden barrel?

Professor: Yes! But not only was she the first woman, she was also the first person ever to do this particular stunt. And what did the article say about a man called Kirk Jones?

Student B: He was the guy who went over the falls in 2003, wasn't he?

Professor: Yes, that's true. But you left out a very important part. He did it without any protection. No barrel, no life preserver. Nothing!

Students: Incredible. Great. Scary. Amazing. Wow!

Professor: But the most famous of all the stunts performed at Niagara Falls was the one performed in the 1860s by Jean Francois Gravelot, who called himself The Great Blondin. He walked to the middle of a wire stretched over the Falls and then did something I would never do in a million years!

Student C: Me neither! The article said that in the middle of his walk on the wire, he cooked and ate an omelette using a small stove and table that he had carried with him onto the wire.

Professor: Right. In fact, he did this stunt several times. And once he even handed down some of the omelette to some passengers on a boat passing below him on the Niagara River.

Students: No way. Way to go. Wow! That's incredible! That's awesome!

Professor: There have been dozens of stunts like these, but since the 1970s, they have been illegal and everyone that has survived their walks or jumps or rides over the Falls have been taken to jail and have paid a very large fine.

Students: Awww. Really? That doesn't seem fair. What for?

Professor: Well, mainly the state wants to discourage anyone from doing daredevil stunts at Niagara Falls in order to save their lives. Many people have been killed taking risks like this. And also they want to discourage a circus atmosphere that occurs when thousands of people gather to watch stunts like these. Kirk Jones was lucky. He only had minor injuries. But after he got out of the hospital, he was taken to jail and fined $3,000. It could have been even more. At first they considered fining him $10,000.

Students: Awww! That's so mean. That's incredible.

Professor: Your response is very typical. To the thousands of people at Niagara Falls on the day that Kirk Jones stepped into the river and then floated on his back casually to the edge of the Falls and then over, and to the millions who later watched him talk about his stunt on the TV talk shows, Kirk Jones was not a criminal. He was a hero. And I'm certain that thousands of young men and women were envious when he was offered a job as a stuntman in a circus and performed daredevil stunts around the world.

Students: (cheer and laugh)

* * *

Professor: OK, OK. So tell me… What motivates daredevils like Annie Taylor, The Great Blondin, and Kirk Jones to risk criminal prosecution, injury, and even death by performing such dangerous stunts? Is it the hope of gaining fame and fortune, the desire for headlines and business deals? It certainly seems so in these cases. But there is another daredevil named George Willig who was nicknamed "the human fly" because he loved to climb straight up the outside of smooth buildings. After climbing one skyscraper, he said he was "amazed at the hullabaloo" he created and insisted that his motives were pleasure, not profit, and increased self-esteem, not glory. He told a reporter that "far above the streets, I was very much alone with myself and at peace with myself… It was a personal challenge; I just wanted the prize of getting to the top."

Psychologists who study what motivates people to take up these kinds of risks agree with Willig. They have categorized stunts such as Willig's as "thrill and adventure seeking"—a subdivision of the larger class of activities called "sensation seeking." According to Marvin Zuckerman, a leading researcher in this field, sensation seeking is a basic human characteristic. That is, sensation seeking is part of the human nervous system, passed on from one generation to the next and encouraged by the social community. He claims that sensation seeking is a major factor that can be used to determine and classify personality types. It was not the desire for fame or fortune that led George Willig to become a "human fly" and climb up the outside of skyscrapers. Instead, it was a need for the intense sensation of a risky activity.

Zuckerman and his colleagues theorize that we all seek different levels of sensation. Some people are most comfortable with a low level of sensation and don't like risky situations. Others require higher levels of sensation to be happy, and without it, they become anxious or bored. And others require unusually high levels of stimulation to be happy. These are the thrill and adventure seekers, the ones who take up extreme sports such as skysurfing, bungee jumping, and rock climbing.

Researchers distinguish four types of high-level sensation seekers. The first type is the thrill and adventure seeker. This type includes people who love activities that involve speed and danger. These physical conditions stimulate intense sensations in the tissues and nerves of the body.

The second type of sensation seeker is called the experience seeker. This type includes people who search for powerful and unusual mental rather than physical activities. Experience seekers may travel to exotic places, listen to the most experimental music, and use mind-altering drugs such as LSD. Occasionally, experience seekers may rebel against established authority. Zuckerman has nicknamed this kind of sensation seeking the "hippie factor," because many of these behaviors were characteristic of the hippies of the 1960s and 1970s.

A third type of sensation seeker is the disinhibitor. The form of sensation seeking at work here is called disinhibition and is nicknamed the "swinger factor." Disinhibitors find their optimal sensation level in activities such as heavy social drinking, frequent sexual encounters, wild parties, and gambling.

The fourth type of sensation seeker is the boredom avoider. Boredom avoiders dislike repetition, routine work, and people who are predictable and unexciting. They frequently feel restless and generally prefer variety over sameness.

***

To determine whether people are higher-level or lower-level sensation seekers in each of the four categories, Zuckerman and his colleagues developed a questionnaire called the "Sensation Seeking Survey," or SSS. The survey requires yes or no responses to statements such as these:

1. I like to ride in open convertibles.

2. I sometimes like to do crazy things just to see the effects on others.

3. A person should have a lot of exciting experiences before marriage.

4. The worst social sin is to be a bore.

Yes responses to all these items on the questionnaire indicate a person who seeks higher levels of sensation. *No* responses indicate someone who is happy at a much lower stimulation level.

Using the SSS as a tool, researchers have discovered several patterns. First, who do you think are higher-level sensation seekers, men or women?

Students: Men! No, no, I think women are! No way. It's *got* to be men! Why is that?

Professor: OK, OK. Let me tell you. Men tend to be higher-level sensation seekers than women, particularly in the first and third subcategories—the thrill and adventure seeker and the disinhibitor. I suppose that's not too surprising considering when this research was done, but somehow I think we might get different results if we surveyed *this* class.

Students: (laugh)

Professor: And what do you all think the results might be according to age?

Student B: I'd bet people our age tend to take the most risks.

Student C: Well, could be. But it could also be teenagers.

Professor: Well, you're *both* right! Adolescents and college students have the highest number of high-level sensation seekers. Sensation seeking tends to decrease steadily as people get older, and very young children very rarely seem to be high-level sensation seekers.

However, excessive and dangerous sensation-seeking behavior in ten to twelve-year-olds and teenagers is a serious problem. For example, two teenage boys jumped off the Brooklyn Bridge. One of them was killed instantly, but the other boy survived. When authorities asked him if he and his friend had understood how foolish this stunt was, he replied that they realized the danger involved but they jumped anyway, "just to see what it felt like." Now by recognizing the creative functions of sensation seeking, doctors are helping children and parents find ways to decrease the self-destructive aspects of sensation-seeking behavior and to increase the self-expressive and creative ones.

Well, that's all we have time for today. Finish reading Chapter 17 and we'll go on with this discussion next time.

PART 3   Saying Yes and No

1 Listening for *Yes* and *No* Expressions page 33

2 Rating *Yes* and *No* Expressions
page 34

Conversation 1

Ted: I'm going whitewater rafting this weekend, Paul, and one of my buddies, Phil—you know Phil, don't you?

Paul: Uh-huh.

Ted: Well, Phil can't go because he sprained his back playing soccer, so there's room for one more. You want to go with us?

Paul: Are you kidding? I've never gone whitewater rafting.

Ted: Aw, come on. There's a mini-course being given by the Explorers' Club Wednesday night this week. Take it and you'll be ready to go with us.

Paul: No way! I'll never learn enough in two hours to go on a trip for a whole weekend!

Ted: Sure you can! The instructor is great. I know lots of people who've done it.

Paul: Well, it's probably not such a good idea, but how much does it cost?

Ted: Well, the trip'll cost you about $150 with everything—food, equipment, everything. The course is only 20 bucks.

Paul: That's not too bad. I'll think about it.

Ted: Don't just think about it; do it! You have the money, don't you?

Paul: I think so.

Ted: Well, then, it's settled. Let's go over to the student union, get something to drink, and then sign you up.

Conversation 2

Terry: Hey Lynn, I saw the greatest trip advertised in this travel magazine I get. It's a mountain-climbing trip in Nepal—you know, in the Himalayas. We'd go all the way to the base camp on Annapurna. That means we'd follow in the footsteps of the women's expedition that climbed Annapurna in 1978! Wouldn't that be great? Let's go!

Lynn: Not on your life! You won't get me up there! I don't even like riding in those glass elevators that go up and down the outside of fancy hotels.

Terry: Come on! Think about it a bit. There's a month-long training program and then the trip is three weeks. Think how strong and brave you'll feel at the end.

Lynn: You may feel strong and brave after a month, but not me! Never in a million years!

Terry: Oh, don't be like that. It's important to overcome your fears. You'll be a better person for it!

Lynn: I won't climb a mountain! Not for all the tea in China, and that's that! Find someone else to go with you.

Terry: But I want you to go. You're my best friend. Besides, there won't be any technical climbing with ropes and all that, just some high-altitude hiking. Really! Come on! It'll be fun. We'll have a good time!

Lynn: I like having a good time, but my idea of a good time is seeing a movie, going out to dinner, or watching a baseball game on TV. Want to go out to dinner?

Terry: Definitely! Maybe I'll even convince you by the time we order dessert.

3 Using *Yes* and *No* Expressions
page 34

Lecturer: To determine whether people are higher-level or lower-level sensation seekers in each of the four categories, Zuckerman and his colleagues developed a questionnaire called the "Sensation Seeking Survey," or SSS. The survey requires yes or no responses to statements such as these:

1. I like to ride in open convertibles.

2. I sometimes like to do crazy things just to see the effects on others.

3. A person should have a lot of exciting experiences before marriage.

4. The worst social sin is to be a bore.

Yes responses to all these items on the questionnaire indicate a person who seeks higher levels of sensation. *No* responses indicate someone who is happy at a much lower stimulation level.

1 Taking Notes to Answer Basic-Comprehension Questions About Specific Details page 37

Sports News Feature

Sportscaster: I predict that extreme sports are soon going to be the number one sports attraction—more popular than baseball, basketball, or even soccer. The first Extreme Games, now called the X Games, were first held in 1995, but in just a few years the X Games have gained an audience of millions, according to ESPN, the sports network that sponsored the games. Extreme sports range from skydiving to deep sea diving, from motorcycle jumping to bungee jumping—and everything in between.

What all extreme sports have in common is an element of danger. The X Games take it one step further, featuring sports epitomized by daredevil stunts performed while traveling at high speed. Many extreme sports are not completely new. They are just new versions of older sports, made possible by technological changes or improvements in equipment. For example, BMX racing and mountain biking are both based on cycling, barefoot water skiing is obviously derived from traditional water skiing, and in-line skating is a form of roller skating.

For the most part, extreme sports originated as recreational activities for individuals, but often in a group context. Individual athletes would show off skills for the rest of the group members to imitate or emulate—or even to "one up"—by doing even more dangerous stunts. Skateboarding is the prime example here. The little tricks that kids used to show off to their friends as they skateboarded down the street have grown into daredevil stunts involving multiple flips high in the air or riding down the edge of stair railings to a magnificent trick landing at the bottom of the stairs.

As they have become competitive, the extreme sports have been at least partly absorbed into the mainstream. Snowboarding was the first extreme sport to become an Olympic event. BMX racing and mountain biking have been adopted as cycling disciplines, and in-line skating falls under the jurisdiction of the international and national governing bodies for rollerskating.

Several extreme sports, such as snowboarding, skateboarding, street luge, and bungee jumping have also been called "outlaw sports" because they have been banned in many areas for being too dangerous. These sports have also been called "alternative sports," in part because they are seen as alternatives to older, more traditional sports, but also because many of the athletes who engage in these sports have also adopted an alternative lifestyle. This lifestyle was known at first as punk and later as grunge. It was characterized by a somewhat grungy or used and torn style of dress as opposed to the conspicuous consumption or "moneyed" fashion look of the yuppie lifestyle.

Bungee jumping is one of the earliest of the extreme sports and also one of the most dangerous. Bungee jumping is based on a ritual practiced by the villagers of Pentecost Island in the South Pacific. Every spring, the villagers collect vines and wind them into long cords or ropes. Then young men climb high wooden towers, tie the vines around their ankles, and jump. A successful jump is considered to be a demonstration of courage and a sign that there will be a plentiful yam harvest.

Bungee jumping is a popular sport among the young, particularly in California, New Zealand, and France. Bungee jumping was once done only by a handful of sky divers, mountain climbers, and other daredevils. Recently, however, thousands of bungee adventure clubs have opened around the world. One club, Bungee Adventures in California, has already sent more than 20,000 thrill seekers over the edge. There have been few fatal accidents so far in the United States. But two French jumpers fell to their deaths when their bungee cords severed. The cords just snapped apart as they were stretched to the limit. A third jumper died when he bounced off the jump tower.

Bungee jumpers claim, however, that the thrills are greater than the risks. Jumpers leap head-first from bridges, towers, cranes, and even hot-air balloons. They leap from 90 to 300 feet above the ground, with only the long nylon and rubber bungee cord to break their fall. The bungee cord is a lot like a giant rubber band. Tied around the ankles or the body, the cord is only long enough to allow a few seconds of free fall before it stretches to the limit, stopping the jumper just a few feet short of the land or water below. The jumper is then thrown skyward as the cord snaps back to its original length.

Unlike other extreme sports, bungee jumping does not require any special physical training or ability. The only strength that is required is psychological. And that, my friends, seems to be the big draw for both participants and spectators in this particular extreme sport. That, and the thrill of seeing someone who has chosen to risk life and limb have a really close call.

Question 1: In what year were the first X Games held?

Question 2: What do all extreme sports have in common?

Question 3: Skateboarding is a prime example of what?

Question 4: Why are some extreme sports called "outlaw sports"?

Question 5: Why do the Pentecost Islanders leap from towers?

Question 6: What kind of a sport is bungee jumping?

Question 7: What do bungee jumpers do?

Question 8: What equipment must bungee jumpers use?

Question 9: In the speaker's opinion, what draws people to bungee jumping?

CHAPTER 3 Gender and Relationships

PART 2 Using Abbreviations

Lecture: I Want a Wife

Students: Hey there. Hi. Nice haircut. Thanks. Can I borrow a pen? Sure. When's the midterm? Don't know, maybe next week?

Lecturer: Good morning. Today we're going to continue our discussion of the metamorphosis that men's and women's roles in relationships seem to be going through. Who remembers what the term *metamorphosis* means? Rick?

Rick: *Metamorphosis* means a change or alteration… maybe even a complete transformation, right?

Lecturer: That's right. And today I'm going to tell you about a very important article that may have had a lot to do with this transformation in male and female roles. It was written by a woman named Judy Brady in 1971. Judy graduated from college with a degree in painting in 1962. By 1971 she had been married for eleven years and was raising two daughters and also working outside the home to support the family while her husband finished his degree at the university. One day, she ran into a male friend of hers who had just gotten a divorce. He had one child, who was, of course, living with his ex-wife and now he was looking for a second wife. Later, as she was thinking about this friend's situation, she wrote down her feelings. These feelings were developed into an essay that was published in a well-known popular magazine and it was titled "I Want a Wife."

Students: What? Really? You're kidding.

Student 1: No, it's true. I read it and it's a terrific article. It really changes your perspective on some things.

Student 2: Right, me, too. It's really famous.

Lecturer: Yes, it is definitely a terrific article and it is really famous. But for those of you who haven't read it yet, or haven't even heard of it and to refresh the memories of those who have… let's break into small groups and discuss the following questions before we launch into the meat of the article, OK? Was Judy Brady's situation typical of those of a lot of other women in 1971? Why do you think meeting up with her recently divorced friend triggered this feeling? What are some of the reasons that Judy Brady might want a wife?

Pause to discuss your answers to these questions with a partner.

Lecturer: OK. Group 1. Do you think that Judy Brady's situation was common in 1971?

Student from group 1: Yes, sort of. I mean there were a lot of women who were working and raising children while their husbands finished their degrees, but we're pretty sure there weren't as many as there are now.

Lecturer: Right. Group 2, why do you think meeting up with her recently divorced friend made her a bit envious?

Student from group 2: Oh my… Have you got a week? We came up with so many reasons, I'm not sure we'll have time in this class to list them all.

Lecturer: OK, OK. I can see that you get it. And I bet group three came up with some similar reasons about why Judy Brady might want a wife, right?

Student 1 from group 3: You got it. Although Joe here didn't quite agree with the rest of us.

Joe: Wait a minute! All I said was, "What's wrong with her helping out a little?"

Student 1 from group 3: A little?!? Are you kidding me?

Lecturer: OK, OK. Settle down. Why don't we go over some of the points that Judy Brady makes in her essay. And, of course, I want you to read the essay in its entirety for homework. We'll discuss it further after that, but today I'll hit the highlights and then I want to share with you a very cute rebuttal to her essay that I happened to come across when I was researching this topic on the Internet.

But first… let's deal with Ms. Brady's essay. Here are some of the things that she'd like to be able to do in her life and why she needs a wife to help her accomplish these things:

1. She'd like to train for a good-paying job, and she'd like a wife to work to send her to school.

2. And while she's in school, she'd like a wife to help her take care of the children and her, too… to do things like make the doctor and dentist appointments, wash the clothes, supervise the children's education and also their playtime with friends. She also wants a wife to take care of her and the children when they are sick, because, of course, she cannot take any time off work to do that. And, of course, there's the shopping and the cooking, and she wants her wife to be a really *good* cook, and do all of the cleaning up while she goes off to study.

3. And while the wife is doing all of this… the wife must also attend to the emotional and social needs of the family. Judy Brady wants a wife who will be sympathetic and nurturing when Judy is not feeling well, but will never ever complain about how tired she is from her wifely duties.

Students: Oh, really? Now that's too much. Oh, no. Sounds about right. I'd definitely like a wife like that. Me, too!

Lecturer: Wait, wait. There's more.

4. Judy Brady would also like a wife who will take care of all the details of their social life, arrange for babysitters or prepare a special meal or dessert to serve to their friends and never ever interrupt when she's telling stories to her friends (even if she's told them before). Ah, you're not laughing now. Am I hitting too close to home? But there's more.

5. Judy Brady would also like a wife that will always remain faithful to her, even though it is understood that Judy's needs may be different and that she will not be held to the same standard as her wife.

And finally, **6**…, and I quote directly from Judy Brady's essay here… "If, by chance, I find another person more suitable as a wife than the wife I already have, I want the liberty to replace my present wife with another one. Naturally, I will expect a fresh, new life; my wife will take the children and be solely responsible for them so that I am left free." And she goes on… "When I am through with school and have a job, I want my wife to quit working and remain at home so that my wife can more fully and completely take care of a wife's duties."

So… now… what do you think? Under these circumstances, who *wouldn't* want a wife? Hmmmm?

Students: Wow! No kidding! Absolutely!

Joe: Wait. There's got to be another side to this.

Lecturer: Yes, of course. Let me share with you the highlights of a very funny essay that I found on the internet that was written by a male student, I think for a high school assignment. It's a kind of parody, but it's got some very valid points in it and it's called… can you guess? "I want a _____."

Joe: Husband! Right?

Lecturer: Yup. That's what it's called. "I Want a Husband." And here are some of the things he says he wants.

1. Someone to work to meet all of the financial needs of me and my children. And it must be a high-paying, stable career so that I can stay home and enjoy my children and not miss a minute of their growing up.

2. Someone to take all of the responsibility of teaching the children how to play sports and to take them to their lessons and team practices because I will be too busy watching my teams on TV.

3. I want a husband who will help the children with their homework, and do all of the disciplining so I can just be their friend and have a good time with them.

4. I want a husband who will never forget our anniversary and will often surprise me with flowers or other gifts on special occasions.

5. And a husband who goes to the gym and stays in perfect physical shape even though he has to work all day. But who doesn't hold me to the same standard and doesn't mind when I haven't showered or shaved for a few days.

6. I want a husband who understands that I am always right and will go shopping with me and never complain about the things I pick out for him to wear.

7. I want someone who will give up going out with his guy friends in order to go with me to romantic movies or walks on the beach.

8. And finally… I want a husband who understands that if I find someone better, I reserve the right to replace him immediately. And it goes without saying that the kids must remain with my husband because I will not have the time to look after them if I am hunting for a new husband.

So… Everyone… all together now… under these circumstances… Who *wouldn't*…

Students: want a husband!

Joe: But isn't that almost like all of the stuff that Judy Brady did for her husband and said she wanted a wife to do for her?

Lecturer: OK. Now you're getting the idea of this parody. So tonight, I want you to find the Judy Brady article somewhere… at the library… on the Internet… borrow it from your mom… wherever. I also want you to read about why this article was so important in 1971 and why it's been reprinted over and over every year in many publications since then. Also try to connect the points being made in this article to the data that I shared with you during our last session on male and female education and pay equity issues.

OK, that's enough for today. See you next week. Goodnight class.

Students: Goodnight Professor. See you tomorrow. Bye-bye.

Joe: I bet that last thing she said about connecting the article to the education and pay equity issues is going to be on the midterm.

Student 1 from group 3: Yup. I'm sure you're right there.

1 **Listening for Expressions of Congratulations** page 53

A: Hi, honey! I'm home.

B: Hi, Maggie. I'm in the kitchen. Come on back here.

A: Guess what! We closed the deal with the small-parts manufacturer and my boss told me I did a terrific job.

B: Congratulations. I'm really thrilled for you. You've worked a long time to impress that guy.

A: Yeah. That's for sure. But he was really grateful for all of the extra time I put in and I think he's going to offer me the promotion we've both been hoping for.

B: Oh, Maggie! That's terrific! Does that mean you'll be getting a raise, too?

A: Yup!

B: This calls for a celebration. What would you like to do?

A: Oh, I don't know. Going out to dinner is nice, I guess. But honestly, I like your cooking better than anything we can get in a restaurant.

2 Listening for Expressions of Condolences page 53

A: Hey! What have you been up to lately?

B: Not much, you?

A: Well, I had the kids last weekend and I took them to Legoland down near San Diego.

B: Sounds like fun, but what do you mean you "had the kids"?

A: Oh, I guess I didn't tell you. Therese and I have separated.

B: Oh, no! I can't tell you how sorry I am. What can I do?

A: Nothing really. We're just going to live apart for a while and see if we can stop bickering over stupid stuff. I'm hoping that after a little while, we'll both get a better perspective and work things out. How about you? You and Josie doing OK?

B: Yeah, we're fine. But her mother passed away last month and she's been pretty broken up over it.

A: Oh, please give my condolences to her and her whole family for me, OK? And be sure to let me know if there's anything I can do, all right?

B: Sure thing. Thanks. You're a good friend.

3 Listening for Sincere and Insincere Congratulations page 54

Conversation 1

A: Guess what! I'm going ice fishing with the guys tomorrow!

B: Oh! Terrific. I'm so happy for you.

Conversation 2

A: Guess what! Louise and I are engaged!

B: Congratulations! I'm so happy for you.

Conversation 3

A: Hey! I've got some news! We're moving to New York.

B: Congratulations. I'm so pleased for you.

Conversation 4

A: Hey, listen to this! I got a raise this week.

B: No kidding! Congratulations! I'm thrilled.

Conversation 5

A: It's my 90th birthday today!

B: Congratulations! May you have many more!

Conversation 6

A: Guess what! I got a leave of absence from my job, and I'm going back to school!

B: Congratulations. I'm so happy for you.

PART 4 Focus on Testing

1 Pragmatic Understanding: Conversation page 57

Sally: Professor Power's class is pretty interesting, don't you think? I especially enjoyed the lecture yesterday on the metamorphosis that's going on with men's and women's roles. How 'bout you, Joe?

Joe: Yeah, I really did, too! But some of that stuff was pretty strange though, right? I mean, Judy Brady writing that article saying she wanted a wife and all… And that guy that Professor Powers told us about who wrote about wanting a husband. Whoa!

Sally: What do you mean?

Joe: Well, I believe that women should get equal recognition and pay for the jobs that they do outside the home and all… But… I can't exactly see *me* doing all the things that women are supposed to do at home, can you?

Sally: What?!? What do you mean by "the things that women are supposed to do?"

Joe: Well, you know, stay home and do laundry, take care of the kids, cook, clean, do all the errands…

Sally: Well, you know what? You're right. When you put it that way, I guess I can't exactly see you ever scrubbing a toilet, that's for sure. I guess you'll just leave that for your wife to do, right? That is, if you ever can find a wife that will put up with that attitude these days.

Joe: Huh?

Sally: I mean, when were you born anyway? I mean, I'm glad that you understand that when we finally graduate and get out of here and go on to our first engineering jobs, that not only *should* I earn as much money as you do, but that I *certainly will*... maybe even more! You realize, of course, that I'm in that group... single female in her 20s... that's already earning more than men my age in the workplace, don't you? But as far as all the stuff you see as just "women's work," I think you'd better take another look at that or you might not find an intelligent woman who'll have you.

Joe: Hang on a minute... I didn't mean...

Sally: Oh... you didn't mean that you expected your *wife* to do it, is that it? Well, who *did* you expect to do it then? And don't say "the maid." And stop smiling like that at me. You know exactly what I'm talking about. And did I say stop smiling at me? Uh-oh! I think I've been had again. What a gullible idiot I am. I wish you'd stop doing that to me, you know.

Joe: Oh, but you're so much fun to tease. And you can't believe I'm that much of a Neanderthal, can you? I know that I can be a bit old-fashioned sometimes, but it's just the way I was brought up. You know, my mom was a doctor and she still did everything for us kids and for my dad at home.

Sally: Old-fashioned?!? I swear, sometimes I think you were born in the Dark Ages.

Joe: Nope. Actually, I was born on a really sunny day.

Sally: Is that so? Well, you could have fooled me.

Sally and Joe: (both laugh)

1. *Listen again to part of the conversation.*

Sally: Professor Power's class is pretty interesting, don't you think? I especially enjoyed the lecture yesterday on the metamorphosis that's going on with men's and women's roles. How 'bout you, Joe?

Question 1: Why does the woman ask, "How about you?"

Question 2: How do you think the man feels about scrubbing the toilet?

Question 3: Which of the following best states the woman's feelings toward men sharing household duties with women?

Question 4: Why does the woman ask the man when he was born?

5. *Listen again to part of the conversation.*

Sally: I wish you'd stop doing that to me, you know.

Joe: Oh, but you're so much fun to tease. And you can't believe I'm that much of a Neanderthal, can you?

Question 5: Which of the following best expresses the man's attitude toward the woman?

Question 6: Why does the man talk about the way he was brought up?

Conference Presentation: Looking Good Matters—Aesthetics as a Pillar of Industrial Design

Speaker: Good evening and thank you for inviting me speak to you at this beautiful conference in this beautiful building in this beautiful city in your beautiful country.

(laughter)

And yes, as you may have guessed, my lecture is about beauty and the idea that looking good really does matter, that the perceived beauty of a product is certainly equal to, and in some cases, more important than, the quality or usefulness of a product. In fact, I propose that the knowledge that industrial designers have about consumer aesthetics is one of the most—perhaps *the* most—important pillar of product success. The customer's sense of what is beautiful may very well be the prime factor that moves the product in the marketplace.

(mumbling)

Now some of you may think I'm exaggerating just a bit, but certainly all of us, being industrial designers, will agree that design is the single most important way a business connects with its customers. It doesn't matter if you design furniture or factories, widgets or websites. It is the design of a product that users invariably encounter first. They see it first, before they use it. And when they see it, the product either has the "wow" factor, or it doesn't. You know, that moment when you say, "Wow! That's beautiful! Gotta have it." Or at the very least, it's that subliminal split second when you choose that product way down there on the lower left shelf rather than the one that's at eye level—right there on the shelf in front of you—because there's something about the one way down there on the left that caught your eye that was simply more attractive than the other product right in front of you.

Now… all of you are familiar with Brooks Stevens, one of the illustrious founders of the Society for Industrial Design who designed every type of product you can imagine, from toasters to trains, but is probably most well-known for his design for the first Jeep and his "wow" factor designs for Harley Davidson. And he, of course, coined that famous, or infamous, term *planned obsolescence*, shamelessly insinuating that design is a mere marketing ploy, a slight of hand, a trick to make consumers think they need the newest model or version of a product and that they "need it *now*."

(chuckles)

He created quite a stir when he first introduced that controversial concept and though most of us have moved beyond, or perhaps back, to a more globally ethical notion of the responsibility of designers, there is one point that he always hammered home that we can all agree on. And that is: that consumer aesthetics, what the end-user, the consumer, thinks is beautiful, really counts—and counts big.

Audience: OK. Sure. All right. Well, certainly.

OK, I can tell that most of you are with me, but just in case we still have any doubters out there… think about this. In the average home, faucets are used in three locations: the kitchen, the bathroom, and perhaps out in the garden, right? Now in each location, you can choose either single handles for your faucet or double handles. OK, now that makes a total of six designs in all, correct? Yet the last time I went to my local home improvement store to pick out a faucet for our kitchen, I counted no less than 158 faucets on display.

(laughter)

I'm not kidding. They were all manner of shapes and sizes and finishes ranging from traditional chrome to copper with a patina that looked like an ancient bronze statue. Beneath their outward appearance, though, faucets are pretty identical as far as function goes. By and large, they all perform excellently and will last for a good number of years. It's obvious then that what sells faucets is how pleasing their appearance is to the eye of the consumer.

I once learned in school that the difference between humans and other animals was that humans could use tools to make things. Anyone who has ever watched a nature program about monkeys or chimpanzees using branches as a device to grab or dig for food, can see that this is not the case. I think, instead, that what really separates us from the chimps is not our ability to design tools, but our ability to design tools that are beautiful. And this desire for beauty in our environment drives us to seek pleasing aesthetics in the cars we drive, the homes we live in, the fabrics that cover us, and even in the boxes that contain our breakfast cereals.

Let me give you another example of how form may be more important than function. And this one might very well be an eye opener for some of you. I have a friend who designs medical devices. Now one would think that the *only* important features of a medical device are safety, durability or strength, and whether or not it performs its intended function well. Does it keep the patient alive or not? Does it provide mobility for the patient or not? Does it allow the surgeon to operate with precision…Well, you get the idea.

Now this is the interesting thing. My friend informs me that looking good matters in this area of industrial design as well as in any other. It turns out that the appearance of a device has a critical effect in the following ways:

First, there is the inevitable "wow" factor. If the device has a high "wow" factor for the user, it will be used more often and more appropriately than if it doesn't. This is true for both patients and doctors. Second, if the user senses that the device is "up to date" (and this is often judged by its looks), then the user will have more confidence in the product. Again, true for both patients and doctors. And third, it has been shown time and again that a more attractive physical environment, including the medical devices used for treatment or rehabilitation, is highly correlated with better patient outcomes. This is especially true for children. If the devices are attractive, they are perceived as helpful and not harmful and the children actually get better faster.

So… now we can get back to the crux of it. If we accept that looking good matters… the problem for industrial designers is how to describe or define "beauty" in terms of the user experience. What makes a product more beautiful to the consumer, more attractive, than another product? Is the perceived beauty of a product merely what's "in" or trendy in a particular culture at a particular time? Or is the true beauty of a product something more permanent? Does the beauty of a product reside in its genius or usefulness? What makes us say it has "timeless beauty"? Is there a type of beauty in a product that could be considered universal?

What do you think? I'd like you to discuss these questions with the three or four people sitting near you for a few minutes. Then I'd like to hear the highlights of your group discussions. In the next phase of today's training session, we'll chart your ideas and see if we can collectively come up with some cohesive thoughts on this most important topic.

PART 3   Admitting a Lack of Knowledge

1 **Listening for Formal and Informal Admissions of Lack of Knowledge** page 74

Conversation 1

Woman: Excuse me, sir, could you give me directions to the Convention Center. I'm going to the Society of Industrial Design Conference that's being held there.

Man: I'm sorry, I don't know. I'm not from around here myself. Sounds like an interesting conference though. Sorry I couldn't help you.

Conversation 2

Veronica: Professor Hill, why did Brooks Stevens go into industrial design instead of architecture? Was it because he flunked out of the Cornell School of Architecture?

Prof. Hill: I'm afraid I don't remember the exact reason why he chose industrial design, but I can assure you it wasn't because he failed at Cornell. I do remember something about a childhood illness and the time he spent in bed making model boats and airplanes. Why don't you look that up for us in a good biography on him and report back to the class?

Conversation 3

Phil: Hey, Bob! When is the next project due in our medical design class?

Bob: Beats me. I haven't a clue. I've been out with the flu for the last week, and I was hoping *you* could tell *me*.

Conversation 4

Carmine: Dorothy, do you know how many different jobs Brooks Stevens had before he finally landed one as a full-fledged industrial designer?

Dorothy: Don't ask me. I haven't any idea. And I don't care. Oh… sorry, Carmine. I know you're just trying to cheer me up because I haven't been able to find a good industrial design position. OK, tell me. But I bet he was never a dog-walker like me, right?

Conversation 5

Chava: Veronica, how come Brooks Stevens never left Milwaukee? Why didn't he move to New York to make a name for himself there? Isn't that what most industrial designers did in his day?

Veronica: I'm sure I don't know! I haven't had time to read anything in that biography that Professor Hill assigned me. Oh… forgive me, Chava. It's not your fault. It's just that I sure could use a little more help around here, OK?

2 **Using Formal Expressions to Admit a Lack of Knowledge** page 74

See Part 2 Cohesion and Reference on page 219 of this audioscript.

PART 4   Focus on Testing

1 **Answering Comprehension Questions with Multiple Answers** page 77

Lecturer: Today I'm going to talk to you about a current controversy in the field of website design. This controversy stems from the age-old debate about the relative importance of form and function, but because websites are part of the world marketplace, the controversy also has a very important cultural component.

First, let's deal with the form versus function part of the controversy. While we hope that website designers try to strike a balance between form and function, there are thousands of websites where we can easily see that designers have chosen sides and that there are two basic camps in this controversy. On one side, in one camp, are those designers who value the aesthetics of a site over its functionality or ease of use. On the other side, in the other camp, are those designers who value the usefulness of a site over its beauty or general attractiveness. Now for some designers, these camps are not located that far apart. Instead of being separated by a great canyon-like chasm, they feel the camps or sides are just a step or two away from each other, across a little stream or brook, and they move freely between the two camps. But as I said earlier, it's not these moderate folks that should concern us. Instead, we should be concerned with the designers that either consciously or unconsciously take one extreme position or the other. Now… before we go any further, let me summarize the arguments on both sides of the divide for you.

Some website designers think their job is all about "looking good." They want to delight the eye of the user with color, shapes, and unusual fonts or types of various sizes. They are more concerned with how the text looks than with what it says. Furthermore, they love to enhance the "feel" and "fun" of the website and the user's experience with all kinds of drop-down menus, roll-over buttons, flash animation, and the like. For these designers, it's all about catching the attention of the user and then taking them for a ride, almost like an entertaining amusement park ride, around the website. They believe that they need to "pretty up" the website or people won't be interested in using it. They ascribe to the idea that, no matter what the function is, it is the visual form and physical feel that users bump into first, and that it's first impressions that count.

On the other side of the divide are the website designers who are convinced that most people do not use the Web for visual stimulation and that they use it to find information, to make contacts with others, and most importantly, to buy things.

These designers think that what users notice is whether they can easily find information, successfully make contacts, and quickly buy whatever it is they want. They do not think that users care very much about the expensive, colorful layout or fancy bells and whistles, menus, animation, and roll-over buttons. They think that these aesthetic elements are not only just frosting on the cake, but also obstacles that slow down navigation through the website and can utterly frustrate users. Therefore, for the designers on this side of the divide, the beauty of a website lies in its function rather than its form—how well it ultimately does its job rather than how seductive it is initially. These designers also insist that it's difficult to convince companies to invest time and money in improving a website that already works. For example, why on earth would Microsoft want to make even one letter of their website "prettier" when they have a product that works and already attracts every web user on the planet?

OK… Now that I've summarized the arguments on both sides of the form versus function debate, let's talk about the inevitable cultural component that exists in the world marketplace. In the field of industrial design, we all know that in the worldwide marketplace there is an ongoing concern about the need to design products that have a wide appeal—that will be attractive to the largest possible number of individuals in the greatest number of cultures. It seems obvious that profits depend on this. But this is not an easy assignment for a website designer. As you are well aware, every culture has its own set of beauty rituals and standards. Things that seem ugly and repulsive to one culture can be alluring and seductive to another. For example, some societies admire fatness while others aspire to be as thin as possible. Some cultures favor big feet while others prefer them small. Some cultures prefer a lot of white space and subtle colors on their websites; other cultures prefer lots of bright colors with very little open space.

So… if you add this cultural component to the form versus function debate… you can see where the difficulty is. For example, will the same website appeal to both Japanese and Saudi users? Will U.S. users be happy using a Taiwanese website designed to appeal to a Taiwanese standard of beauty? And think about this: if a Japanese website user doesn't care how ugly a U.S. site is as long as it functions well, will the same Japanese user feel the same way about Japanese sites? So then… if we are concerned with form, the look and the feel of the website, do we have to find a universal standard of beauty, a form that will appeal to all cultures before we can create a successful website for the world market? Or should companies invest in creating multiple sites for multiple markets. I'll leave you with these questions. I'm very interested in what you think and we'll pick up there with a discussion of this topic next time. The debate is far from settled and I'm looking forward to hearing your opinions and seeing how they will continue to stir things up in the field of website design.

Question 1: Which of the following websites might appeal to a user or a designer that is primarily concerned with form rather than function? Choose two answers.

Question 2: Which of the following would not be a concern of the designer or user who is more concerned with function than form? Choose two answers.

Question 3: According to the speaker, what is the current controversy in the field of website design about? Choose two answers.

Question 4: Why do you think the speaker is interested in this topic? Choose two answers.

Question 5: What might the speaker talk about next time? Choose two answers.

CHAPTER **5** **Transitions**

Radio Program: The Stages of Life—A View from Shakespeare

Grace Powers: In some ways, life is like a giant puzzle. To construct a puzzle, you have to gather and put together the parts. Similarly, we gather and piece together our life experiences as we learn and grow and change.

Hello. This is Grace Powers and welcome to *Transformations*, the show that talks about change—in ourselves and in our society. Tonight we are pleased to have with us the distinguished professor of English literature, Fred Alley, who will speak about Shakespeare's view of the stages of life.

We hope you'll enjoy the program. We'll have a call-in discussion afterward as usual. Our newsletter has a speech from Shakespeare's play, *As You Like It*, in the latest issue. Professor Alley will be referring to this speech in today's presentation.

And now, Professor Alley.

Prof. Alley: Thank you, Grace. Now… most people look forward to changes in the future. We hope that these changes will bring good fortune, yet we also know that not all changes are good. We want to see time and change as positive, but let's face it—we also see time and change as negative because they always bring our decline and eventual death.

In my view, the ways people react to change are more important than what actually happens to them. Frankly, I think that some people waste time worrying about what they weren't able to do or what they didn't become. Other people take a more positive view and learn to accept and take pleasure in what *is*—in what they *were* able to do and what they *did* become. For example, if they've lived an ethical life and been kind to others, they don't worry about the fact that they've never sailed around the world, earned a million dollars, or won a Nobel Prize.

People who have positive feelings toward humanity tend to believe that a lifetime is a period in which we must work hard to develop and perfect ourselves. On the other hand, other people aren't as optimistic about the intelligence and goodness of people. To put it bluntly, they don't generally like or trust people. Those who believe that humankind is not worthy of trust, and therefore not worth caring about, are known as misanthropes.

There are many ways people view the stages that they go through in life. A Buddhist would probably see transformation or change as an opportunity for spiritual growth. A business executive might be concerned with the financial aspects of change. Honestly, there are as many ways to deal with the transformations in our lives as there are points of view. In Western civilization, we seem to be afraid that all our planning and struggling for success are simply meaningless moves in a game that can't be won. We fear that our efforts will produce, as Shakespeare wrote, merely "sound and fury, signifying nothing." One of the most disturbing visions is the idea that we are just actors playing out roles created for us by genetics, the choices our families made, or any number of other circumstances. Or even worse, what if we are just puppets whose strings are pulled by forces beyond our control? I'm sorry to tell you that if this is the case, we do not have any freedom. Each and every moment, every move, every gesture, and every thought is decided for us.

Of course, when we are young, we don't like the idea of being puppets, because this limits our freedom. As we grow older, though, we are often willing to settle for less freedom. We agree to play roles that are predetermined by our own characters and society's expectations of us. These roles sometimes make us feel that we're in a rut—stuck in a boring, repetitive world—but for some reason, we do not rebel. Eventually, we might even become cynics—people who do not believe in free choice and who distrust human nature and people's motives. Cynics believe that most people basically are selfish. And when the cynics describe our failures, we listen eagerly. Why? Well, the truth is that the cynics' view of humanity reassures those people who are weak. You see, if that's the way humanity is, then the weak just can't help themselves. They have the best possible excuse for their behavior: That's simply the way all people are. Cynics also criticize authority in society, because people, especially those in power, always make a mess of everything. I'm sorry to say however, that the cynics offer nothing constructive, no positive suggestions or solutions. They merely whine and complain about the poor condition of the world and how it's all our own fault.

Because we are so aware of the fact that we will all die eventually, the dark visions of the cynics and even darker visions of the misanthropes can be fascinating to us. One of the most famous speeches in literature about the stages in life that we all pass through is the one given by Jacques in Shakespeare's play, *As You Like It*.

Let me tell you a little about Jacques. Jacques is one of the lords serving the duke in the play. He also presents himself as a philosopher who wanders from place to place, has no connections with other people, and no desire for them. At the drop of a hat, though, he will comment freely to anyone and everyone about the state of the world.

As I read the speech, you can decide for yourselves whether you think Jacques is a cynic, a misanthrope, or a realist. Now please follow along on your handout:

All the world's a stage,
And all the men and women merely players.
They have their exits and their entrances,
And one man in his time plays many parts,
His acts being seven ages.

So, Jacques says that we are all simply actors going through our lives as if they were real, when actually we are only playing roles already determined for us. He says the seven stages of life are like acts in a play. In the next few lines, he describes the first two stages:

At first the infant,
Mewling and puking in the nurse's arms,
Then whining schoolboy, with his satchel
And shining morning face, creeping like a snail
Unwillingly to school.

Jacques is so cynical that all he has to say about the sweet, innocent baby in the first act of life's drama is that he cries (that's the "mewling") and he spits up his milk, or "pukes." And the next twelve years don't get any better. The child is sent off to school with his face washed and his books in his "satchel," in his bag. He does nothing of importance but continues to whine and complain as he goes unwillingly to school. The only choice he makes is to go to school slowly, "creeping like a snail." Soon he reaches adolescence—his teenage years—and his interest in girls grows quickly:

And then the lover,
Sighing like a furnace, with a woeful ballad
Made to his mistress' eyebrow. Then a soldier,
Full of strange oaths, and bearded like a pard,
Jealous in honor, sudden and quick in quarrel,
Seeking the bubble reputation
Even in the cannon's mouth.

So, now, in this third stage of life, our hero burns with desire ("sighing like a furnace") and not much else. He becomes possessed by the passion he feels for his sweetheart. Jacques makes the youth seem foolish by having him write a poem about the beauty of his girlfriend's eyebrow. That is certainly silly stuff, but it is all the lover has to say.

The next stage of his life, however, is not as amusing nor perhaps as understandable. The youth soon grows beyond love and sexual desire into anger, jealousy, and the most forceful emotion: ambition. And to him, fulfilling the ambition of becoming a man means becoming a soldier. His language changes. It becomes coarser; to put it bluntly, he swears a lot. He begins to hate his enemies more than he loved his sweetheart—his "mistress." He grows a beard, hoping to look as fierce as a "pard," that is, leopard. He does this to intimidate his enemies. He fights, "quarrels," in order to make a name for himself, to improve his reputation. He is so driven by his ambition for recognition that he doesn't care if it endangers his life. That is, he pursues the "bubble of reputation" even in "the cannon's mouth," even if someone is about to shoot him. He ignores the fact that he is mortal and puts glory and reputation before reason and thought.

If the youth manages to survive these years, he will achieve the fifth stage, making a career for himself and accumulating things and ideas. He will shift from liberal to conservative, from adventurous to cautious, from passionate to self-controlled. Listen:

And then the justice,
In fair round belly with good capon lined,
With eyes severe and beard of formal cut,
Full of wise saws and modern instances,
And so he plays his part.

So, you see, now our young man has become a justice—a court judge. He has become fat from eating chicken (that is, lining his belly with "capon") and other tasty foods. His beard is no longer bushy and fierce-looking but is now well trimmed. Furthermore, he is full of sayings and examples. OK, let's not beat around the bush. He's boring. If this were the last stage, he might be quite content, but there are still two more stages. And the next stage brings the trouble of aging:

The sixth age shifts
Into the lean and slippered Pantaloon,
With spectacles on nose and pouch on side,
His youthful hose, well saved, a world too wide
For his shrunk shank, and his big manly voice,
Turning again toward childish treble, pipes
And whistles in his sound.

Here our man puts on the clothes of old age: loose, comfortable pants and warm slippers. His eyes are weak, and he wears glasses on his nose. He carries his tobacco and perhaps his money, too, in a pouch or purse at his side. There it will be easier for an old man to reach and to guard. The colorful stockings that he once wore on his strong, youthful legs are too large to fit his small thin legs now. He no longer has the clear voice of lover, soldier, and judge, but speaks in a high, childlike voice, often whining like Scottish bagpipes. To add insult to injury, his missing teeth give a whistling sound to his words. His life has almost come full circle, and the next stage ends the play:

Last scene of all,
That ends this strange eventful history,
Is second childishness and mere oblivion,
Sans teeth, sans eyes, sans taste, sans everything.

And so he returns, without teeth, without sight, without taste, without any of the senses, to the emptiness from which he first came into the world.

We all travel the same path. Sometimes our lives are disappointing, even tragic; sometimes delightful; sometimes they are merely routine. We might be glad to be alive, or uncertain of life's value. In any case, only when we die is our role in the play completed.

And let's face it, whether we are simply actors in a play that we have not written or are in control of our own fates is a fascinating question. If you found the answer, would it make a difference in the way you lead your life? I'll leave you with that question.

Grace Powers: Hello again, listeners. This is Grace Powers. Professor Alley's question seems like a good place to start the call-in segment of our program. Our phone lines are now open. If you knew for certain whether or not you could control your own fate, would it make a difference in the way you live your life? Go ahead, Salim in Milwaukee, you're on the air.

PART 3 "Telling It Like It Is"

① Listening for Tone of Voice page 93

Conversation 1A

Mickey: Gloria, have you seen my Uncle Ted lately?

Gloria: Yeah, I saw him last week at the club meeting.

Mickey: Oh, really? How was he?

Gloria: Well, to be honest with you, I don't think he looked very good. He seemed so thin and pale and… well, just old.

Mickey: Well, he's been working very hard, and let's face it, he's no youngster anymore. I've been trying to persuade him to retire, but he just won't do it.

Conversation 1B

Mickey: Gloria, have you seen my Uncle Ted lately?

Gloria: Yeah, I saw him last week at the club meeting.

Mickey: Oh, really? How was he?

Gloria: Well, to be honest with you, I don't think he looked very good. He seemed so thin and pale and… well, just old.

Mickey: Well, he's been working very hard, and let's face it, he's no youngster anymore. I've been trying to persuade him to retire, but he just won't do it.

Conversation 2A

Miranda: Dad, I've something to tell you.

Dad: Well, what is it, sweetheart?

Miranda: Joseph asked me to marry him.

Dad: And?

Miranda: And I said yes. We'd like to be married right away. What date this month would be best for you?

Dad: To tell the truth, if you go ahead with this plan, you'll have to get married without me.

Conversation 2B

Miranda: Dad, I've something to tell you.

Dad: What is it, sweetheart?

Miranda: Joseph asked me to marry him.

Dad: And?

Miranda: And I said yes. We'd like to be married right away. What date this month would be best for you?

Dad: To tell the truth, if you go ahead with this plan, you'll have to get married without me.

Conversation 3A

Paul: Well, how do you like it? I know it's not professional quality yet. I've only taken one course. But what do you think? Should I quit my job and become a photographer?

Jane: To tell the truth, I can't make out what it is.

Paul: It's a bird soaring over a rainbow. See the little point here? That's the beak. Well, what do you think?

Jane: Well, not to beat around the bush— don't quit your job just yet.

Conversation 3B

Paul: Well, how do you like it? I know it's not professional quality yet. I've only taken one course. But what do you think? Should I quit my job and become a photographer?

Jane: To tell the truth, I can't make out what it is.

Paul: It's a bird soaring over a rainbow. See the little point here? That's the beak. Well, what do you think?

Jane: Well, not to beat around the bush— don't quit your job just yet.

2 **Listening for Expressions that "Tell It Like It Is"** page 94

See Part 2 Figurative Language on page 223 of this audioscript.

PART 4 Focus on Testing

1 **Sorting and Classifying Information** page 98

Professor: Many cultures divide a person's life into stages and create images or ideals of each stage. In other words, they have a *topology* of life-stages, a system used to metaphorically trace the "shape" of human life. For example, the ancient Greeks composed the famous riddle of the Sphinx:

What goes on four feet, then two feet, then three But the more feet it goes on, the weaker it be?

The mythological figure Oedipus is said to have solved the riddle. It refers to a person, Oedipus answered. He or she crawls on all fours as an infant, walks upright during youth and middle age, and then leans on a cane or walking stick when old.

This is what I call a *functional* topology of life's stages. The stages are defined by how a certain function—walking, in this case—is performed. A culture could, theoretically, build a functional topology around any activity that is, for most people, affected by changes in age. For example, if I wanted to focus on the function of chewing food, I might divide life into a sucking stage (babyhood), a losing-teeth stage (pre-teen), a "braces" stage during which one can't eat sticky food, a full-toothed chewing stage, and a gumming stage in later life. This topology may sound a little silly, but it works. Not every person would go through every stage in the same progression, but not every ancient Greek lived long enough to use a cane either. The point is that the image works broadly enough to ring true.

Closely related to functional topologies are *maturational* schemes. These trace the stages of life in terms of mental, physical, or even spiritual changes. The most obvious and common maturational topology divides life into childhood (pre-puberty), adolescence, adulthood, and old age. With our current knowledge of body chemistry, we can say that the outward signs of these stages of life are traceable to hormonal changes. But even without that specific knowledge, cultures throughout history have recognized these stages.

One well-known maturational topology that is not quite so obvious is a Hindu system that focuses on spiritual maturation. Life is divided into four stages, depending on one's progress towards being spiritually full-grown. The first stage is studentship, or *Brahmacarya*, which lasts from initiation into the Hindu community at five to eight years of age until marriage. During the second stage of the ideal life, *Grihasthya*, one marries, raises a family, and takes part in society. *Vanaprasthya* is the third stage. It is during this stage, after one's children have grown up, that the Hindu leaves the household and prepares for the spiritual search or quest. The fourth and final stage is *Samnyasa*, renunciation. This is when one gives up attachment to all worldly things and seeks spiritual liberation.

Most cultures take maturational topologies one step further and establish ceremonies, called rites of passage, to mark a person's entrance into a new stage. Stage-of-life topologies that focus on these ceremonies are called *ritual* topologies. Typically, ritual topologies include celebrations at birth, puberty, marriage, and death. Countless cultures have rituals for these occasions, often because of religious or philosophical traditions. Confucian thought, for instance, helped establish this kind of ritual topology in many East Asian cultures and helped determine the materials (rice, water, etc.) used in the rituals. Christianity—with baptism, confirmation, and other life-stage rites—did the same in European cultures and cultures elsewhere that are based on European models.

Functional and maturational topologies are almost poetic in their ability to create images. This stands in contrast to what I would call a *bureaucratic* topology, one based purely on where a person falls into some scheme invented by a government or another organization. Take, for example, the stages by which Americans gain greater status under the law. For most purposes, one becomes a legal person at birth. In most states, the age of 16 is the age of consent, the point at which someone can agree to marry or enter other relationships. Eighteen is the age at which one can vote and enter the military, and at 21 one can legally drink alcoholic beverages. Cultural traditions have influenced this topology, but it is supported mostly by law and not by belief. Why do people pass from one stage to another? Purely because the law says so. Some aspects of a bureaucratic topology may actually conflict with widespread cultural beliefs. For example, many Americans firmly believe that no one should get married at the age of 16, even if the law says they may.

Narrator: Open your book and use your notes to complete the table. For each item, mark an "X" in the appropriate box, to indicate which of the four topologies each statement goes with best, according to the lecture. To simulate a real test, give yourself only five minutes to complete the table.

CHAPTER 6 **The Mind**

PART 2   Comparison and Contrast

1 **Listening for Comparison and Contrast in Informal Conversations** page 107

Conversation 1

Otto: I really like that cheese shop on Second Street, Henry. You know, the one with the giant mouse on the roof holding a chunk of cheese?

Henry: I don't think I've ever been there, Otto. Why do you like it?

Otto: They make cheese the same way my grandfather used to. It makes me daydream about my childhood on my grandfather's dairy farm in Wisconsin.

Conversation 2

Judy: Paula, do you think we should drive or take the train to the concert in Chicago? I can't decide. There are advantages and disadvantages to both.

Paula: Well, let's see. Driving means that we can leave whenever we want. On the other hand, Judy, taking the train means we don't have to worry about parking and we can both sleep on the way home.

Judy: That would be great! Then I could finish that dream I was having about becoming a famous musician.

Conversation 3

TA: I've talked with Professor Thornton and there are going to be some changes this week. What do you want first—the good news or the bad news?

Students: Oh, no! What? Wait, what's up?

TA: Well, the good news is, we're not going to have a quiz today.

Students: Really? That's great! No kidding?

TA: And the bad news is that this means that next week we'll have two quizzes—one on the mind on Wednesday, and one on dreams and the dream state on Friday.

Students: Oh, no. Great!

3 Listening for Comparison and Contrast page 108

Lecture: Dreams and Reality

Professor: Hello, everyone. Well... how did you do with the reading for this week? Any problems?

Student 1: Oh, yes. I thought that the textbook was really hard to understand.

Student 2: Yeah, me too. I thought I knew something about the topic for this week, you know, "Dreams and Reality," until I started doing the reading.

Student 3: I agree. I finally went to the library and got another book on the subject.

Professor: OK. How many others had problems? Yes, well, it looks like about half of you had some difficulty. So let's not use the textbook today. Instead, let's talk about one of my favorite science fiction books. It contains some great examples of the concepts in the textbook.

Last summer, I read a science fiction book called *The Lathe of Heaven*. My lecture is based on some of the ideas in this book. And I'm very interested to hear your reactions. So let me just share a few ideas with you; then we'll open it up for discussion. OK?

Students: Sure. Yeah. Great. Sounds good.

Professor: Most of us have had intense dreams. While we are sleeping, these dreams seem very real, but after we wake up, the dream images break up and become much less intense, perhaps like photographs of something way off in the distance. Even though the dream images have become much less intense, they still stay with us as we go about our daily activities. We may be only partly aware of these images and only partly aware of the changes in perception that they may cause. But our dreams can affect our lives during the day without our conscious awareness. This is because our dreams influence our decisions and choices even though we don't realize it.

Often, however, our dreams seem trivial and useless. On the other hand, many breakthroughs in science and in the arts have originated in dreams. In the sciences, for example, a German chemist, F. A. Kekule von Stradonitz, dreamed about a snake with its tail in its mouth. He said that this dream led him to visualize the benzene molecule. The dream helped him to conceptualize a model of this molecule.

Samuel Taylor Coleridge wrote a poem titled "Kubla Khan." Coleridge said that he created the poem during a dream and that the minute he woke up, he began to write it down. While he was doing this, a visitor came to see him and interrupted his writing. Later, when he tried to finish the poem, he couldn't. He had forgotten the end of it. That's sad but, on the bright side, critics still consider it one of his best poems, even though it is not finished.

So dreams can be very important. My dreams, however, do seem pretty silly. For example, the other night, I dreamed about buying a suit, something I had actually done that day. And one night last week I dreamed about hot dogs piled up on a bridge—no useful images for scientific discoveries or artistic creations there that I can figure out. But at least I do dream. And we know that dreaming, any kind of dreaming, is necessary for both physical and mental health.

So the mind can create two basic types of dreams: On the one hand, the powerful and intense images that can change our lives, and, on the other hand, the fleeting, chaotic, meaningless images that contain no important messages.

Ursula LeGuin, a popular and highly respected science fiction writer, explores the world of dreams in *The Lathe of Heaven*. In this book, she looks at the relationship between dreams and reality in a fascinating way. Let me briefly summarize the story for you.

George Orr, the main character in the story, has a problem. When he has certain kinds of dreams, the world changes according to his dream. So he frequently awakens to a different world from the one that existed when he fell asleep.

Student 2: Wow! That would be neat.

Student 3: Yeah! Cool!

Professor: Yes, that's quite an extraordinary power. But as you can imagine, it frightens him because he doesn't believe that it is right to use his dreams to change reality. His fear grows bigger when he realizes that no one else knows that he is changing the entire world, night after night. Everyone else changes completely to become a part of the new world that George creates in his dream. Every time George dreams a new reality, each person has a new set of memories to fit this new reality. They remember nothing of the old reality that existed the night before.

Student 1: That sounds awful!

Student 2: Yes it does, but just think of the power he has to change the world!

Professor: Right, and it's interesting that you should point that out. You see, George is extremely upset. He is afraid to go to sleep and dream, so he goes to a psychiatrist named Haber. Fortunately, Dr. Haber believes George and does not think he is insane. However, Dr.

Haber wants to use George's power for his own purposes, so at first he does not tell George that he knows that the dreams really change things. But in the end, someone else finds out that George can actually change reality through his dreams, and Dr. Haber is forced to admit that he is not trying to cure George of his fear of dreaming. Instead, Dr. Haber is trying to use George's dreams to change the world.

The upside of this is that the doctor wants to change the world into a "better" place. He wants to do *good* things for the world by controlling George's dreams.

Student 4: That sounds OK, but I bet there's a downside, right?

Professor: Right. Dr. Haber builds a special machine that records George's dreams, so that he can transfer George's brainwave patterns during dreams to his own dreams. Dr. Haber thinks that this machine will give him the power to change the world by himself, through his own dreams, without George.

This technique works, sort of. Dr. Haber does, in fact, gain some power to change reality through his own dreams. But he fails to understand what is real and what is unreal. Because he sees only the concrete, material world as real, his dreams produce nightmarish realities with no flexibility. For example, Dr. Haber decides that he wants complete equality in the world. He wants all people to be absolutely equal in all ways. So he dreams, and when he wakes up, everything is gray. People's skin, their clothes, the houses, the trees, the animals—everything!

Students: Oh, no! What a shock! It figures!

Professor: Everything is certainly equal, but only in a material sense. But things could be worse. Just imagine if Dr. Haber were an evil person rather than a basically good man. Eventually, Dr. Haber goes mad from the stress of never getting it quite right.

Students: (laughter)

Professor: Well, now. What's the point that LeGuin is trying to make in this story? One clue is in the title, *The Lathe of Heaven*. A lathe is a machine on which objects are turned and shaped into new forms. If the wood or the metal is not flexible, it will crack when it is shaped by the machine. The same thing happens with the lathe of heaven. If a person is not flexible and accepts only one part of the mind—the rational, logical part—he or she will be destroyed by the lathe.

In this novel, Dr. Haber represents the inflexible, rational, materialistic person who thinks that he can control nature, that he can bend nature to serve himself. His mind is never still, never quiet. Instead, his mind is always active, looking for new ways to change reality. George, on the other hand, is mentally quiet. He never thinks of manipulating reality. His dreams are powerful not because he wants power but because he is in tune with nature.

But LeGuin suggests that George, even though he's in harmony with reality, will still suffer. Imagine what it would be like to wake up to a new world with a new history every few days and to be the only one who can remember the old world.

Likewise, the lathe of heaven forms and re-forms the world and plays with time like a child playing with a recording. Time is moved forward or backward like fast forwarding or rewinding.

LeGuin asks us to let go of our concept of time, which is the idea that time continuously moves forward, inch by inch, as on a ruler. Instead, she wants us to see time in relation to a central point. George represents that central point and all of time depends on him. Perhaps LeGuin wants us to see that change cannot be pushed from behind along a straight course, but only exists in relation to a stable central point.

Uh-oh. I can see there are mixed reactions to this idea. So… let's take a short break and then open it up for discussion. I'm really anxious to hear what you think.

PART 3 Expressing the Positive View

1 Listening for the Positive View
page 115

Conversation 1

Gary: Hi, Julius. How's it going?

Julius: Hi, Gary. I'm really tired. I didn't sleep much last night because I had this terrible dream. I dreamed that I got the second-to-lowest grade on the history final.

Gary: Oh, yeah? And who got the *lowest* grade?

Julius: Henry Mitchell. Wow, what a horrible dream!

Gary: Oh, yeah! But it could have been worse!

Julius: Yeah? How?

Gary: Well, you could have woken up and discovered *you* were Henry Mitchell.

Conversation 2

Christine: Oh, shoot, Eric! It's raining again, and I was looking forward to going to the soccer team picnic.

Eric: Yeah—too bad—but look at it this way: Now we'll have time to go see that dream therapist I was telling you about.

Christine: Oh, well—maybe…

Eric: Now come on, Christine. You said you wanted to stop smoking, didn't you?

Conversation 3

Clara: Hi, Joyce. What's up?

Joyce: Hi, Clara. I'm on my way over to my study skills class. We're starting a unit on speed reading, and I'm not looking forward to it.

Clara: Really? Why not?

Joyce: Well, I'm afraid that those speed-reading techniques might interfere with my reading comprehension. And I already have so much trouble understanding a lot of the material in my classes.

Clara: Oh, but just think. You'll learn to read everything so quickly that you'll at least read everything once. You *were* having trouble completing all the reading assignments on time, weren't you?

Joyce: Yes, but remember what the comedian Woody Allen said a speed-reading course did for him?

Clara: No—what?

Joyce: He said: "Well, after the speed-reading course, I really improved. I was able to read Tolstoy's *War and Peace* in five minutes… Yes, uh huh—it's about war."

Clara: OK, OK! Well, to improve your comprehension, how about learning that new dream technique we heard about instead? You know, study like crazy before you go to sleep and then dream all night about the topic?

Joyce: Sure, that sounds better. Where do I sign up?

2 Summarizing the Positive View
page 116

See Part 2 Comparison and Contrast on page 227 of this audioscript.

PART 4 Focus on Testing

1 Answering a Realistic Mix of Question Types page 119

Angie: Hi, Brian. What's up?

Brian: Huh? What? What?

Angie: Oh, sorry. I didn't mean to startle you. Am I interrupting anything?

Brian: Oh, Angie. It's you. No, no, you're not interrupting anything. I was just dreaming. Or at least I *think* I was dreaming.

Angie: What do you mean *think*?

Brian: Well, I'm so tired. I think I may be losing touch with reality. You know, I've been studying for final exams and it's really important that I get all *A*s and *B*s this semester. I want to get into a really good law school, and my scholarship money is about to run out, and my psychology professor said she can't write a letter of recommendation for me unless I get at least an A minus in her course, and you know that my parents haven't been too happy about my grades lately... . Anyway, I've been up for about three nights straight now. And just before you came in, I was reading this psychology book, and I guess I sort of drifted off. Only I didn't realize it until you came in.

Angie: What do you mean? What happened?

Brian: Well, I was studying for my psychology final in my room, or I thought I was, and then this girl comes in and she says that I really need to rest and that I should go with her into the garden and sit there and relax for a while and that she'll bring me some refreshments.

Angie: Refreshments? Nobody uses that word any more. Sounds to me like you just fell asleep for a few minutes and you were dreaming.

Brian: Yeah, but it seemed so real. She took my hand in hers and it was so soft. I...

Angie: Soft hand, huh? Softer than mine?

Brian: No, no, don't go there. You're missing the point. See... then I follow her out into the garden and she sits me down at the table right here. Then she leaves for a minute... I guess to get me some refreshments.

Angie: (chuckles)

Brian: Now, c'mon. Don't laugh. Listen to the rest first. Then I lean over to smell the roses, you know, right there and I pick a really beautiful pink one to give her when she comes back. Then all of sudden, she appears again in the doorway. She almost floats over to me, she's so delicate the way she walks and all... and then she gives me a cup of tea and the most delicious-looking cookies. Well... that's it. I was reaching for a cookie and just about to ask her name when... when... I guess that's when you came in. Did you see her? Do you know who she is?

Angie: Hmmm. I honestly don't know who she is, Brian, but these cookies are really great. Where'd you get 'em?

Brian: What? What cookies? I didn't have any cookies here a few minutes ago!

Angie: Relax, Brian. I brought you the cookies. You're not losing touch with reality. You were just dreaming.

Brian: Yeah, I guess you're right. It sure was a great dream, though.

Angie: Sounds like wishful thinking. You know, that's what Freud said about dreams—that they can represent what we hope for or what we need.

Brian: Well, after this dream, I'm sure Freud was right. A lovely lady to share some cookies with me is exactly what I need right now.

Angie: Well, here I am.

Question 1: What was Brian doing when Angie arrived?

Question 2: Why is Brian so tired?

3. *Listen again to part of the conversation.*

Angie: Oh, sorry. I didn't mean to startle you. Am I interrupting anything?

Brian: Oh, Angie. It's you. No, no, you're not interrupting anything.

Question 3: Why does Brian say to Angie, "It's you"?

4. *Listen again to part of the conversation.*

Brian: You know, I've been studying for final exams and it's really important that I get all *A*s and *B*s this semester. I want to get into a really good law school, and my scholarship money is about to run out, and my psychology professor said she can't write a letter of recommendation for me unless I get at least an A minus in her course, and you know that my parents haven't been too happy about my grades lately… . Anyway, I've been up for about three nights straight now.

Question 4: Why does Brian say, "anyway"?

Question 5: Fill in the following chart by putting the number of each statement in the correct category. Two of the statements will not be used.

Question 6: What didn't the girl in the dream do?

Question 7: Why was Brian surprised and a little anxious about the cookies?

8. *Listen again to part of the conversation.*

Angie: Relax, Brian. I brought you the cookies. You're not losing touch with reality. You were just dreaming.

Brian: Yeah, I guess you're right. It sure was a great dream, though.

Angie: Sounds like wishful thinking. You know, that's what Freud said about dreams—that they can represent what we hope for or what we need.

Brian: Well, after this dream, I'm sure Freud was right. A lovely lady to share some cookies with me is exactly what I need right now.

Question 8: What does Brian want to do?

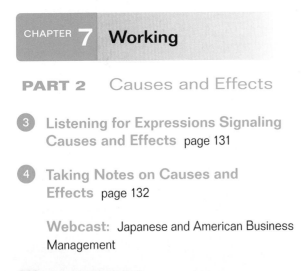

CHAPTER **7** **Working**

PART 2 Causes and Effects

3 **Listening for Expressions Signaling Causes and Effects** page 131

4 **Taking Notes on Causes and Effects** page 132

> **Webcast:** Japanese and American Business Management

Technician: Phil, you're on in ten seconds.

Phil: OK, thanks. Are we ready, everybody? Here we go.

Technician: Five, four, three, two, one. You're on the air.

Phil: Good evening. I'm Philip Grant, and I will be your moderator for tonight's Downlink Discussion. As usual, we have a live audience here in our broadcast studio.

Audience: (applause)

Phil: Tonight's discussion is "Japanese and American Business Management." And we are fortunate to have two very knowledgeable people on this topic here—Laura Gordon and Brian Mani. Laura and Brian are management consultants and have worked for over 15 years with corporations in Japan and America.

First, Ms. Gordon and Mr. Mani will give us some background information and then we will open up the discussion to participants from our studio audience and all the Downlink sites. So, without further delay, Laura Gordon and Brian Mani.

Laura: Good evening. Let me begin by saying a few familiar, well-loved words: Nikon, Honda, Mitsubishi, Sony…

Audience: (laughter)

Laura: Yes, these names are household words to Americans. They demonstrate the success of Japanese goods in the American marketplace.

From cars to cameras, from video recorders to violins, we are surrounding ourselves with more and more products "Made in Japan." We choose them because they are easy to get, well made, and not too expensive. Consequently, the demand for Japanese goods has cut deeply into the sales of American companies, and they are losing a lot of business.

In response to this situation, some leaders in business, labor, and government want to have protective taxes and import quotas on Japanese products. Other leaders, however, have suggested a different approach. They say that instead of trying to keep the Japanese out, we should learn from them by studying and using Japanese methods for producing better goods at lower cost.

What are these methods? What are the differences between Japanese management techniques and our own? Before I answer these questions, let me ask you a few. Take a look at the blue handout in the study packet. It says "Audience Survey" at the top. And the title is "How Would *You* Run a Doorbell Company?"

OK. Everybody got it? Good. Look at the handout. As you read it, imagine that you are the manager of a large corporation that is setting up a new electronic doorbell assembly factory. For each item, decide which of the choices, *A* or *B*, you would use to increase productivity at your company. On your handout, mark *A* or *B*, depending on which choice you think is better.

We'll give you a few minutes to complete this survey, and then Brian will go over the handout with you.

Brian: OK. It looks like everybody is just about finished. So, if you haven't figured it out already, let me explain what we've got here.

The *A*s and *B*s describe the two systems of management, Japanese and American. All the *A*s describe one system, and all the *B*s describe the other system. Which is which? Do you know? How many of you think that the *A*s describe the American system of management?

Well, you are right. If you chose mostly *A*s you picked the American management system. And, of course, if you chose mostly *B*s, you picked the Japanese management system.

Let's look at the *A*s first, the statements that describe typical American management. If you are a typical American manager, you encourage and reward individual initiative. Therefore, you separate the people who are moving up in a company from those who aren't.

On the other hand, if you are a typical Japanese manager, illustrated in the *B* statements, what you do is encourage the group to work together. You reward the group for working together. You don't focus on individual initiative. So, what you believe is that long-term job security for everyone in the company is important. In addition, you feel that it is absolutely necessary to keep the organization as stable as possible. Therefore, you don't try to make rapid changes. Furthermore, you believe it is unnecessary to keep a clear division between management and labor. In fact, you encourage strong identification between management and labor.

Now just why are the Japanese and American business management styles so different? Over the last 20 years or so, many researchers and management specialists have studied the contrasting styles of Japanese and American managers. What they have found is that the different styles of management reflect the different traditions and values of the two countries. While the Americans have treasured the values of individualism, self-reliance, and freedom from rules, the Japanese have preferred group identity, the interdependence of all workers, and the interdependence of workers and management along with a complex system of rules.

The researchers believe that the contrast between these two management styles has its roots in the geography, history, and the traditions of the two countries. Japan, as you know, is small, isolated, and poor in natural resources. As a result, it is necessary for Japan to bring together the available wealth and labor in a cooperative effort to succeed economically. The United States, in contrast, is large and has many areas that are still unpopulated. In the past, the United States had unlimited natural resources and populations that moved from place to place. In addition, the people in the United States seem to love breaking rules. They also love competition.

So researchers are now seeing that the American tradition may not work as well for modern industrial production as the Japanese system does. This is because modern industrial production demands supportive cooperation among workers and between workers and management, not competition within the company. Did you know that the word *corporation* comes from a word that means "a single body"? Now, both scholars and businesspeople believe that a shift in the direction of the Japanese cooperative system is just what American industry needs to improve its performance.

Laura, why don't you talk about Ouchi's work now? He's a great example of what I'm talking about.

Laura: Yes, great idea. I was just thinking the same thing.

As Brian mentioned, one scholar who has taught the principles of Japanese business management to American managers is Professor William Ouchi. He asserts, in his widely-read book, *Theory Z: How American*

Business Can Meet the Japanese Challenge, that if U.S. managers take steps to strengthen close relationships between workers and their firms, U.S. productivity will increase dramatically and eventually be greater than Japanese productivity. Four important steps that he mentions are: (1) lifetime employment contracts, (2) promotions in small but regular steps, (3) nonspecialization of executives, and (4) consensus decision making with input from all employees—at all levels.

Although these measures suggest a slowing down of three corporate processes—innovation, advancement, and decision-making—Ouchi claims that in the long run, these changes will lead to higher levels of agreement, morale, corporate strength, *and* profits.

Phil: Excuse me, Laura. I've heard that many American companies have already adopted the Japanese corporate model. Could you name some of the well-known ones, please?

Laura: Of course. There's IBM, Intel, Procter and Gamble, Hewlett-Packard, and the Cadillac and Saturn divisions of General Motors, to name a few. Oh, and lots of power companies such as Wisconsin Power and Light and Florida Power and Light.

These firms have divided employees into project teams that manage their own jobs, and they have protected jobs during bad economic times by cutting back everyone's working hours so they do not have to fire anyone. They have also allowed workers to manage quality-control procedures. These changes have produced encouraging results. There has been a decrease in complaints among workers and also a decrease in disputes between labor and management along with gains in both quality and productivity. If this trend continues, it may turn out that Japan's most valuable export to the United States is a philosophy of business organization.

Phil: But didn't some of the Japanese management practices get started in America?

Laura: Yes, in a way. W. Edwards Deming, an American, brought many innovative management concepts to Japan after World War II. The Japanese quickly put them to use, but American companies just weren't ready until recently.

Phil: Laura, Brian, I think this would be a good place to take a short break. OK?

Laura and Brian: Sure. That's fine.

Phil: OK. We'll take a short break, and when we come back, we'll open up the discussion to everyone in the audience here and at the Downlink sites. And thanks so much to Laura Gordon and Brian Mani for doing the background presentation tonight.

Audience: (applause)

Executive: Our company is one of the most successful of its kind in Japan. We are sure to be successful here as well.

City official: That will be good for your company, but exactly how will it help our town?

Executive: Well, first of all, we will hire only local people to work in the factory.

City official: Does that include all the employees? Even those in management positions?

Executive: Yes, for the most part. We will, of course, have some of our personnel from Japan in management positions to get things started and to teach our management system.

City official: That sounds good. Now what about your waste products? What will you do about them? We don't want any industrial waste problems here!

Executive: There really isn't any waste to speak of. Not only that, the industry is very quiet as well. So you will have no noise pollution from us.

City official: I'm sold. It sounds like an ideal situation. How about you, Mayor? What do you think?

Mayor: Well, I'd like to know more about your management system. I'm not so sure the people in our town will be happy with that system, not to mention the fact that I have my doubts about how well your product will sell over here.

Executive: You may have a point there. But our company is willing to take that chance. What's more, if the management system is not satisfactory, we're willing to change it if necessary to keep the employees satisfied and to keep our production rate up. And I might add that our company is willing to pay top dollar to the city for the use of that land by the railroad tracks where we want to build our factory.

Mayor: I see. In that case, you've talked me into it!

3 **Listening for Expressions**
Introducing Persuasive Arguments
page 139

See Part 2 Causes and Effects on page 232 of this audioscript.

PART 4   Focus on Testing

1 **Responding to an Integrated-Speaking Prompt** page 142

Professor: June Randolph of the University School of Business is an expert on the work of W. Edwards Deming. She has developed a very accessible, down-to-earth explanation of Deming's seven-step quality improvement process. I'd like to summarize this for you in today's class.

The seven-step process helps people look at a problem or a project in a very systematic way. They analyze the situation, take steps to deal with it, and then check their results. If the results are satisfactory, the problem-solving group uses what they have learned from the process to keep improving their operations.

She points out first of all that Deming's system is useful for small businesses as well as very large corporations. Size of the organization is irrelevant, as long as the group needs to get a job done well. To illustrate that this process works for smaller entities, she shows how it has been useful even in her family.

Randolph gives a great example of using the seven-step process to help train a family dog. The dog, named Gracie, kept getting into the family garbage. Now, the first step in Deming's improvement process is to understand the reasons for improvement. In this case, with Randolph's dog, they were pretty obvious: (1) Gracie was making a big mess in the kitchen every day, and (2) she was eating things that were not good for her. The second step is to collect data on the current situation. Randolph's family counted exactly how many times a month Gracie got into the garbage. They even tried to note the exact times of the day, but sometimes this was difficult because she usually only caused a problem when no one was home.

The third step in the Randolph family's process was to analyze the data. They found that Gracie got into the garbage only about three times a week. That was somewhat surprising, because it had seemed to the Randolphs like Gracie was doing it all the time. It turned out, however, that the problem only occurred after the Randolphs had eaten meat.

Deming's fourth step toward quality improvement is to plan and implement a solution to the problem. With the dog, that was easy. Every time the Randolph family ate meat, they gave Gracie a little bit of it in her bowl and then took the garbage out right away. That way, the dog didn't keep smelling meat in the garbage.

The fifth step is to check results, and the sixth step is standardization. That means you have to see if your efforts have worked, and then make sure that successful results will continue into the future. To accomplish the sixth step, the Randolphs all agreed to take turns taking the garbage out on time—and giving Gracie some meat in her bowl if she kept out of the garbage. The seventh step involves making plans for the future. In the case of the Randolphs, this meant looking out for other family habits that might encourage Gracie to misbehave.

Narrator: How does information from the lecture illustrate principles described in the reading? Your response should include specific examples from both the reading and the lecture. You have 30 seconds to prepare your response and 60 seconds to speak.

CHAPTER **8**   **Breakthroughs**

PART 2   When You Don't Understand the Concepts

2 **Practicing Seven Ways to Approach Difficult Concepts** page 150

Lecture: Discovering the Laws of Nature

Student 1: You know, I don't usually have trouble in science classes, but I'm having a really hard time understanding all this stuff. How about you?

Student 2: Yeah! Me, too. Let's get together later and compare notes, OK?

Student 3: Hey! Are you guys talking about comparing notes later? Great idea! This class is impossible! I just don't get this stuff.

Student 1: Yeah, I know. But I think that together we can probably figure it out.

Student 2: Right. Come over about 6:00. I'll order a pizza.

Students 1 & 3: Sounds great!

Student 2: Shhhh. Here he comes.

Professor: Good morning. I'm going to tell you a little about the history of physics today. You know, physics has not always been a separate science. In fact, long ago physics was part of the religious and metaphysical study about the nature of the cosmos. So is our current view of physics the one true and final view? Or is it like other views of the past, just a temporary belief about nature that may change in the future?

If we look at history, we find many examples of common beliefs about nature that turned out to be false or foolish. For instance, for many centuries, millions of people believed that the Earth was the center of the universe. Others believed that lead could be turned into gold… or that doctors could cure sick people by bleeding them.

Let's look at some ideas about physics and how they changed over time. The first great age of physics began with the ancient Greeks. They developed many theories about the beginnings of the universe. These theories were based on the four basic elements of nature: earth, air, fire, and water. The Greek philosopher Plato caused a revolution in physics by showing the connection between nature, the physical world, and philosophy, the ideas of humans. He also did not think the Earth was the center of everything. In contrast, another Greek, named Aristotle, imagined the universe with the Earth at the center and the sun and the planets traveling around it in never-ending circles. Ptolemy, an Egyptian astrologer, confirmed this view.

As ridiculous as it might seem now, this view was accepted by most people for the next 1,800 years, until the work of Sir Isaac Newton. Of course, before Newton's time, there were some philosophers and scientists who had serious doubts about Aristotle's ideas. For example, Copernicus, Kepler, and Galileo all attempted to prove that the sun, and not the Earth, was the center of the solar system.

However, it was Newton who finally demonstrated that the sun is the center of our solar system by using mathematics. He also showed that mathematics was the key to understanding the unity of nature. He showed that the stars in the distant skies as well as the Earth under our feet obey the same mathematical laws. What's more, for Newton, the mathematical principle of gravitation was the unifying idea, the *paradigm* that explained all events in the physical world. Gravitation was *the* unifying principle, or unified field theory of its time, the principle that provided the model for all other forms of knowledge.

Surprised? That's nothing. Listen to this… While Aristotle's paradigm lasted 1,800 years, Newton's lasted only about 200 years before it was seriously questioned. The problem with Newton's theories was not that they were wrong, but that they just didn't cover everything. When scientists began to look at atomic and subatomic particles, they found that Newton's mathematical equations simply did not explain what they were observing. So again there was a need for another unifying theory to explain how the objective world works.

The person who was able to come up with this theory was Albert Einstein. In the early 20th century, Einstein gave us a new way of describing natural events. He gave us a new way of perceiving the world. His Special Theory of Relativity proposed that time and space were not constant and separate. He said that time and space were not independent principles of nature. Rather, they were relative to each other and even interchangeable. The unifying principle that Einstein proposed was light, because the speed of light remains constant, remains the same no matter where it travels.

Einstein went on to develop a General Theory of Relativity that joined elements of gravity, space/time, and matter into a cohesive or unified system. This theory was later used as a basis for theories of the origin of the universe. But Einstein was not completely happy with his work. He did not believe that his theories explained the events in the world of subatomic particles, such as electrons. You see, an observer cannot say that an electron is in a certain place at a certain time, traveling at a certain speed. An observer can say only that there is a *probability* of finding an electron in such and such a place at such and such a time when it is traveling at such and such a speed.

Einstein was puzzled by this problem most of his adult life. He tried and tried to find a unified field theory that could explain all electric, magnetic, optical, and gravitational events and locate them in space and time. He died, as we know, without succeeding. Nevertheless, he tried until the end of his life to prove his belief that "God does not play dice with the universe," that everything is not just left to chance.

So how long will Einstein's paradigm last? You think it will last a long time, don't you? It certainly does explain some aspects of our world very well. Ah, yes, but so does the mathematics of Newton.

So where do we stand now in terms of a unified field theory? Is it a myth, or perhaps a religious notion that we inherited from our ancestors? Or is all of nature truly unified in ways we can't see yet, but may discover one day. Is the unified field theory within reach, or is the search for it just a wild goose chase? Neils Bohr, one of the fathers of quantum theory, has suggested that we simply may not be looking in the right places. He believes that mathematical models are not able to describe all events in nature. Perhaps now we must use symbols and metaphors from other areas of human interest to explain the world. And this brings us back to where we started: combining physics, the study of nature, with religion and myth or metaphysics.

Well, I think this is a good spot to break. Next time, we'll continue our look at the search for a unified field theory. So be sure to review the chapters on Einstein's Special and General Theories of Relativity and begin the next chapter on quantum mechanics.

PART 3 Giving and Receiving Compliments

1 **Listening for Appropriate and Inappropriate Compliments** page 154

Conversation 1

Ron: Mr. McGovern, you are such a very good teacher. I like your class so much. I think I've really made some major breakthroughs. I'm learning so much. I like you so-o-o much.

Mr. McGovern: Oh, uh… thank you, Ron. Well, I'm on my way to an appointment right now. I'll talk to you later.

Conversation 2

Sandra: Oh, Mr. McGovern, that was a great class. I never understood the second law of thermodynamics before, and now I feel like I could explain it to someone else who might not understand it.

Mr. McGovern: Thank you, Sandra. I appreciate your saying that.

Conversation 3

Martin: Larry! Helen! Hello! Who's winning?

Helen: Oh, hello, Martin.

Larry: Hi, Martin. Not me! I can never seem to beat Helen at checkers. Just between you and me, she's definitely the checkers champion around here.

Helen: Oh, I wouldn't say that. I just win a few games now and then.

Martin: Oh, no, Helen, Larry's right. You're definitely the best player here.

Helen: Well, thank you both very much. I guess I have made a breakthrough lately in my efforts to pick up a few new strategies.

Larry: Hey, Martin, you were looking pretty good last night at the party. I couldn't believe how well you danced! I didn't know you knew how to do all that.

Martin: I don't! It was my first time—my daughter pulled me out onto the dance floor and I had to do it. But I wasn't really any good. In fact, I was terrible. You know that law of nature that says, "You can't teach an old dog new tricks"!

Helen: Come on, Marty. That's not a law of nature! This is the generation dedicated to the principle of lifelong learning! And I don't mind telling you that you looked just fine out on the dance floor. And what's more, your daughter looked simply beautiful!

Martin: Well, thanks. Coming from you, that means a lot. You're quite a dancer yourself.

Helen: Oh, I can't take all the credit. My partner helped some.

Larry: Oh, no, I hardly did anything. Helen really is a wonderful dancer. She's so graceful and light on her feet. She should give lessons. Better yet, she should go on stage in New York or be in the movies. She's as good as any of the dancers you see there.

Helen: Now Larry, flattery will get you nowhere today. You're losing this game of checkers, and I'm not going to let you win no matter how many compliments you give me.

Martin: That's telling him, Helen!

Conversation 4

Larry: Martin, what's wrong? You look a bit worried.

Martin: Well, I'm not worried exactly, but I am confused and feeling very old. I wish I had Helen's attitude about the principle of lifelong learning. You always seem so in touch with current ideas, Helen.

Helen: I appreciate your saying that, but what brought all this on?

Martin: Well, I was trying to help my grandson with his physics homework, and I'm afraid I wasn't much help at all. I don't really understand some of the new theories.

Larry: Well, if you ask me, Martin, you were wonderful to even try to help him. A lot of grandfathers wouldn't take the time.

Martin: Thanks, I needed that. But I still wish I knew more about what's happening in the field of physics these days.

Larry: Why is that so important to you?

Martin: It seems to me that young people today have a different view of the world than we did when we were young, and I'd like to understand it.

Helen: Well, that's admirable, Martin. Sounds to me like you are interested in lifelong learning after all. In fact, I've been meaning to tell you that you're one of the brightest, most stimulating, most adventuresome, and forward-thinking men I know.

Martin: Why, thanks, Helen! That kind of flattery will get you everywhere!

② **Giving and Receiving Compliments** page 157

See Part 2 When You Don't Understand the Concepts on page 235 of this audioscript.

PART 4 Focus on Testing

① **Basic Comprehension: Biographical Narratives** page 161

Professor: I'm almost embarrassed to lecture to you today about Albert Einstein. After all, he's probably the best-known scientist of the past couple of centuries, if not of all time. He has had an immeasurable impact on the human understanding of physics. Very few, if any, of you would fail to recognize a picture of him from his later life if I showed it to you.

Of course, he wasn't always an elderly man with a big bushy moustache and wild hair. Even Einstein had to be a baby first. He was born on March 14, 1879, in Ulm, Germany. Some people mistakenly believe that Einstein could not talk until the age of three. I haven't seen any evidence for that. What his family actually remembered about him was that he didn't talk *very much* during those first three years, not that he couldn't talk at all. There is also a nasty rumor that he was a poor student in his younger years. Not true. He wasn't always interested in what went on during class hours, but who is, right? Don't answer that.

He grew up in Munich, Germany, where his family had moved shortly after he was born. The family business, selling electrical supplies, fell on hard times during Einstein's early teens, and his family relocated to a town near Milan, in northern Italy. At that time, Einstein was unhappily studying in a Munich secondary school. His dissatisfaction with this rigid academy is probably the source of that bad-student rumor I mentioned earlier. It's not that he disliked education but that the memorization he was forced to do in his Munich school was stifling. For someone with a mind like his, the school's restrictive environment could only be a nuisance. He finally quit this German high school at 15 and joined his family in Italy.

He actually tried to skip the remainder of high school altogether by applying to the electrical engineering program at the Swiss

Federal Institute of Technology (the SFIT) in Zurich. However, he failed the liberal arts part of the entrance exam and had to change his plans. It was about a year after quitting school in Munich that he finally enrolled in a high school in Aarau, Switzerland, from which he graduated without any particular honors at the age of 17. After graduating from Aarau, he eventually did enter the SFIT, from which he graduated in 1900 with a degree in physics.

For the next couple of years, Einstein taught secondary school. He also married Mileva Maric, a Serbian mathematician with whom he had fallen in love during their days studying together at the SFIT. Another big change in his life was that he officially became a Swiss citizen in 1901. In 1902, with the help of one of his father's friends, he obtained a position at the Swiss patent office in Bern. During his two years clerking at this office, he completed an astounding amount of work in theoretical physics. For the most part, the papers he produced were written in his spare time and without the benefit of books to read or colleagues to talk to. Einstein submitted one of his scientific papers to the University of Zurich, which awarded him a Ph.D. degree in 1905. In 1908, he sent a second paper to the University of Bern and was offered a position as a lecturer there.

Physicists still look back at the year 1905, when Einstein published four brilliant papers in physics, as a kind of marvel. Some of science's toughest questions—about the nature of light, about molecular motion, about the relationship between time and physical space, and so on—were tackled by Einstein and brought into a theoretical whole. It was as if someone figured out in May of this year how to make cars run on water and then in July described exactly how the brain produces language. The scientific world was astounded. By 1909, Einstein was recognized throughout the German-speaking part of Europe as a leading scientific thinker. He worked for a brief time as a professor at the German University of Prague and at Zurich Polytechnic. In 1914, at the age of 35, he advanced to the most prestigious and best-paying post that a theoretical physicist could hold in Central Europe: professor at the Kaiser-Wilhelm Gesellschaft in Berlin, Germany. Einstein remained on the staff in Berlin until 1933. It was also during this time that he divorced Mileva Maric and married Elsa Lowenthal, who was actually one of his cousins.

It was not easy for him to remain in Berlin after the National Socialist Party (the Nazis) began consolidating their power in Germany. Einstein was Jewish, which made him a prime target for Nazi hatred. He was also an outspoken pacifist, someone who opposes war as a means to solve problems. The war-hungry Nazis saw this famous spokesperson for peace as an obstacle to their plans. At that time, he came to the United States and took a research position at the Institute for Advanced Study in Princeton, New Jersey. He died in 1955.

Question 1: When was Einstein born?

Question 2: Why did the Einstein family move to Italy?

Question 3: Which of the following is a likely source of the rumor that Einstein was a bad student, according to the professor?

Question 4: Which of the following is *not* a job that Einstein held, according to the lecture?

Question 5: What did Einstein do in his spare time during his two years as a patent-office clerk?

Question 6: Which institution gave Einstein a Ph.D. degree?

Question 7: Why, according to the lecture, is the year 1905 greatly significant in Einstein's life?

Question 8: Which of the following best states why, according to the professor, Einstein left Germany in the 1930s?

CHAPTER 9 **Art and Entertainment**

Part 2 Distinguishing Between Fact and Opinion

2 Listening to Get the Gist page 171

3 Listening for Facts and Opinions page 172

Radio Program: Reality TV: Really Good or Really Bad?

Announcer: Welcome to "Media Watch", a production of Wisconsin Radio. This is program number six: "Reality TV: Really Good or Really Bad?"

Lecturer: So far in our "Media Watch" series on current trends on TV, we've talked about recent changes in newscasts, sitcoms, and dramas, including soap operas... although in my opinion, soap operas belong in the sitcom or even comic satire category... but that's a topic for another day, hmm?

Today we're going to take up the topic of reality TV. Sociologists agree that reality TV is a phenomenon that can't be stopped. Reality shows now far outnumber all other types of shows on television and not only sociologists, but also doctors, are concerned about the influence these shows have on the viewing public. But before we get into what the pundits are saying about either the beneficial or evil effects of reality TV, and before I share with you a few of my own thoughts on the subject, let's backtrack a little to define exactly what we're referring to by the term *reality TV* and to see how this runaway train got fired up, shall we?

Wikipedia defines *reality television* as "a genre of television programming that presents supposedly unscripted dramatic or humorous situations and events that feature ordinary people instead of professional actors and that these shows are produced in a series which distinguishes them from documentaries, newscasts, and sports shows." Well... it seems to me that someone should go online and edit this definition because we all know that actors, singers, models, athletes, and many other types of celebrities with aspirations to be professional actors have managed to snag their own reality show either for the publicity or just to make a living when they can't get work elsewhere, right? But what you *can* read on Wikipedia that *does* ring true, however, is that reality television is a modified and highly influenced form of reality that uses sensationalism to attract viewers and thereby increase advertising revenue. Participants in reality shows are often placed in exotic locations or abnormal situations (or as is the case with celebrities, are themselves exotic or abnormal in some way) and then are persuaded to act in specific scripted ways in these contrived situations by story editors or producers. Furthermore, after filming has been completed, this so-called reality can be manipulated further during the editing process. It is obvious that only a small portion of what is filmed ends up in the show and the choices concerning which scenes to show and in what order can considerably change the reality presented to the viewers.

So... this is reality TV now, but was it like this from the beginning? Well, yes... and no. Most researchers agree that Allen Funt's show *Candid Camera*, *Ted Mack's Original Amateur Hour* and *Arthur Godfrey's Talent Scouts* were the precursors, or shows that inspired the style and format of shows like *Punk'd*, where hidden cameras capture the reactions of unsuspecting ordinary people to pranks or outrageous joke situations and *American Idol* or *The Voice*, where supposedly amateur contestants compete for huge recording contracts based on both judges' and audience's votes. In 1948, the audience voted live in the television studio using an applause meter that measured the loudness of their clapping and the number of people who voted was limited by the number of seats in the studio. Nowadays, of course, people text or e-mail their votes and the number of people who can vote seems limitless.

In the 1950s and 60s there were countless game shows such as *Beat the Clock* and *Truth or Consequences* that involved contestants in wacky competitions where they had to attempt difficult physical feats or perhaps crawl through slippery green slime to reach the prize which might be a set of dishes or a refrigerator. Nowadays, we have shows such as *Survivor* or *The Amazing Race* where the prize can be a million dollars or more.

The first reality show in the modern sense may have been the twelve-part series *An American Family*, which was produced in the 1970s. In documentary style, it depicted a family going through a divorce. It was supposedly not scripted, unlike many of the reality shows today, and many viewers were shocked, even appalled, by what this family allowed to be revealed about them. Today, we barely blink or raise an eyebrow when celebrities or ordinary individuals who'd love to become celebrities, tell us about the most personal aspects of their lives.

In the late 1980s, a show called *COPS*, which came about partly in response to the need for new programs created by a writers' strike, showed real police officers during their normal scheduled duties catching real criminals. This show introduced the handheld camera technique that makes so many of today's scripted dramas such as *Law and Order* as well as supposedly unscripted reality shows seem like they are taking place in real time and in real places, as if the camera were our own eyes.

In the 1990s, MTV launched their series *The Real World*, the first show in the United States (very likely inspired by a show called *Nummer 28* produced in Holland) to put strangers with obviously conflicting values and personalities together in the same environment for an extended period of time and record the drama that naturally takes place. This show was also the first in the United States to use a music soundtrack that suggested particular emotions and also after-the-fact confessionals or commentaries by the participants about their own feelings or behavior in particular situations. These techniques were also used by the previously produced *Nummer 28*. Since the producers of *The Real World* deny that *Nummer 28* influenced them at all, I suppose we'll never know for sure, but I believe that either it truly did influence them or there was some sort of universal magic in the air that launched these groundbreaking reality TV techniques one right after the other merely by coincidence.

So here we are in the new millennium where reality shows have pretty much taken over the majority of TV airtime. I bet that you can name just about any topic and any situation and there is a reality show about it. There are shows about fat people, skinny people, tall people, and little people. There are shows that take place in jungles, in New York, and in "Smalltown" USA. There are shows about animals in the wild and pets that have gone wild at home… Shows about young mothers, older mothers, families that can't have children, and families that have *Eighteen Kids and Still Counting*, still expecting more. There are shows about killing animals, eating animals, and stuffing animals as well as shows about saving the whales and raising pandas in captivity. There are shows about bachelors and bachelorettes looking for love and others about looking for work. There are contests for people who want to be America's *Top Chef* or *Top Model* or *Top Designer* or even *Top Dog*. And then, of course, there are the "how to" shows. Just one click and you can learn how to paint your house, train your dog, cook like a pro, plant a garden, and save your marriage. Do you want to buy a house or at least dream about buying one, then *House Hunters* may be the show you're looking for. Or sell your grandmother's dishes? Then tune in to *Antiques Roadshow* where experts tell you the value of inherited or found objects. Or do you thirst for adventure? Then how about *The Most Dangerous Catch*, a show about Alaskan Crab fishermen? I said before, it's as if you and your friends can think of a funny or dramatic idea for a reality show and the very next day… there it is on the TV lineup.

So… what now? Can too much reality be a bad thing? Can't some of these shows help us to learn new skills or about other parts of the world? Or even help us learn about other parts of ourselves? Or are they just trash for the most part as some people say? Before I open the phone lines to callers, let me share two opposing views with you just to get us started. First, let me tell you what a blogger named Austin Cline has to say about the downside of reality shows. Then I'll share some surprising things that *Time* magazine TV critic and blogger James Poniewozik has to say on the subject.

Cline says that we tend to delight in or are at least be entertained or fascinated by the failings and problems of others. For example, we laugh at someone slipping and falling on the ice. If they are seriously hurt we are still fascinated by their painful situation. What causes us to be entertained in some way by the suffering of others? Are we relieved that it is not happening to us? Cline suggests that this may be true if it is truly a real situation. But why do we watch when something painful is deliberately scripted and staged for our amusement? Can a steady diet of this type of reality TV be good for us? I think not.

Cline also raises the issue of how reality TV tends to perpetuate or reinforce class and racial stereotypes. For example, in many shows there is a similar black female character. In reality, they are all different women, but they share similar characteristics… or at least the so-called reality show is scripted so that they do. This black female character is loud, aggressive, points her finger at people, and is always lecturing others on how to behave. Personally, I feel Cline is right since I, myself, have seen at least half a dozen reality shows that have this type of character. Then there's the sweet, naive person from a small town looking to become famous while hanging on to his or her smalltown values, and the party girl or boy who's always looking for a good time. These are stock characters, typical characters we see in works of fiction. So is it art imitating life in the case of the fictional shows, or life imitating art in the case of the reality shows?

A third point that Cline raises is the morality of a production company that creates a show with the intention of trying to make money from the humiliation and suffering which they create for unsuspecting people. And what about the participants? Should we question their morality if they humiliate themselves for money? And what about you, the viewer? Cline is not saying that you shouldn't watch reality TV, but that you should examine your motivations for watching some of these programs. I must say that I completely agree with Cline here.

In addition to what Cline says are the negative aspects of reality TV, I must mention one more—and that is that doctors are reporting an exponential increase in the amount of plastic surgery young people are requesting in proportion to the amount of reality TV that they habitually watch. That is to say, that the data shows that young people, women and even young girls in particular, are convinced that they should look like the models or actors or other supposedly ordinary people on these shows. They don't seem to realize that what they are seeing takes hours and hours of careful make-up application and very artful lighting. What they are seeing is not really the way these women look when they get out of bed in the morning. That's for sure. And psychologists are concerned that reality TV is just one more factor that is contributing to the poor self-image of the average viewer.

Poniewozik, however, has a more positive view of what reality TV has to offer. He thinks, and I quote, that "reality TV is the best thing to happen to television in years." He says it has given people at work something to connect to, something to talk to each about other during their breaks. It has reminded viewers that TV can be exciting, not boring, and it is teaching us a new way to tell engrossing human stories. He asks us, "When was the last time that a regular network show caused you to call your best friend in the middle of the show and say 'you've gotta see this' or to yell back at the people on the show?" Well, he's got a point there. Reality TV shows do get you to sit up

and pay attention. As Poniewozik says, these shows may provoke us or even offend us, but at least they do something more than just help us get to sleep. And if they get us to talk to each other again instead of sitting silently watching the same old boring sitcoms or police dramas that propose to be based on real cases, but aren't nearly so fascinating as the real thing, what's the harm in that? Probably, we love to laugh and judge and judge and laugh, and then gossip about it. And Poniewozik adds that, for all the talk about humiliation on reality TV, the participants seem very good-humored about it all. The *American Idol* audition rejects are still stubbornly convinced of their own talent, and the players on *Fear Factor* walk away from boxes of snakes and insects like Olympic champions.

OK, listeners. The phone lines are now open. Let's hear what you have to say about reality TV? Really good or really bad? And I'd love to hear from anyone out there who has ever been on or worked on a reality TV show. We'd love to hear the truth about what *really* goes on behind the scenes. Now *there's* an idea for another reality show, eh?

Part 3   Expressing Doubt or Disbelief

1 **Listening for Expressions of Doubt and Disbelief** page 177

Conversation 1

Emmett: Professor Brandt, I'd like to talk to you about my art project for my senior thesis.

Professor Brandt: No time like the present, Emmet. Have a seat. What would you like to do?

Emmett: Are you sure it's OK? I know how busy you are.

Professor Brandt: It's fine.

Emmett: Well, I'd like to do something really imaginative and creative, something like my friend Howard did for his master's thesis.

Professor Brandt: What was that?

Emmett: He filmed himself sleeping every night for a month and then edited it and added a soundtrack and called it a reality show. He sent it to all the networks and then filmed himself reading all of the rejection letters out loud.

Professor Brandt: And he got his master's for that?

Emmett: Yes, he did.

Professor Brandt: I find that hard to believe. You'll have to think of something else, Emmet, another type of project to fulfill the requirements for your media and communications degree.

Question 1: What expression does Emmett use to express doubt?

Question 2: Why do you think he uses that expression?

Question 3: Professor Brandt expresses disbelief twice in this conversation. Is she polite to Emmett?

Question 4: The first time Professor Brandt expresses disbelief through intonation alone. What words does she use?

Question 5: What expression does she use the second time?

Conversation 2

Amy: My twelve-year-old daughter is on a show called *Making the Band*, and I'm sure that she's going to win and get into the band. The producers told her that the band could make $30 million dollars next year.

Jen: Get outta here. The Rolling Stones only make $58 million in a whole year!

Amy: Yes, they really will. And the most amazing thing is that they already have a twelve-year-old manager. She does all the contract negotiating for the concerts.

Jen: Oh, sure!

Amy: Yes, and she's really first-rate. These twelve-year-olds are booked for concerts in New York, Chicago, Denver, Los Angeles, Atlanta, Detroit, and Philadelphia in the next four weeks alone.

Jen: Yeah, right, and I'm Mick Jagger.

Question 1: Is this conversation formal or informal?

Question 2: When the second speaker says "Get outta here," does she sound amused or angry?

Question 3: How does the second speaker sound when she says, "Oh, sure!"?

Question 4: When the second speaker says "Yeah, right, and I'm Mick Jagger," does she sound rude?

Question 5: Why do you think the second speaker expresses disbelief this way?

Conversation 3

Thea: I'd really love to be one of the professional dancers that get to dance with a celebrity on that reality show *Dancing with the Stars*.

Nick: Well then, you'll have to do more than take lessons once a week. I bet the professional dancers on that show dance in those high heels until their feet bleed, and then keep on dancing some more.

Thea: I find that hard to believe. How do you know that?

Nick: I saw it in a reality show about what goes on backstage and during rehearsals for that show. This one dancer was so dedicated you wouldn't believe it! With bleeding feet she just danced and danced and danced. I saw it all on the show.

Thea: Come on. Did she really do that?

Nick: Absolutely, it was the most incredible thing I've ever seen.

Question 1: Are Thea's expressions of disbelief formal or informal?

Question 2: Is she polite or rude?

Question 3: What are some expressions Thea uses?

Conversation 4

Professor Pickering: Today I'm going to talk about Mozart, the musical genius who performed concerts on the pianoforte for European royalty at the age of eight. I don't think anyone has ever matched that achievement.

Rose: Oh, come on! Have you seen those kids on *America's Got Talent*?

Professor Pickering: Well no, but he not only could play the pianoforte, but was also composing music at the age of five. I'm sure that the children on that show cannot compose their own music.

Rose: You've got to be kidding. Those producers wouldn't invest so much time and money in those kids if they weren't geniuses like Mozart, too.

Professor Pickering: Well, why don't you see me after class if you'd like to discuss the matter further? But for now we'll concentrate on a discussion of Mozart's music.

Question 1: Are Rose's expressions of disbelief formal or informal?

Question 2: Is she polite or rude?

Question 3: Does the professor seem impatient with Rose?

Question 4: What are some expressions Rose uses?

② Listening for Opinions page 179

See Part 2 Distinguishing Between Fact and Opinion on page 239 of this audioscript.

Part 4   Focus on Testing

① Answering Questions about Facts and Opinions page 183

Reviewer:

Bethel, New York, August 29, 1969.

The Woodstock Music and Art Fair in Bethel, New York was advertised by its youthful New York promoters as "An Aquarian Exposition" of music and peace. It was that and more, much more. The festival, quickly nicknamed "Woodstock" for short, may have turned out to be history's largest "happening." As the quintessential moment when the American youth of the '60s openly displayed its strength, appeal, and power, Woodstock may rank as one of the most significant political and sociological events of the age.

By a conservative estimate, more than 400,000 people, the vast majority of them between the ages of 16 and 30, showed up for the Woodstock Festival. Thousands more would have come if police had not blocked off some of the access roads. Other roads turned into long, ribbon-like parking lots as spectators simply left their cars, rather than wait for hours in a traffic jam. If the festival had lasted much longer, as many as one million youths might have made the pilgrimage to Bethel to participate in the Woodstock Festival. The concert promoters had originally sold tickets in advance, but on the first day, overwhelmed by the feeling of the crowd just wanting to gather together to share, to listen to, and to speak their common language of music, they decided to let everyone in for free. Authorities worried that having so many people sitting in traffic jams on the highways would lead to violence, but one police officer remarked that this was certainly the most peaceful bunch of frustrated people he'd ever witnessed. Imagine what would happen today with the speed of cell phones and social media such as Facebook. I wonder how big the crowds would get and if everyone would remain so peaceful.

What lured our country's youth to Woodstock? An all-star cast of top rock artists, including Janis Joplin, Jimi Hendrix, and Jefferson Airplane to be sure. But the good vibrations of good groups turned out to be the least of it. What the youth of America and their worried elders saw at Bethel was the potential power of an entire generation, a generation that in countless disturbing ways had rejected the traditional values and goals of the United States. Over 400,000 young people, who had previously thought of themselves as part of an isolated minority, experienced the thrill of discovering that they were, as the saying goes, "what's happening." They were the current voice of America. They were the generation that was determined to put a stop to war and bring corrupt governments to their knees without firing a shot. And they were the generation that would accomplish all of this through peace and love.

To many adults, the festival seemed like a monstrous Dionysian orgy, a wild party where a mob of crazy kids gathered to take drugs and groove and move to hours and hours of amplified noise that could hardly be called music. The significance and power of Woodstock, however, cannot be overestimated. Despite the piles of litter and garbage, the hopelessly inadequate sanitation, the lack of food, and the two nights of rain that turned Yasgur's farm in Bethel, New York, into a sea of mud, the young people found it all "beautiful." This was the pinnacle of the Peace Movement, and the beginning of the end of the Vietnam War. The historical significance of this youthful, yet peaceful, energy in one place can never be forgotten. One long-haired teenager summed up the significance of Woodstock quite simply: "The people," he said, "are finally getting together."

Question 1: According to the speaker, which of the following statements describes the festival?

Question 2: What was the nickname for the festival?

Question 3: Approximately how many people went to the festival?

Question 4: According to the speaker, why did the promoters decide to let everyone in for free?

Question 5: According to the speaker, what was the main reason people went to the festival?

Question 6: Which of the following was not a problem at the festival?

7. *Listen to part of the music review again.*

Reviewer: To many adults, the festival seemed like a monstrous Dionysian orgy, a wild party where a mob of crazy kids gathered to take drugs and groove and move to hours and hours of amplified noise that could hardly be called music. The significance and power of Woodstock, however, cannot be overestimated.

Question 7: What does the speaker mean when he says that the power of Woodstock cannot be overestimated?

8. *Listen to part of the music review again.*

Reviewer: This was the pinnacle of the Peace Movement, and the beginning of the end of the Vietnam War. The historical significance of this youthful, yet peaceful, energy in one place can never be forgotten.

Question 8: What is the speaker's opinion about Woodstock in relation to the Peace Movement?

CHAPTER 10 — Conflict and Resolution

PART 2 Exam Questions

2 Listening to Predict Exam Questions page 192

Resident Advisor Training Session:
Dealing with Conflicts

Head Resident Advisor (RA): OK, guys! Today's the last session before your final test to qualify to become a resident advisor. Next week's test will be on today's topic—conflict resolution—and then the week after next, the students arrive. This year, we have a record number of international students entering the university. I understand that many of you are international students, too. That will be a great help, I think. Let's see, how many of you are international students? I see seven hands up. That's about 30 percent. Great!

Now, how many of you have had previous training in conflict resolution? Six out of 20—that's pretty good. Well, today's session may be old hat for you. So please feel free to interrupt if you've got any information to add.

But before we go into conflict resolution, let's review the principles of making friends we talked about last week. These principles can be useful if you've got a student who's having trouble making friends and even with students who are having serious conflicts with others. Believe it or not, these principles are based on Dale Carnegie's 1937—yes 1937—bestseller *How to Win Friends and Influence People*. And I think they're still as true now as they were then. Giving students this information can definitely help prevent conflicts. Look at your handout on the seven principles of making friends that you got last week as we review. Now, although these principles have some things in common with what we'll cover today, be sure not to confuse the seven principles of making friends with the seven principles of conflict resolution which I'll get to in a bit. OK? So... here we go.

Principle #1: Try to praise people. And be sure to speak honestly about how or why you appreciate them.

Principle #2: Be indirect when you talk about someone's mistakes.

And **Principle #3:** Talk about your mistakes first, not others'.

Principle #4: If possible, try to ask questions; don't give orders.

Principle #5: If people make mistakes, let them save face by praising all improvements.

Principle #6: Give people a fine reputation to live up to, that is, set a good example.

And finally, **Principle #7:** Always try to be encouraging.

So now that we've refreshed our memory about these seven principles of making friends, let's look at the steps to take if you're going to do conflict resolution with, for example, two roommates, or any two students in the dorms who have a conflict. Conflict resolution is one of your prime duties as an R.A., and you can be sure these steps will be on next week's test.

The first step is to get the two people who are having the conflict to cool off or chill out. Anger is the emotion that people have the most difficulty controlling, and when people are angry they don't make good decisions. Therefore, it is not surprising that anger sometimes leads to rage or violence. How can you get people to cool down? Here are a few ways:

- Well, you can distract them. For example, tell a joke. It's hard to stay angry when you're laughing.

- You can also encourage them to exercise, such as playing a game of basketball or another sport. Anger is a high-arousal state, and exercise changes a high-arousal state to a low-arousal state.

- A third thing you can do is you can get them to write down their angry thoughts instead of saying them to the other person. Verbalizing anger may feel satisfying, but it increases the arousal state, which will certainly not help resolve the conflict.

Now... OK... After you've gotten the angry person to cool off, go to Step 2: Get the people to talk and listen to each other.

Hmmm. How do you do that? Well, first, have one student state the problem completely. Then the second student should restate what the first is saying to make sure he or she understands. Encourage the second student to begin these restatements with things like, "What I hear you saying is... ," "One concern you have is...," "What bothers you is... ," or "What you're afraid of is... " Then have the students change roles. The second one should state his or her view of the problem, and the first one should restate what is said to make sure he or she understands. During the process, you, as the advisor, should keep asking, "Is there anything else?" until there is nothing else either of the students wants to say.

OK. Now this takes us to the third step, and that is to be clear about what each student needs. To be sure that each student's interests are being considered, make a list. Be sure you give the person time to think about what his or her most important needs or priorities are in the situation.

Remember the old Jack Benny joke. Do you guys know it? Jack Benny was a famous comedian who was very stingy with his money.

Group of RAs: Hmmm, not me. No, I don't think so. No, never heard it. Which one? Huh?

Head RA: Well, a robber comes up and pulls a gun on Jack Benny and says, "Your money or your life," and Jack Benny hesitates. The robber becomes impatient and says again and again, "Your money or your life." Finally Jack replies, "I'm thinking ... I'm thinking."

Group of RAs: (laughter)

Head RA: In other words, give each person time to figure out what his or her priorities or most important needs are.

But there's one thing you have to be careful about during this part of the process. When students in conflict are talking about their feelings, tell them to make "I" statements. In other words, they should talk about themselves and their feelings and concerns, not the other student's faults. They should say for example, "It bothers me when people don't look at me when they talk to me," instead of "You never look at me when you talk to me." They should say, "I feel confused when people say 'you know' and I don't know," instead of "You always assume I know things that I don't." And here's one more example: They should say, "I get nervous when people make plans for me without consulting me," instead of saying "You're always trying to tell me what to do."

OK, so now what do you do after the two students have heard and restated each other's views of the situation and made lists of what they each need? Step 4 is when you help them brainstorm solutions. The rule to follow here is that these solutions must honor all of their concerns.

Then consider each of the brainstorming ideas. Make these ideas into trial balloons and test them out. Discuss each solution in turn and see which one will fly by discussing the consequences of actually doing it. Remember: the real solution may be a combination of several ideas. So at this stage in the process, you must keep asking both people, "Are you still feeling happy about the process?" Remember that there is no one right way. At this point, you are just generating ideas, and you want to make sure that both students trust that you are not choosing sides.

The fifth step is to evaluate the solution. Each step is important, and this one is no exception. In fact, this one is so important that it's worth writing it out in black and white. Yes, put it on paper. Each student takes a sheet of paper and writes out the pros and cons for each of the brainstormed solutions. Just the action of putting all of the possible solutions and the advantages and disadvantages of each of them on paper can help both people clarify their views. At this time, let people express their reservations. Listen for statements like, "I hear what you're saying, but... ," "I have a problem with... ," "I guess so, but... " "one drawback I feel is... " or "I'm not sure that will work for me because... ," Remember, Socrates said, "Know thyself." It's very good advice and is really important in conflict resolution. Unless you are really clear about what you want, it's difficult to come to a compromise.

There's something else that's also very important at this stage and actually for all of the steps. When you are doing conflict resolution, notice the body language. For example, is the speaker talking with folded arms or hands on the hips? Does the speaker shake a fist or wag a finger? Does the speaker move into or back away from the other person's space? Good. I can see from your nodding heads that you all know what I'm talking about here.

Next is Step 6: this is where you help the students choose one of the solutions or make a combination solution. In this step, both people must agree on a solution, one that is acceptable to both of them. This step will take some more negotiation. There must be some give-and-take. Be sure to have both parties buy into the agreement. If you hear one person say, "I trust you completely," that's good, but if you hear "Do whatever you think is best" or "Whatever you say" watch out. It's a sign that someone has acquiesced but hasn't really bought into the situation. The person does not really like the agreement, and that could mean trouble later. To make this step in the process work, start with the big picture, that is, the basic problem and all its consequences and the best solution and all its consequences. Each person should restate what he or she thinks the big picture is. Then help the two students create a shared vision and make commitments to action within a time frame. Work on the agreement until everyone is satisfied.

Finally, the last step: agree on contingency plans, which are ways to monitor how things are going, and agree on a time to reevaluate. Of course, you must realize that no matter how good your agreement is, how well intentioned each person is, and how clear both people are, circumstances change and there must be a way to deal with these changes. An unexpected event could happen after your agreement, but before you can start to implement the new plan. Part of providing for such contingencies should include finding a way to get out of the agreement, specifically a way to get out without loss of face. And be sure to agree on some way to measure the outcome. It should be a yes/no measure. Either they did accomplish various parts of the agreement or they didn't. And be sure to discuss how the agreement will be monitored. Everyone has to agree on this. And when will the agreement be reevaluated? Everyone should agree on this too.

So there you have it guys—seven steps to conflict resolution. It's a lot to think about, I know. I'll stick around for a while to answer any questions, OK? The test is next Wednesday. Good luck; and I'll see all you 'round the dorms.

PART 3 Acquiescing and Expressing Reservations

1 Listening for Acquiescence and Reservations page 197

RA: I'm glad you guys have agreed to get together to resolve your conflict. Let's start with James. What's the problem, James?

Mohammed: Why should he start? I'm the one who was insulted.

RA: Whatever you say. Then let's start with you, Mohammed.

James: If you think that's best.

Mohammed: I want a new roommate because James hates me.

James: What do you mean I hate you? I don't hate you. Where did you get that idea?

Mohammed: Well, you always sit facing me with your feet on the desk.

RA: Oh! I see what the problem is. James, in Mohammed's culture, if you show someone the bottoms of your feet, it is a great insult.

James: Oh, OK. I didn't mean anything insulting by that. I was just comfortable with my feet up while we were chatting. I can move my feet. *Not* a problem.

Mohammed: OK then.

James: Yes, but the question really is, is that enough? I don't know enough about Mohammed's culture and I'm afraid that I'll do something wrong again… at least from *his* point of view.

RA: OK, then. If there were a lecture on Middle Eastern culture or perhaps a discussion group where you could discuss your feelings about this, would you be willing to go?

James: Sure, but shouldn't Mohammed have to learn about my culture, too? But I don't think there are any lectures or discussion groups about my culture.

RA: Yes, you're right. It's difficult to find such a thing about the majority culture. I have an idea though. Would you and Mohammed be willing to begin a cross-cultural discussion group?

Mohammed: Yes, I would be very interested in that.

James: Yeah, me too.

RA: OK, then. In the meantime, I think you guys should give being roommates another month. If there are still problems, after a month we can see about changing roommates. What do you think?

James and Mohammed: I'm willing to go along with that. OK, let's try it.

2 Listening for Suggestions About Conflict Resolution page 198

Excerpt is taken from Part 2 Exam Questions on page 245 of this audioscript.

RA: The first step is to get the two people who are having the conflict to cool off or chill out. Anger is the emotion that people have the most difficulty controlling, and when people are angry they don't make good decisions. Therefore, it is not surprising that anger sometimes leads to rage or violence. How can you get people to cool down? Here are a few ways:

- Well… you can distract them. For example, tell a joke. It's hard to stay angry when you're laughing.

- You can also encourage them to exercise, such as playing a game of basketball or another sport. Anger is a high-arousal state, and exercise changes a high-arousal state to a low-arousal state.

- A third thing you can do is you can get them to write down their angry thoughts instead of saying them to the other person. Verbalizing anger may feel satisfying, but it increases the arousal state, which will certainly not help resolve the conflict.

3 Listening for Ways to Express Reservations page 199

Excerpt is taken from Part 2 Exam Questions on page 245 of this audioscript.

RA: Now… OK… After you've gotten the angry person to cool off, go to Step 2: Get the people to talk and listen to each other.

Hmmm. How do you do that? Well, first, have one student state the problem completely. Then the second student should restate what the first is saying to make sure he or she understands. Encourage the second student to begin these restatements with things like, "What I hear you saying is… ," "One concern you have is…," "What bothers you is… ," or "What you're afraid of is… " Then have the students change roles. The second one should state his or her view of the problem, and the first one should restate what is said to make sure he or she understands. During the process, you, as the advisor, should keep asking, "Is there anything else?" until there is nothing else either of the students wants to say.

PART 4 Focus on Testing

1 Listening for Information and Point of View in Classroom Interactions page 201

Professor: Let me review what will be on the final exam next Monday. The exam will definitely cover the history of the conflicts in South Asia, in the Middle East, and in Northern Ireland. I'm not sure whether it will also cover the conflicts in Africa. Sorry I can't say for sure, but I just have to see how long the rest of the exam is. Unless you'd like to add another hour to the exam time and have an extra-long one.

Students: No! No, please. Come on!

Professor: You will be responsible for everything we've covered in lectures and discussion sections as well as the readings, of course. In addition, you will be responsible for the class presentations your classmates made. I see a hand up here.

Student 1: Yeah. What kinds of questions will there be?

Professor: The first part will be definitions, either in a matching format or short answer. I don't know because I haven't written it yet. The second part will be true/false and short answer, and the third part will be an essay in which you have to synthesize the concepts we've covered so far. You'll have to take a point of view and defend your position with specific examples. Question?

Student 2: Short-answer *and* an essay? Really?

Professor: That's right. Life is cruel.

Students: (laughter)

Student 3: You mean the essay will cover all the concepts we've studied? We have to put them all together?

Professor: Well, not all of them. That would be pretty hard to do. Let me just say that I'll give you very specific directions about what to cover. But you'll have to wait until the exam to find out which concepts I'll target.

Student 4: Can we ask you questions now about the material?

Professor: Let's hang on a minute and see whether there are any more questions about the format of the exam. Anyone?... OK, I guess I'll take content questions for... uh... a couple of minutes. Yes?

Student 2: I was wondering about the effects of deforestation. It shows up over and over again in my notes, but I have to say I just don't see the point. If you don't have forests you have conflict?

Professor: I wouldn't put it that way, but think about the regions we've been discussing. A lot of them are in the sub-tropical desert belts between about ten degrees of latitude and 30 degrees. Rain is not very common in many of these places. Still, these are societies that traditionally built a lot of things from wood, burned wood for cooking, and so on. People use up all the wood, cut down all the forests, and then what happens?

Student 1: No rain?

Professor: There wouldn't have been much rain anyway. Look deeper. And what effect would sparse rainfall have on the forests?

Student 4: They can't grow back very fast.

Professor: Exactly. And then all these people who need wood to live as they have always lived are scrambling for access to the few remaining trees. Conflict! This is a good clue to what you should focus on as you study. Which factors influenced events and how? Think about geography, culture, religion, minerals, soil resources... all sorts of factors.

Question 1: Which topic may or may not be on the final exam?

Question 2: Which of the following is *not* mentioned by the professor as a possible source for material on the exam?

3. *Listen again to part of the exchange.*

Student 3: You mean the essay will cover all the concepts we've studied? We have to put them all together?

Professor: Well, not all of them. That would be pretty hard to do. Let me just say that I'll give you very specific directions about what to cover. But you'll have to wait until the exam to find out which concepts I'll target.

Question 3: What is the male student's concern about the essay?

4. *Listen again to part of the exchange.*

Student 2: Short-answer *and* an essay? Really?

Professor: That's right. Life is cruel.

Students: (laughter)

Question 4: Which of the following best states the meaning of the professor's comment, "Life is cruel"?

5. *Listen again to part of the exchange.*

Student 4: Can we ask you questions now about the material?

Professor: Let's hang on a minute and see whether there are any more questions about the format of the exam. Anyone?... OK, I guess I'll take content questions for... uh... a couple of minutes. Yes?

Question 5: Why does the professor ask the female student to wait?

6. *Listen again to part of the exchange.*

Professor: I wouldn't put it that way, but think about the regions we've been discussing. A lot of them are in the sub-tropical desert belts between about ten degrees of latitude and 30 degrees. Rain is not very common in many of these places. Still, these are societies that traditionally built a lot of things from wood, burned wood for cooking, and so on. People use up all the wood, cut down all the forests, and then what happens?

Student 1: No rain?

Professor: There wouldn't have been much rain anyway. Look deeper. And what effect would sparse rainfall have on the forests?

Student 4: They can't grow back very fast.

Professor: Exactly. And then all these people who need wood to live as they have always lived are scrambling for access to the few remaining trees. Conflict!

Question 6: Which of the following best describes the situation?

Chapter 2 Part 3

Talk It Over pages 35–37

Question	Strong yes	Weak yes	Maybe	Weak no	Strong no
1.	4	3	2	1	0
2.	6	5	3	2	1
3.	5	4	3	2	1
4.	6	5	3	2	1
5.	7	6	4	2	1
6.	2	1	5	0	0
7.	3	2	1	.5	0
8.	6	5	3	2	1
9.	7	6	4	2	1
10.	7	6	4	2	1
11.	9	8	6	4	2
12.	7	6	4	2	1
13.	10	9	8	4	2
14.	8	7	5	3	1
15.	10	9	8	4	2
16.	10	9	8	4	2
17.	5	4	2	1	0
18.	4	3	2	1	0
19.	5	4	2	1	0
20.	9	8	6	4	2
21.	8	7	5	3	1
22.	7	6	4	2	1
23.	3	2	1	.5	0
24.	2	1	.5	0	0
25.	7	6	4	2	1

Vocabulary Preview　page 169

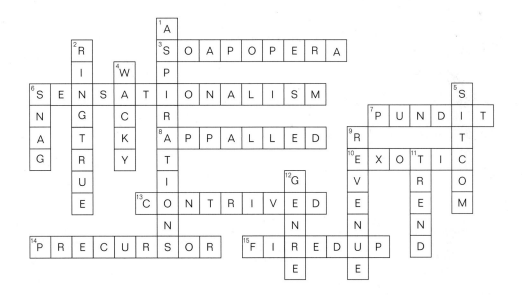

Vocabulary Index

Chapter 7

assemble
consensus
consultant
dispute
individualism
initiative
innovation
interdependence
quota
top dollar

Chapter 8

bleed
cosmos
matter
metaphysical
paradigm
relative
such and such
wild goose chase

Chapter 9

appalled
aspirations
contrived
exotic
fired up
genre
precursor
pundit
revenue
ring true
sensationalism
sitcom
snag
soap opera
trend
wacky

Chapter 10

arousal state
big picture
chill out
contingency
cool off
generate
give-and-take
honor
old hat
rage
trial balloon
well-intentioned

Skills Index